WITHOUT ME YOU'RE NOTHING

The Essential Guide to Home Computers

Frank Herbert

WITH

Max Barnard

Simon and Schuster

NEW YORK

SIMON AND SCHUSTER and colophon are trademarks of Simon & Schuster

Manufactured in the United States of America

Library of Congress Cataloging in Publication Data

Herbert, Frank.
   Without me you're nothing.

   1. Microcomputers.   2. Minicomputers.   I. Barnard,
Max, joint author.   II. Title.
QA76.5.H46   001.64.04   80-22315

ISBN 0-671-41287-6

The GRAPHIC COMPUTER SYSTEM AND KEYBOARD (appearing herein as
PROGRAMAP) that is described in this book is the subject of one or more claims of
a patent application now pending in the U.S. Patent & Trademark Office.

Grateful acknowledgment is hereby given to the following companies for usage of
materials from their catalogs and manuals in this book:
Apple Computer, Inc.
Atari, Inc.
Cromemco, Incorporated
Heuristics, Inc.
Micropolis Corporation
North Star Computers, Inc.
Vector Graphic, Inc.

Contents

List of Illustrations

Precede

You have in your hands a book that can change your life, that can help you organize those dull routines most of us dread, a book that can save you days of time every year while it converts drudgery into fun—all of that and much, much more.

This is a book about computers. By the time you have finished it, you should know how to use your own computer. You will find it rewarding and fun if for nothing else then for the freedom it gives you from tedious and boring jobs.

To help you learn how to use your own computer, we have developed a new approach to programming based on a new kind of flow chart that we call PROGRAMAP. It is rooted in plain English and in easily understood graphic symbols that are no more difficult to learn than road signs. The shape of the symbol tells you immediately where something is being done. The picture in the telltale shape gives you a specific direction. We see the PROGRAMAP system as a new computer language, but that does not belong in this primer. For this book we have held ourselves to a four-stage presentation:

1. A discussion of what's happening and about to happen with computers—why it's urgent that you develop these skills.

2. An introduction to your new machine with simple explanations of how a computer works.

3. A Buyer's Guide—how to get a computer you will like.

4. Step-by-step instructions for soloing with your own computer—using it for yourself.

We are not saying you can gain this skill without any investment of time and effort. Quite the contrary. In fact, a general rule about computers is that there is no time saving up front. It takes just as long, for example, to put your checking account into a computer as it takes to put the information into a handwritten ledger. It's at the other end where you get the marvelous payoff in time saving and automatic recall of useful information.

What we assure you is this: The payoffs are enormous. And there exists a starting point for you to understand computers, a starting point well within your experience. But that starting point has been so confused by misinterpretations and outright lies that we must begin once more at the beginning.

1

What's Happening

We will start with a promise.

In this book you will find the essential things you need to know to run your own computer. Those essentials are easy to understand.

It is our belief that you have been lied to about computers as part of a conspiracy—sometimes deliberate, sometimes unconscious—to keep them in the hands of an elite few. We are here to help rid our world of an elitist mystique that has acted as a barrier to your understanding.

Somewhere in the course of this book you should use a computer. It's the best way to learn. We promise that it will be easier than you may think. Let's cross that bridge when we come to it.

First, to give you an idea of how we have separated the essentials from the chaff, we will tell you a true story that has little to do with computers but a great deal to do with what you need to know before you can run one of these machines.

A young furniture salesman, closely observed by his boss, was selling a used refrigerator to an older woman. This was more than twenty years ago. The woman asked how the refrigerator defrosted.

Using the manufacturer's handbook, the young salesman took twenty minutes to explain how the refrigerator performed. Satisfied, the woman paid for her refrigerator and left the store.

At this point, the boss stepped in and angrily chewed out the young salesman for "wasting so much time on that customer."

"But she wanted to know how it defrosts," the young salesman protested.

Said the boss: "You tell her it defrosts at night!"

We don't intend to go quite that far in simplification, but there will be points in this book that we will flag. You will be able to skip across the flagged sections with full confidence that what goes on there happens "at night." It may be interesting, but you really don't need to know it.

You will also find in this book an appendix for information you may want. The stuff there is, for the most part, more complex and beyond the primer level to which we are holding the core of this book. There are also a glossary and bibliography for those of you who may wish to go deeper into the subject, but you will not have to read them to follow the central thread. That central thread will teach you how to use your own computer.

Things are happening in our world that make a necessity of the skills we are about to share with you. Before long it will at least be a matter of self-defense for you to have your own computer and be able to use it. You are already being taken advantage of by people with computers. You will not be able to meet that challenge or keep up with other changes unless you acquire a computer yourself.

Luckily, very powerful small computers are already priced within the range of most household budgets. Competition in this field is intense. Computer power is going up while the price is coming down.

Please take our warning to heart. Very soon, if you don't have access to a computer, you're going to be racing in something equivalent to the Indianapolis 500—only you'll be on foot. An elementary look at what computers do makes this obvious.

It is often said that computers are "number crunchers," that they can handle large and complex mathematical problems very rapidly. In fact, this common description of computers has been repeated so often that it forms a barrier against a deeper understanding of them even among scientists.

In the general population, though, this description acts as a "big lie" that keeps most people from looking into them or even considering the purchase of a personal computer.

How does something like that happen?

There are many reasons, but here is one of the most powerful:

Most teachers in the United States don't understand mathematics. It is not surprising, then, that many students don't understand mathematics. The whole idea of "math" in our world is much like what was once considered "knowledge confined to the priesthood." That plus the common description of computers as "just math machines" have built a strong barricade around the elite few.

It's just that the word *computer* makes so many people feel their own weakness in "mathematics." '

Okay—here's a demystification for you:

YOU DON'T NEED TO BE A MATHEMATICIAN TO RUN YOUR OWN COMPUTER.

The most important fact about computers is that they do things very, very rapidly. Few people latch onto that key word *rapidly*. We want you to focus your attention on it. That single fact contains the unguent that can take the sting out of your "future shock." We say flatly that computers will have more influence on what people do than all of the effects laid at the door of both fire and the wheel.

We have said that people with computers are taking advantage of you. There is no doubt that your historic rights of privacy and freedom have been violated by business and government through their use of computers. This is well enough known that it no longer can be questioned.

Private information about your life, information stored in government and other data banks, has been sold (sometimes under the counter) to people who use it for their own private gain. It is used to plan assaults on your wallet and on your liberties.

Billing departments in major industries use their computers in a system designed for regularly overcharging you on your monthly accounts. This is done under the guise of "cyclic billing." Your bill goes out on a set day each month, a day carefully planned to miss the posting of your previous payment. These overcharges, which most people miss, don't amount to much individually, but they are enormous collectively. The effect is that these businesses get the use of large sums *without paying interest*.

Your own computer will make the foiling of this gimmick a ten-second operation at bill-paying time.

Computer crime is on the upswing. Clever programmers are stealing millions of dollars each year through their inside knowledge of computers. If you have a business and it uses computers in any way, it would not hurt you to know a few of the basics that we will come to in this book.

Computer automation may be creeping up on your job. That makes it a matter of survival for you to know how *you* can benefit from these machines.

We are already surrounded by people who use the computer as an excuse for avoiding personal responsibility. How many times lately have you heard the following excuse?

"We are very sorry about the mistake in your account. It was a computer error."

That is a lie. It leads to a kind of mental parasitism, a destructive dependency. Every time you hear this excuse, you should tell the person who uses it: "You are a liar."

COMPUTERS DO NOT MAKE ERRORS.

All so-called "computer errors" lead back to some human being. People make errors. People produce inadequate programs. Manufacturers produce hardware that breaks down.

These few comments don't begin to plumb the accumulating problems of the "Computer Age." That would take another book plus many sequels. We are just touching on a few high points to emphasize the urgency.

Right now there is an explosive growth of the number of computers and things they can do. Not only are their numbers increasing at a dazzling rate, but the storage of information in giant data banks is growing in the same explosive way.

We have no way to control this now and none in sight. In fact, the very nature of this growth says that all controls will lag far behind computer developments. Any attempt to ban them will only drive computers underground. Never lose sight of the fact that computers "crunch time." The speed at which computers can operate tells us that laws cannot keep up with them. The person with a computer can dance rings around you while you react as though you were embedded in molasses.

What can you do?

Get your own computer. Learn how to use it. We are here to help you make that first step: how to find the one that fits your needs and your pocketbook, where to put it, how to program it—all of the essentials. If you don't do this, the Bill of Rights is dead and your individual liberties will go the way of the dodo.

2

You Can Do Wonderful Things

To give you a better idea of what's happening with computers, we're going to take a brief excursion through some present and potential uses. Some of the potential uses may appear "far out," but we assure you that the real potential will be farther out, far beyond anything we now imagine. It's the nature of the beast: Computers also amplify creative imagination.

In the arts and in our own special requirements for aids to writing, this is especially exciting. No matter how sophisticated, a computer is, after all, only a tool. A pen is a tool. A typewriter is a more sophisticated pen. A library is a tool. A painter's easel is a tool. It's the creative mind behind the tool that is important.

Musicians are already using computers in the digital composition of music. A digital recording of a composition allows you to change one note or even a fractional note in a full symphonic performance. This is extremely fine creative detail. And what separates any truly memorable artistic event from the ordinary is just that—attention to detail. This is true in all areas of artistic creativity. The thing of spontaneous beauty comes from long hours where the artist concentrates on the fine details.

With a computer a calligrapher can create any desired shape on the screen and then transfer that shape to paper with exact precision.

The same is true in printing. The printer can choose any typeface he wants and have the computer reproduce it. The cold type for this book was set by a computer.

The writer, too, can turn over to a computer some of the housekeeping chores of his profession. Newspapers already use computers for some

17

of their proofreading and editing chores. Reporters now write their stories directly into a computer.

In health and medicine present uses and the obvious lines of development are staggering. A Nobel Prize has just been given for developments in the use of computers to read X rays. That's only a bare beginning. Computers can obviously give us another quantum leap in longevity.

Many hospitals around the world now link their computers in a data-sharing system that submits current treatments for certain diseases to a combined analysis on a very large scale. This shows up new and/or improved ways of treating many medical problems. The system already has made significant contributions in the treatment of cancer, massive burn damage, transplant rejection, heart diseases, and some diseases carried by insects—to name just a few.

The ability of a computer to store, index, and cross-check massive amounts of information very rapidly is of particular interest in medicine. This means that any breakthrough in medical treatment can be available worldwide with minimum delay and, what is more important, the feedback from a wide experience with a new treatment can be shared at the same high speed.

The medical profession is already excited by the potential that computers have in scanning the deluge of publications for special information. A pediatrician will be able to have his computer scan only for information that applies to his specialty.

At an even more personal level, your home computer can already keep track of your medication as well as assist in diet planning, diet control, *and* exercise management. Your computer can be linked to a system that will warn you against taking incompatible medicines. Major hospitals already use such a system. And there is little doubt that your home computer, linked to a larger central system, will soon be able to monitor your physical status and statistics through blood and urine analysis, actual physical measurements, and the like.

The development of increasingly sophisticated optical scanners is of particular interest to medicine. High-resolution scanners capable of detecting extremely fine detail and miniscule variations in such things as color tones are already available. The application of such devices and systems for automatic chemical analysis to medical detection and diagnosis can only be a matter of time.

The bookkeeping tedium, such as keeping patient records, is already being turned over more and more to computers. But this only scratches the surface of the medical potential. The pharmaceutical applications are legion. It is highly unlikely that anything like the thalidomide tragedy, with its thousands of deformed infants, could occur in a society with a computer-managed drug-monitoring system. The rapid sharing of treatment information and results would show up the problem and the likely cause with extreme rapidity. In fact, with widespread linkage of everyday medical information, the detection of problems in medication can become routine.

Human gullibility being what it is, this does not mean that all over-the-counter nostrums will vanish, but it does mean that hard data on all medications will be readily available for anyone who wants it.

In certain specialized medical applications the computer potential is a banner of hope. Sufferers from aphasia—the inability to translate printed words into intelligible meaning—can get a computer to read to them. Many people afflicted with aphasia fill important posts in our society—in medicine, law, engineering, and the like. In each instance these people keep a hired reader on hand. Aphasia blocks only the visual channel to the written word. Such sufferers understand the spoken word quite well. How much more convenient to carry a small portable computer which will break through this visual barrier for them.

The deaf can expect equivalent aid from a computer. The computer will translate sounds into visible words.

If you're blind, a computer will give you an auditory "picture" of your surroundings—read signs and traffic lights, recognize friends, warn of dangers, identify addresses, and provide the time of day.

The deaf *and* blind can expect a "tactile translator" that will spell out necessary information on a sensitive patch of skin.

All of this means that the self-driving vehicle will be developed—a fact of poignant interest to people whose physical problems confine them to bed or wheelchair. A computer will make such people mobile by voice or touch control—or by control through any movement of which the person is capable.

To all of these people, the computer's potential means a new kind of freedom.

It is said with some truth that modern society has built a technological trap with life-support systems based on highly sophisticated manufacturing and on vulnerable energy resources with their distribution networks. Computers are not *the* solution to an escape from this trap, but they do offer us manageable ways to deal with our technological environment on our own terms. We can do this individually with a home computer.

Here are some of the present and potential home developments:

Existing house wiring can transmit signals for control and monitoring of household management. You can have your own computerized life-support and alarm system with fire, smoke, and burglar detection. An automatic system that calls for appropriate assistance—fire department, police, or medical—already is available. The system detects the problem and makes the call without your intervention.

By extension it seems obvious that systems to detect harmful substances in food, water, and air will be a logical next step for home installation.

Today's home computers can control your household lights, the heating and cooling, and the music and communications systems as well as perform some maintenance chores. Turning elevator and door controls (including fire doors) over to a computer is already routine in many buildings. It is already possible to talk to your own personal computer from anyplace on earth through telephone, radio, and satellite linkages. Think about that.

You're driving to dinner with friends. Suddenly you ask, "Did we lock the garage?" No sweat. You can lock the garage from your moving car while you continue on your way to the dinner. Did you forget to turn off the iron, the sprinkler, the stove, the lights—whatever? Same solution: You solve the problem from your moving car. And the scrambler code system for doing these things is exclusively your own.

Not only can a computer manage your household heating and cooling systems for maximum efficiency and economy, but it can be programmed to the actual needs. It can be set to detect when people are not using a particular room and can shut off the heat for that room when it's not in use. A computer also can monitor your fuel supply and alert you when you need more. With an automatic calling system it could call your fuel distributor on its own.

What you're looking at with a home computer is a personal secretarial service with potentially infinite capacity and infallible *memory*. (Computers don't really remember things the way you do, but their storage systems serve a similar function at your demand.) Your computer will store records of all your important dates—birthdays, anniversaries, and the like. It will act as your appointment calendar. It will store your correspondence and provide you with form letters, contracts, and mailing lists for such things as your Christmas cards. Through legal-advisor programs, it will compare your needs to those laid out in proposed contracts offered for your signature. It will cross-index all of these things and sort through them very rapidly for potential conflicts.

You will get up in the morning, punch the bedside calendar key, and while you dress, your computer will list for you the things you need to do that day.

While doing all of these things, your computer will also test the moisture content of your lawn and, when appropriate, will turn on the sprinkler system for precisely the time required to provide needed water.

Management of routine household chores is just the kind of thing a computer does best. In fact, this is sure to provide us with a new interpretation of the word *routine*. It will become synonymous with *automatic*. Take a quick scan through these routines:

A computer can list all of your insurance policies and their provisions, what they insure, when those policies need upgrading or other changes, and when they must be paid. A computer can manage your household budget with exquisite detail, keeping bank and tax records with special attention to your unique needs and, through legal-advisor programs, indexing whatever require your attention.

All of this involves a "special instruction" capability that computers can provide. The extensions of this are too numerous to list here, but just look at a few of them:

Your home computer will give special instruction to shut-ins. It will tailor home-study education for the particular needs of the student. It will make games out of educational projects. It will test your skills, increasing the performance demands as you improve.

The thing you must remember is that a computer can control any system that can be automated. The sophisticated watering system that tests the soil and irrigates accordingly has profound implications for the interacting chemistry of land and food—plant or animal. This not only has applications to lawns but to pastures, forest, and croplands, to floral plantings outdoors, in greenhouses, *and* in your own home. This ability to test, monitor, and control automated systems with preprogrammed instructions will transform many areas of our world.

With appropriate sensors a computer can be applied to pest control. With weather-satellite linkages it can be applied to soil improvement and management either on a small and local level or over wide regions and with high-resolution emphasis on fine detail. It's easy to see how this can influence ranching—feed, pasture, fertilizing, planting, and irrigation—but it also applies to the medical monitoring of stock, to the storage and recovery of veterinary information at the point of use.

"What made this leaf curl?"

Given the appropriate diagnostic program, your computer will require only that you pass the leaf under a scanner and subject part of the leaf to computer-monitored microscopic analysis.

There appears to be little doubt that ranchers and farmers will someday get their informational alerts and updates from the Department of Agriculture through a home computer. Once that starts, the improvement of the informational network will be only a matter of time.

With optical scanners and other sensitive means of probing, this is sure to have far-reaching implications for disease diagnoses and pest identification—not just for farmers and ranchers.

We're sure you can see the parallel implications for the control of human diseases and pests.

For much of this discourse, we've been talking about business applications, but you must remember that running a home has many aspects of business management. A computer can only help you bring a businesslike attitude and facility to that management. A machine that can monitor all of the applicance and mechanical parts of a home, that can monitor the internal and external requirements for maintenance of the building itself, gives its users a powerful economic advantage. This alone could pay for your computer.

In the business world computers are already past the first development phase, now there are increasing refinements. Computers keep track of inventory and payroll. They control production and manage work and manufacturing schedules. They take charge of such things as selecting which steel plate will be used next and where in the construction of an ocean liner. Computerized management of government forms and other paperwork is already routine in many businesses for a very good reason: This is the cheapest and most reliable way to do these things.

Computers allow very precise and very fast profit analysis. They can provide a quick performance assessment of salesmen, with attendant route management and the flagging of probable areas for best sales improvement.

You, the potential buyer, are the target for much of this business shift into computers. Do you think you can protect your own interests without your own computer?

How far will the use of computers go in our government? All the way. The White House now has at least two computer centers. The U.S. Department of Transportation is already far along the road to being fully computerized. Other bureaus and departments are following this same path. The computer is seen as a superb decision-making tool because it can store and sort through enormous amounts of information at extremely high speed.

You won't be able to vote intelligently or have even the vaguest idea of what's going on in any of these areas unless you can tap large sources of data with your own computer system.

These business and government uses of computers in organizing and indexing needed information, including published literature, will have immediate home applications. Just as the professional may use his computer to keep an index of magazine articles and technical books and journals, scanning them for particular attention to personal needs, the homeowner has particular needs for specialized information. The automated search of information at the home level may only tell you which book to ask for at your library, but it will "home in" quickly on the information.

Scientists and technologists will "crunch" numbers and play their specialized computer games. But this is already part of a developmental system with its own built-in course of changes that will filter down to the average home computer user. Don't be surprised at anything that comes out of this system.

The analysis and storage of information on materials for architects and engineers—stress formulas and applications analysis automatically translated into forms for use by the construction trades, including automatic blueprint reading—are already accomplished fact. This is sure to become increasingly sophisticated.

Marine architects and landscape architects use similar computer facilities.

Not only do building architects use computers for shape and stress analysis, they also project a proposed building into its setting with a computer. This gives them the building's relationship to sun, wind, and the views from within it. Architects also use computers to provide the drawings for standard shapes and installations, such as trees and plantings, the placement of 2×4 studs in wood construction, and the like. Marine architects test the flow lines of proposed boats in computer simulation. Aircraft designers do the same with proposed wing and fuselage relationships.

From all of this will come improvements for your home and office building.

Out of this same system of development will come new methods of mapping and navigation. That, too, has personal applications. How would you like a screen in your car that tells you where you are in relationship to your destination? No more squinting at maps or stopping at service stations for bewildered questions.

How would you like your own news sheet and magazines printed in your own home with attention to your personal interests and requirements?

Would you like a personal and portable device that would link you with larger and more sophisticated computer networks and information services? The next time someone tries to take advantage of you with a computer, how would you like to say, "My computer will talk to your computer"?

Some of these developmental steps, of course, come under what's generally called "futurism"—the analysis and projection of trends with highly accurate probability readings. Politicians use this computer facility regularly. Manufacturers are turning to it more and more in attempts to determine what you will buy tomorrow and how much you will pay. Some mail-order houses are using their computers in an interesting twist on this "futurism" concept. They are computer-linked to production facilities. The item you order today isn't even produced until your order reaches the mail-order offices. A computerized order for the item is transmitted by the clerk who reads your letter. The clerk merely punches the item number and your order number into a computer terminal. Your order is then filed by the computer. When the item comes into the warehouse, the computer matches it with your order number.

We have saved some of the major political implications of computers for the last part of this chapter. This is an extremely sensitive, complicated, and difficult area for prediction. People in positions of power tend to react strongly against anything they see as a threat to their power. There is little doubt that the widespread, intelligent use of personal computers threatens any power structure based on deception or concealment. Legislative attempts may be made to ban, restrict, or otherwise hobble certain uses of computers, uses not only by businesses but by individuals.

Remember that your computer will list and index anything you want to put into it. Your own computer will keep track of voting records on any politician you want to observe. The computer will give you an immediate readout on that record, testing it against any requirements you may name. Such a use of computers promises to sensitize legislators to those power blocs that make this use of the machine. That is not altogether an immediate entry into Utopia—but it could very well happen.

The routine political uses of a home computer hardly need mentioning—automatic reminders on your calendar for voting dates, places, times, and the candidates. Your home computer will provide that service with rapidity and ease. It's only when you start making special political use of your computer and when you link it to special attachments that things become complicated and sensitive.

For example, if you incorporate an automatic recorder and voice-stress analyzer in your computer, the machine's potential in politics and other public activities enters another dimension. It's well for you to note that some people are making it a matter of routine to monitor important speakers with a voice-stress analyzer. Don't make the mistake of assuming that this provides you with an infallible lie detector. It does not. It is, however, a sensitive stress detector—and if you possess other essential information, you may also learn the reason for the stress: It could be that the speaker is lying.

The complexity and sensitivity of this computer use cannot truly be appreciated until you test it against a real example. At that point, you see the difficulties but also the importance of this additional information. Here is such an example, and we warn you not to jump to any conclusions about it.

Before and after the Begin-Sadat talks at Camp David, which resulted in their signing of a peace agreement, both Begin and Sadat joined President Carter in speaking publicly about these events on U.S. television. Both Begin and Sadat addressed themselves to various key matters in the peace talks with varying degrees of stress or lack of it. On one subject, however, the difference was dramatic when their voices were subjected to a voice-stress analyzer. Every time Sadat spoke of wanting peace, his voice showed no stress whatsoever. But every time Begin spoke of this desire, his voice showed extreme stress.

Do *not* assume from this that Sadat was being truthful and that Begin was lying. You do not know this, and the evidence of the voice-stress analyzer does not say it. Without inside information about the parties concerned, any analysis you make must be inconclusive.

For example, if you have nothing but the voice-stress evidence, here are some of the limits to a possible analysis:

It is possible that Begin has a deeper and more stressful need for peace, perhaps based on his own lifetime involvement in violence and counterviolence.

It is possible that Israeli intelligence activity in the Middle East, perhaps superior to that of the United States or of the Arabs, has convinced them that the survival of their state requires military conquest of the region. The stress in Begin's voice could then be laid to the necessity for him to conceal an essential part of his motivation. He *truthfully* would not see peace as a real way for Israel to survive, and *quite properly* the survival of Israel is his first concern.

Also these men were speaking English when monitored by the voice-stress analyzer. English is for both of them a foreign language. Speaking a foreign language introduces its own stress patterns. The answer to these observations may simply be that Sadat finds it more comfortable to speak English than does Begin.

As you can see from this brief and incomplete analysis, attaching a voice-stress analyzer to your computer does not solve problems. Quite the contrary: It introduces another problem. It requires that you assess the information. The value of the information depends on how well you can analyze it. There is no doubt, though, that voice-stress analyzers are coming more and more into use. Frequently, they have the application described by one man who uses a voice-stress analyzer in all of his business and other public negotiations. He said:

"When I see stress, I am alerted to the need for caution. I must try to find out why."

We have explored this political and economic use of computers to point up some essential facts. The machine is only as good as its information *and your judgment of that information.* The thing to remember is that a computer amplifies information. Depending on how you use it, the machine will filter out some things while concentrating on certain other things. That is a matter of how it is programmed—for which we have some relatively simple solutions in this book. Just keep in mind that computers amplify. Without discrete and intelligent intervention on your part, your computer may give you nothing but loud "noise."

3
Meet Your New Machine

The Apple II computer. Here is a personal computer system with keyboard and CRT. The computer is in the foreground cabinet with the keyboard. The display screen is a standard TV set. The top of the computer cabinet lifts off, giving access to the plug-in components. *Photo courtesy of Apple Computers*

The Atari 400 computer. This personal computer system uses a cassette tape recorder as external storage. The CRT is a special unit providing both capital and lower-case letters in a large dot-matrix system. *Photo courtesy of Atari Computers*

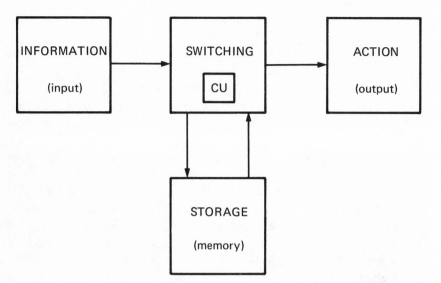

Your personal computer. A keyboard much like that of a typewriter at INFORMATION; a screen similar to that of your TV at ACTION; a disk driver or cassette tape recorder linked by cables to an insulated box containing switches and lights. Note that we have changed the accepted labels in order to give you a better handle on what your machine does.

This is your personal computer. It looks much like a typewriter and may weigh less than a portable. It has a keyboard similar to that of an electric typewriter and, yes, you can use it if you only "hunt and peck." It is hooked to a cathode ray tube (CRT for short) with a screen like that of your TV. We don't mind a bit if you call your CRT a screen. In fact, we often prefer that.

Your new machine is also linked to a *disk driver* or to a *cassette tape recorder,* which you use for storage and recovery of information.

Look at the accompanying diagram. There are some clues in this diagram to one of the best-kept secrets in the computer business.

THIS MACHINE IS AN ASSEMBLY OF SWITCHES.

That's it. The simplest computer is an electric light with its wired-in power source and switch. The light tells you in which position the switch has been placed—on or off.

We are assuming that a switch in its simplest form is something very familiar to you—a door open or closed, which stops you or through which you can pass—a common, everyday device that you push, pull, turn, or toggle to control such things as lights, TV sets, and telephones.

Take the switch in your telephone. It works automatically when you lift the handset.

The switch in your TV is turned to select the tuning system for the channel you want to watch.

These are examples of what are called *two-state switches*. Even the multichannel TV switch is two-state at its roots because for any channel there is only an "on" or "off" condition. Your world has countless examples of such two-state switches. When the switch-activated device is "lit," "hot," or making appropriate noises, we say the thing has been "turned on" or simply is "on."

So it is with your computer. It's an assemblage of two-state switches that can be arranged in many patterns. And those patterns can be recognized. Just as when we recognize that the letter *s* stands for a sibilant sound, we also can say (because that's our choice) that one particular switch pattern stands for the letter *s*. This pattern will reproduce a letter *s* on your screen or on paper.

It's a code. It is *our* code because we have agreed on what the patterns represent.

Now, it's one thing to have a machine that can flip a lot of switches for you, but it's another thing to make a generally acceptable code that everyone can learn and use. That's a language. We'll get to the special languages of computers later. Just accept our promise here that we know of a computer language that will be easy for you to learn. The words in this computer language stand for things that are very close to their meanings in the language you already speak—English.

What we're concerned with here is that you need to know about the hardware that flips the switches.

Back when the first modern computers were being built, the designers went to much trouble making certain that the things could add numbers. The designers were driven by a powerful motive, the desire to build a machine that could handle more numbers than they felt they could hold in their heads. Right away, before they even got close to the automatic, electronic adding machine that they all had in mind, they were forced to face a very big problem.

How could they make the thing automatic?

To do this, they had to build in a selective storage system. That raised a new problem: the need for the machine to "write" things internally into temporary storage. Then there had to be a way to select particular automatic operations. Thus, the keyboard became the gadget of choice. That is why we begin your introduction with the keyboard. Let us assure you, however, that your keyboard is nothing more than a preselected arrangement of switches. Each time you press a key on your keyboard, that switch, *which you select,* turns on more switches for you. This gives you a place to enter the machine's preset, built-in switch patterns.

Everything a computer does is based on the simple fact that a switch can be turned on or off. Always keep in mind that computers respond to only one thing: the presence or absence of electrical currents. This *presence* or *absence* is controlled by switches.

This is a primary reason why we have changed the more commonly used labels in the boxes of our diagram. We want you to have firm handles on what happens in your machine. Take the time now to impress this diagram upon your memory.

The box that we have labeled INFORMATION is commonly called INPUT. We, too, will often call it INPUT, making our usage agree with what you will read in your manufacturer's manual. What we want to emphasize is that you put information into the machine here—in small bits and strings.

The box we call SWITCHING is sometimes called PROCESSING. We want you to remember at all times that what you're doing is flipping switches, not canning peaches or making lumber—although a computer can help control those kinds of "processing."

You will notice a smaller "CU" box inside the SWITCHING box. We'll explain that one presently.

The ACTION box is often called OUTPUT. We want you to remember that this is where your machine does something. The machine does things automatically, and its results come out here as symbols on a screen, words printed on paper, or control of some other device.

STORAGE in our diagram is most often called MEMORY. We think that is a serious error. Computer STORAGE is only remotely similar to your human memory, usually faster in response but far more limited. We'll go into some very enlightening comparisons in a later chapter.

Before we go on, it's obvious that there are things about computer languages and the English language we must use in this book that require our special attention.

We've already indicated that you'll be learning some new words, those in the diagram for example, and others that are mostly a special kind of shorthand. You may already use similar shorthand tricks if you write such things as *nr* for "near" or *w* for "with." Good examples of such computer jargon are CPU for "central processing unit" or CLK for "clock." You should not have any trouble with such terms because we're going to explain them carefully as we go along, and the jargon will always contain some letters of an original word that you will know.

Occasionally, it will make things easier for us if we are allowed to bring up a few specialty words, such as *anthropomorphic*. This is like a longer switch pattern to which we can give a shorter *code* meaning. The longer pattern for *anthropomorphic* is "things that are confined to human shape or human behavior."

Because of a bad habit that has developed around the manufacture and programming of computers, we must use anthropomorphic words to describe what goes on in these curious machines. Kicking and screaming, we will go along with that bad habit. The necessity to use these anthropomorphic words, such as *memory* and *decision* and *talk* and *write* and the like, is equivalent to saying we will have to write this book in English. The illusions carried in this jargon have been welded to the machine.

DON'T LET YOUR FAMILIARITY WITH SUCH WORDS FOOL YOU.

Your computer has no *will*. It does not *think*. It is not *conscious*. It does not *know* anything. It does not *want*. It does not *plan*.

Think for a minute about what you do when you plan. You use language according to your own judgments. Your judgment controls what you include in your plan. But more than that, you remake your plan to fit new information and the new demands that develop out of your plan— more and more complex judgments. This is a high level of information juggling, which requires that you create new theories and that you test such personal creations outside the simulation play of your computer.

To say that your computer *knows* it's time to add *A* to *B* and store the answer in *C* is about the same as saying that when you're drunk, your car knows the way home. Both thoughts are dangerous; we don't want you telling your friends that we said computers *know* anything.

When you put a prejudice into a computer, what you get out the other side is a prejudice that has come through a computer.

In a very real sense your computer tells you what you order it to tell you. Computers do not "disagree" with their programmers.

A computer is simply a tool that handles information. The information is given to it in ways that it has been built to store and use. It uses the information according to your plan. You turn over to the machine the things it can do rapidly and automatically. What the computer does with your information can range from nothing (usually frustrating to you) to everything, which is our term for a computer "going berserk"—paper flipping out onto the floor, tapes spinning, a lot of random nonsense flashing on the screen—again, a source of frustration, but not a "computer error."

At the heart of all this comparison between you and the machine is a little-understood faculty that, no matter how we cut it, cannot be included in our diagram: EMOTION. It can be argued that people employ logic and intuition (which may not be labels for the same thing), but emotion is something altogether different. Emotion goads you to action. Computers don't have such a self-starter. You are what starts a computer.

What we have paused to discuss right now is probably the single most important barrier to the widespread useful development of individual computers. It involves a lot of people blathering about their fears of "computer intelligence." According to this scare story, "computer intelligence will win out someday over human intelligence, and then we're all going to be in deep trouble."

That makes good science fiction drama, but it ain't gonna happen. Just the briefest comparison between the computer and your brain exposes the idiocy of this scare story. Each computer switch has only 2 interconnections, whereas your dendrites (the equivalent switch branchings in your brain) can have as many as 300,000 interconnections. This is a difference of enormous magnitude. The comparison also presupposes something else not in evidence: that your brain's functions can be reduced to mechanical rules.

But the idea of intelligence has been tied up with our brains for so long it has come to have *only* a human definition. Ruling out our own snobbery about that definition may be the biggest barrier standing in the way of a workable description of what your computer does. It was a serious mistake to use those anthropomorphic words in describing the things this machine does. It was such a serious error that we intend to return several times to this critical analysis.

For the foregoing reasons, and for other reasons, the labels we attach to computers, to the things done by them and by their accessories, are often confusing if not misleading. Seemingly conventional uses of language are at the core of the problem.

Sometimes you can identify a computer attachment in a simple, direct way. The keyboard, for example. This is an INPUT device. That means that with it you can put things into your computer.

The screen is another example. This is an OUTPUT device. That means this is an attachment by which computer SWITCHING sends signals to you. It is geared to your abilities.

But now consider a cassette tape recorder attached to your computer. It can be called a STORAGE device. It is also both an INPUT and OUTPUT device. You can "play" things into the computer from it. You also can "record" things from the computer onto the cassette's tape. You need a specific interpreting system to do this. If you play one of your computer tapes over your stereo system, you will hear bursts of beeps and gurgles and other strange sounds.

Then there is SWITCHING itself, the core of your computer. This, too, is both an INPUT and OUTPUT device.

That is why we want you to put all the anthropomorphic nonsense out of your head while you study our diagram from an operational viewpoint. What is the thing doing at any given moment? Any label then becomes only a temporary signal to you. Your attention is focused where it ought to be—on what the thing is doing.

There is one other critical fact worth mentioning: You often will see the word *computer* used where SWITCHING (the PROCESSOR) is meant. Try not to be too hard on people who do this. You might even say that *we* are doing it when we tell you that things are "put into your computer" and what we're actually doing is describing the uses of the keyboard. Technically, the keyboard is part of the computer itself. We hope that you are adaptable to the jargon and that you see the value of our operational approach to labels.

We know that we are entering a time of wild confusion where our human brain *and* computers are concerned. Most present approaches to this confusion are dominated by the idea that a single unchanging law (or rule) can be found at the root of everything in our universe. That is the province of religion, not of logic. And computers remain logic machines no matter how "intelligent" you may believe them to be. Use the funny words if you must, but depend only on the operational labels as laid out in our diagram:

> INFORMATION
> SWITCHING
> ACTION
> STORAGE

Those are the things your machine can handle at your command.

Go back to the diagram now and look at that small box in SWITCH-

ING. That "CU" is the central working area of your computer, often called a CPU (for central processing unit) or MPU (for microprocessing unit). That sounds as exotic as a Chinese recipe, but you already have the key to it: No matter what we call it, the thing is just switching electrical currents on and off.

At the heart of SWITCHING are silicon chips containing very tiny (microminiature) electrical circuits—wires and electronic switches. The comparison is often made between computer SWITCHING and a railroad switchyard. If you allow for a very complex yard, this is a useful comparison. Each branch line in your computer takes trains of electrical switch patterns. You can imagine a "yardmaster" obeying your commands to make up trains of different lengths and carrying different "cargoes." These are different combinations of *bytes* (which we will explain presently).

All of this SWITCHING and mingling of branch lines is regulated by your computer's *control unit* (CU), the "yardmaster." This unit, sometimes called simply the CONTROLLER, is to SWITCHING as SWITCHING is to your entire computer. It is the "wheeler-dealer" behind the whole operation, the thing which causes every internal activity of which your computer is capable. The CU is directly tied to STORAGE and makes use of an arithmetic logic unit (ALU), which we have not indicated on the diagram. This is a most essential piece of business, which we will be coming back to after explaining bytes. For now, just remember where it is—in the CU, or attached to the CU, and both of them in SWITCHING.

The diagram relates the basic devices you can use to assemble, disassemble, and reassemble your trains. With these devices you can form enormously complex patterns of trains moving through your switchyard.

The orderly movement of your trains is accomplished by subdividing SWITCHING into many sections. This is necessary because the system acts on only one instruction at a time and because SWITCHING can interact with STORAGE in random ways.

All such movement is conducted in *bits* and *bytes*.

Bit stands for "binary digit," the smallest unit of information that your computer can use—one switch in an "on" or "off" position, indicating a "1" or a "0." (The "binary" system carried in those 1s and 0s is actually very simple, and we'll get to that, too. One step at a time.)

A byte is eight bits in a string. The reason for this particular number will become clear as we proceed. All you need to know right now is that a bit is the smallest response unit of your computer, and a byte is eight of those tiny units. Each bit is a "1" or a "0," and eight "1s" and "0s" in a train are a byte.

At the core of your CU is a synchronizing pulse, a counting system: "Now you, now you, now you," etc.

This pulse regulates the timing of each thing the yardmaster does in making up the trains. The CU holds everything to a steady, although very rapid, pace. To give you some idea of that pace, at four million cycles a second (a common pulse rate), a computer could handle four million bytes a second. That's four million actions every second.

Perhaps now you can begin to understand what we mean when we call the computer "a time cruncher." Pause for a moment and consider that. If a computer had your time sense, it would be as though it accepted your problem, followed your instructions to produce an answer, and then had to wait seven or eight years for you to pick up the answer and get on to the next instruction. If you took a few minutes to read a "printout" while composing the next steps in your head, the computer would be counting off a wait of centuries. And that's for computers with millionth-of-a-second responses. Computers are now in the works with trillionth-of-a-second responses.

Your first computer probably will accept only one byte at a time, eight of those 1s and 0s in a string. It is said to have "an eight-bit format." Each byte can contain one piece of useful information (an instruction) used by SWITCHING. SWITCHING uses a byte's pattern to transmit a particular instruction. "01100110" is not the same instruction as "01000110." How those patterns are set up in the simplest switching arrangement is the internal vocabulary (the machine language or instruction set) of your machine. This language sets up all of the possible things your computer can do. When the switch pattern for one of those machine instructions is in the CU, an automatic sequence of events is started. This is the way your computer talks to itself. You don't need any knowledge at all of that vocabulary. You just need to know that it's there and will respond to your commands.

The different ways those eight bits can be arranged give you 256 combinations $(2 \times 2 \times 2 \times 2 \times 2 \times 2 \times 2 \times 2)$. This does not mean there are 256 basic instructions in your computer's vocabulary. Many instructions are duplicates using a different group of switches. Most eight-bit formats provide fewer than 80 different sorts of instructions. That's pretty impressive when you consider the variety of things your computer can do.

Many computers are built with more than eight bits in their basic format. However, such machines are generally set up with a section that deals with eight bits. This lets them *talk* to eight-bit computers. Even with an eight-bit limit, there's another way your computer can share more complex information and instruction with larger machines. It can, for example, be rigged to simulate sixteen digits. What we're saying is that an eight-bit computer, used imaginatively, has an extremely large potential.

Let's make a quick review of that first diagram now. Time spent with it here will be time saved later. The diagram illustrates relationships within a machine that does something (ACTION or OUTPUT) in a predictable way. It does this when you do something at the INFORMA-TION (INPUT) stage—either when you type on a keyboard or activate an attachment to the machine.

All of the problems you put into your computer are broken down by it into arithmetical steps—the bits and bytes—everything controlled by the hardware and the programs.

This brings us to the arithmetic logic unit (ALU), which we noted earlier is closely linked to SWITCHING. The ALU is at the heart of the controller. In most machines the ALU can add, subtract, complement (change 1s and 0s) negate, and rotate (push selected contents of STOR-AGE to the left or the right), and here is where your computer deals with AND and OR. These are the most important instructions you can program into your machine. Remember these things that the ALU lets your computer do:

SUBTRACT
MULTIPLY
ADD
DIVIDE
COMPARE

Just like the control unit that directs it, the ALU accepts only one instruction at a time. This is an extremely important thing for you to remember. In a sense, SWITCHING and all of its components contain a large number of mazes, all obedient to a simple on-off code and always operating just one action at a time, one track at a time—certainly a fast track, but we hope you're beginning to sense its limits.

What separates your computer from all previous attempts to make such a machine is its ability to work automatically. One reason it can do this is found in its ability to store instructions and partial answers. This is a most vital function of STORAGE. Your machine can set aside the required parts of a problem and come back to them when they are needed *in the logical steps of a solution.*

If your program carries the right instructions, the computer will even adjust to some changes—"if this happens, then do that"—all through the process of solving a problem you have given to it.

Because these things have been built into it, your computer takes your original INFORMATION and puts it through long strings of SWITCHING/STORAGE mixtures with marvelous rapidity. You never need to look in on what your computer is doing until the answer(s) pop out at ACTION. All you have to do is feed it the INFORMATION and push the key that tells the machine the information is there. The hardware and the program(s) do the rest.

The ACTION may be presented to you in a wide variety of ways: displayed on a dial or other indicator, printed or punched on paper, plotted on graph paper, flashed as lighted symbols on a CRT, spoken aloud through a speech simulator, presented as raised Braille dots for the blind, or as a change in some control mechanism. The potential is enormous.

Just remember that when you get to the level of the electronic gadgets in SWITCHING, there's nothing more complicated than a refrigerator light and its push-button switch that turns off the light when you close the door. All of the electronic gadgetry is just various mixtures of two-position switches. In one way or another, each switch is controlled by a train of other two-position switches. The train reaches back to an original INFORMATION and forward in a continuous line through more trains of two-position switches to a final response (ACTION).

These are the keys to how your machine handles numbers and symbols other than numbers. Keep in mind that it can switch on groups of tiny glowing spots that will appear on your screen. Those glowing spots can be made to merge and form any symbols you may require.

Given the logical limits it must follow, your computer's potential accuracy approaches absolute. It will not make arithmetical errors. Thus the symbols controlled by the internal arithmetical system will be a precise response to your instructions at the keyboard. If you require that kind of accuracy, this is your machine.

But don't let that fact go to your head. "GIGO" should be your constant reminder of human failing: "Garbage in—garbage out." The answers you get will be no more accurate than what you put in at INFORMATION. Your computer has to be directed by you or by a program that you set up through every step of a problem. You not only give it INFORMATION but what it is to do with your INFORMATION.

Depending on how you define them, all of this is done with fewer than a dozen electronic devices. The key is found in the fact that these devices can be wired together to produce a very large number of effects. And the number and variety of things you may automate in your computer is limited only by how many switches you want to string into how many trains and how you put together those trains.

SIMPLE STEPS—COMPLEX JOBS

At its roots the machine itself is simple. The wide variety of automated jobs it can do depends on the almost unlimited ways the available pieces can be put together. This elementary truth about computers guided the challenging format we chose for our book. We insist that the machine must fit your needs, not the other way around. And we are presenting what you need to know in a way that simulates the computer's own switch-oriented increased complexity. We are doing this to carry you along on a tide of increased understanding that will let you grasp and make your own those skills heretofore reserved for the elite few.

Review

You should now have a good start on the following jargon and, more important, what the named things do. Referring to the diagram where necessary, see if you can describe what is done by the following:

INFORMATION (INPUT)
SWITCHING (PROCESSOR)
CU (CPU or MPU)
ACTION (OUTPUT)
STORAGE (MEMORY)
ALU
CRT
Two-state switch
CLK

Can you explain the following terms?

dendrite
bit
byte
machine language

4

Intelligence

It is very common in computer texts to start with simple, basic ideas and then to inflate them until they completely lose touch with their roots. We already have exposed for you one of the engines driving this system—the desire to keep computers in the hands of an elite "priesthood." Another driving force in this is the computer industry's long refusal to reexamine some of its most prized ideas, the ideas concealed in their jargon, especially the arguments that the machine is somehow intelligent or capable of intelligence.

When applied to computers, the word *intelligence* is really a measure of automation, how much the computer can be programmed to do automatically during a run. This word *intelligence* is often introduced into computer jargon as a sales pitch. Apple computers, for example, calls its accessories Apple Intelligent Subsystems. From the semantic viewpoint, you can say, "That's not very smart." From an advertising department viewpoint, however, you have to agree that this goes along with current mythology.

Whether you accept the idea of "machine intelligence" depends in large part on how you define intelligence. As you probably know, one of the most common tests for this illusive factor in people is the Stanford Benet Intelligence Test. Who in our society has not heard of the "IQ Test"? Who has not been awed by such a statement as "She has an IQ of 180"?

Ahhhhh, but the insiders know something about IQ tests they don't often share: *What they test for is nothing more than an artificial concept they have called "IQ."*

IQ TESTS TEST "IQ"

That's it. The tests do not measure intelligence, not even "native intelligence," whatever that may be.

But the label "intelligence test" creates a marvelous illusion. It suggests that the testers understand the thing they are testing. After all, that thing has a name that is part of the test's own name: intelligence.

We all know what *intelligence* means, right?

Some of the IQ testers will admit that they don't understand intelligence. The most they will say is that their tests flit around the edges, giving an occasional foggy glimpse of something that may be intelligence.

Thus it is with these funny words that describe what computers do. They inflict us with illusions and with illusions built on illusions.

Intelligence has to be a measure of self-starting and success in the things you self-start. That is why, no matter the jargon, we keep returning to that operational question:

WHAT IS THE THING DOING?

We think it's vital that we face up to this problem at once because we are dealing here with the sudden and explosive growth of a vernacular.

Vernacular comes from a term used by the Roman historian, Marcus Terentius Varro (ca. 116–27 B.C.). Varro's term was *vernacula verba*. It was translated as "unilateral expressions used by slaves or serfs." This idea moved into other societies to mean, loosely, "the native language of an unlettered peasantry." A vernacular can often be identified by its grammatical simplicity, its "pidgin" character.

But there was no day in history when someone went to bed one night speaking either classical or vernacular Latin and woke up the next morning speaking French, Italian, or any other "Romance language." Those languages came about through the explosive demands of change—the very thing that's happening right now with computers and computer jargon.

In point of fact, French, Spanish, and Italian evolved from a mixed vernacular called Camp Latin. Camp Latin picked up valuable expressions in the field. The original language was modified by necessity—the necessity to say new things and the necessity to be understood by people who did not share the original linguistic tradition. Camp Latin was in a sense a "trade language," a compounded lingo worked out by camp followers and others as a domestic convenience between conqueror and slave, between native and invader, and for the use of travelers and merchants.

Such languages have occurred many times in our history. A good example was the language called Chinook, which originated in the Pacific Northwest of North America long before the first European arrived on the scene.

Chinook was a linguistic sponge that absorbed meanings and usages wherever and whenever they were needed for communication. It was the language of slaves and conquerors and of traders. When French trappers arrived, Chinook absorbed what it needed from French. When other Europeans came along, Chinook treated their languages the same way. It was impartial, taking on such words as *kitty* and *bouche* and making them its own. Prior to European contact Chinook had a word *hyas* (meaning "bigger," "louder," or "amplified"). *Kitty* entered Chinook as the name of that new thing, the domestic cat. This new thing altered an earlier meaning, and *hyas kitty* took over as the name of the mountain lion. *Bouche* is preserved today in the name of the Washington coastal community of La Push, which is at the *mouth* of several rivers. (*Bouche* means "mouth" in French. The indigenous people had no *b* sound; thus *push* was their closest approximation of *bouche*.)

We're sure you can see the connection between this brief historical excursion and what's happening right now in computer lingo. You can be sure that computer jargon will happen no matter what any of us may desire. It will grow out of necessity—a new vernacular. We have no argument with this. It is an exciting development, a sure sign of ferment and change. We are seeing the growth of a "trade language" not only between elite and elite but also between elite and you "invaders." What we want you to watch with care is the carrying over of misleading illusions into the new lingo. This has largely been an activity of the elitists, and we don't think it's very intelligent.

5

What's Your Name, Funny Machine?

At the start of writing this book, we entertained a personal conceit about what we should call computers. We were not the first people to face that problem.

Some people have called it the "organization machine." Not a bad idea. We'll discuss later some of the advantages found in using your computer as an organizer.

"Computer" was not the best choice, but we're stuck with it. That name suggests mathematics too strongly.

Some of the first computer users wanted to call it the "all-purpose machine" or the "everything machine." Very suggestive. After all, a computer is anything you can make it do.

We focused on the maze character of the internal switching system and went around for a time calling it the "maize machine." The pun on *maze* and the reference to corn were intended. Aside from the fact that it was a corny idea, there was some sense in it. Corn, as some of you may know, cannot survive or adapt without us. If people didn't plant and cross-pollinate corn, the plant, as we know it, would die out. We have developed what scientists call a "symbiotic relationship" with corn. It depends on us and we depend on it.

Well, that's the way it is with computers. Without our intervention, they are useless junk. We are the ones directing the computer evolution . . . and the computer revolution. We may use computers to help us do this, but we are doing it. We are responsible for what is happening.

We definitely do not want to call them "electronic brains." That is the most misleading name to come along. It is highly unlikely that computers ever will "think" the way you think, or that they will possess thought structures even vaguely similar to yours. People have experiences that a computer, by its very nature, cannot share.

The complexity of our universe necessitates animal adaptations (such as your brain), which can work without words. Some survival reactions must happen too fast for words to have any effect. But without words there can be no program. Without a program, your computer cannot communicate—with itself or with you.

Not a "brain," then.

Maize machine is too corny.

The "relativity machine," perhaps? After all, we do owe something to Einstein. And the computer is giving us a leg up in the multistep universe of relativity.

But that's kind of pretentious.

One thing certain in the name quest: Your interaction with your own computer will be unique, just as you are unique. You already have a whole bag of things you enjoy doing or want to do. You can very well decide to make your computer do things no one else has ever done with one. If you're a little whacko, your computer may very well do whacko things.

How do you put a name on that?

Names are important, though, and we should not give up too easily. And we have seen many computer specialists playing a remarkable identification game with the machine.

Each of these specialists imposes upon his computer a mirror image of his own personality. It's fascinating and well nigh universal. Psychologists call this "transference behavior." That means that the person gives to the machine a personality that originates in the user's unconscious.

Now, we all know (especially in our folk wisdom) that such behavior is not confined to "computer freaks." It can be seen in the man-auto relationship and in the ways we deal with other machines.

"Tin Lizzy" is not a chunk of metal devoid of personality!

Look at the popularity of individualized decoration on cars and the pet names people give them—even to painting the names on the cars or putting the names on license plates.

We know of a milling machine operator who calls his machine Esmerelda. Why? "Because it performs better when I call it by name."

This has a great deal to do with naming the device because people seldom observe the other side of the coin: *How you identify the machine determines how you will use the machine.*

Computers are extremely susceptible to this unconscious "name game." SWITCHING works so fast that it can create an illusion of human behavior. But the thing is still just switches and electric currents. Illusion remains illusion.

How about calling it the "illusion machine"?

This ability with creative illusion is at once a danger and one of the most attractive characteristics of computers. When we get into the section of this book dealing with images on screens, you will understand even more of that fascination with creating illusions that correspond to our "real world." One of the most exciting things about computer screens has to be that ability to create illusions of reality.

But there is a gossamer and transparent quality to such creations. Just for the preservation of your sanity they require that you think "illusion . . . illusion . . . illusion . . ." When the play is over, you come back to a quite different world.

We suspect, however, that the interaction between illusion and what we call "reality" will undergo profound changes because of computers. Many philosophers have warned us that reality, too, has a way of shifting under our feet. Let's just remember that yesterday's reality is today's illusion. It's worth noting that when unworkable illusions merge with whatever we're currently calling reality, that's a good definition of insanity.

There's something in this, though. We all know that the closer we bring our illusions to the way the universe performs around and within us (based on a hard reading of consequences), the better we are at predicting what's going to happen next. Accurate prediction, after all, is the real name of the scientific game.

Should we call it the "prediction machine," then? Or perhaps "reality machine"?

They sound even cornier than "maize machine."

Let's get back to the fact that this device is a tool, and by the best operational definition it is anything you can make it do. Let's go ahead and be a little bit anthropomorphic, as long as it's all in fun. And let's name it in a way that keeps the thing in its place. Let's call it "Hey, you!" or anything else that suits you at the moment you're using it.

One more thing in this same vein. Just to make very sure that you keep the relationship between you and your computer in the proper perspective, the first time you prepare to use it, stand there for a moment and address it sternly. Say, "You stupid, inanimate chunk of hardware! Without me, you're nothing!"

We guarantee that unless somebody is playing a very difficult joke on you, your computer will not answer back. After all, computers don't argue; they just don't forgive.

6

Inside Information

For this next step you should have your own small computer or have access to one. We are going to take you on a guided tour under the lid of the computer. Don't be afraid. Your friendly native guides will protect you from all the dangerous flora and fauna in here. All you really need is a general understanding of what's under that lid. This also gives us an excuse to familiarize you with some of the buzzwords behind which the "experts" are hiding.

First, unplug the machine. An electrical shock is at least a painful experience, and we want this tour to be enjoyable. Now, following the manufacturer's instructions, take off the lid, which conceals and protects the "working parts" of the computer.

The biggest box under that lid will be a large container (usually metal) that encloses the power supply. The contents of this box feed a constant, steady electrical current into the computer. Your TV and radio have similar devices, but they are not designed to quite the tight requirements of your computer. Don't try to open the power supply box unless you're deeply into electronics. Just understand that this is what changes your household electricity into "juice" that the computer can use.

Your computer itself and the essential parts are mounted on a thin plastic board (most often green, black, or rust brown) manufactured by a photographic and etching method that leaves plated copper lines sealed on both surfaces of the board. Those lines are the "wires" of your computer.

If you look closely at this plastic board, you will see little metal dots here and there on the plated copper lines. These are dollops of solder at

Vertical view of computer. With lid removed, the inner works of an Apple II computer are revealed. The large metal box at left is the power supply. RAM and ROM chips plug into the printed circuit board. Note that the keyboard reveals a strong similarity to that of a portable typewriter. *Photo courtesy Apple computers*

points where circuits go from one surface of the board to the other surface. The dots mark the places where your computer's electrical lines cross.

At some location on the plastic board you will see a series of thin parallel "wires"—all of the lines fairly close together and in stacked rows. The presence of these rows locates the internal STORAGE area of your computer. The small rectangular boxes in this area contain the switches with which the computer juggles its signals.

Those little boxes are called "chips" in the computer industry. A chip is a plastic sandwich in a very small package. Sealed in it are a great many very slender imprinted "wires" and electronic switches. Some of those switches are stuck in one position—on or off (a 1 or a 0). The preset patterns of those switches, either stuck or changeable, identify what that particular chip can do.

One of the largest chips under here will be the *microprocessor,* SWITCHING in our first diagram. You already know what happens in this box.

A code number on each chip identifies the manufacturer and what the chip does. Some of them also may be identified as ROM or RAM. We'll explain that presently.

Remember that your computer is basically a juggler of coded signals. In a sense, all of those signals are sent darting around through a maze, and they are always subject to a simple on-off code. Long sequences of such juggling are carried out automatically in these chips. The internal STORAGE holds an essential key to how your computer solves your problems. Note the RAM and ROM.

RAM stands for *random-access memory.*

ROM stands for *read-only memory.*

Aside from the fact that STORAGE is only remotely comparable to your memory, this computer jargon is even more misleading. Both RAM and ROM can really be used as random-access devices. Furthermore, both can be described accurately as *direct-access* devices. The really distinguishing thing about ROM is that it is *permanent* storage.

Your friendly native guides will now try to lead you through this dangerous part of the computer jungle. Stay close and pay very strict attention. If you fall off, you're on your own.

What *random* really means here is "non-predeterminable." There is no way for you to know in advance which switch or which pattern of switches in RAM will be selected for a particular job. It makes no difference how you identify any particular bundle of switches here. They

48k RAM board. This printed circuit board (PCB) contains part of a computer's circuitry that can be plugged into an S-100 bus system. This board holds the "read and write" portion of internal storage (RAM). *Photo courtesy Vector Graphic, Inc.*

can be numbers one time and letters another time. The pattern that you label "stroganoff" today can be "violin" tomorrow and "$E = mc^2$" the day after.

ROM on the other hand really stands for "stuck switch." It's as though the light switch on your wall were always either "on" or "off," always locked down in a preset pattern. Your computer cannot change that pattern, it can only read the pattern, only respond to the pattern.

Keep in mind that your computer does everything, even printing letters, by the numbers. Every switch has a number attached to it. And you are sitting there giving this machine commands to shift information around—move this over there; find that thing; compare these items; select the biggest, the smallest, the longest, the shortest; find the stored meaning for that word . . . a great many commands.

Since important information must be taken from one place and put into another place, your computer makes temporary copies in RAM. The bits and bytes go in here. You will recall that if the same sequence and number of switches are always used for a specific symbol, then you not only can identify (decode) that symbol (repeat it correctly every time), but you also will know where each symbol starts and stops just by how many switches have been used since the start of the message. For the math-minded among you, it requires seven two-position switches to give you a different on-off code for one hundred different symbols—a powerful "alphabet." With one extra switch for important internal instructions, this gives you eight switches per symbol—one of the reasons there are eight bits in a byte.

But now you are finished working with your computer, all answers received, all the important stuff stored on tape or disk or paper. You turn off your computer. RAM is gone—instant amnesia. Ahhh, but ROM remains. The switches are stuck, remember? And the next time you fire up your computer, the basic patterns for operating your computer are already there in ROM.

Very handy.

However all of that *randomity* makes it necessary that you use addresses when you're operating this machine. *By the numbers*—never forget it. The addresses are easy, and your computer will store them for you if you like. We'll *address* this more directly in the section on programming.

Meanwhile, more about what happens in ROM and RAM.

Fixed patterns are available to you in ROM in what is called a *random selective process*. That means that whenever your computer needs a particular thing that has been stored in ROM, that thing can be yanked out at random. You do not need to know in advance where that thing has been stored.

With RAM, on the other hand, your computer can both store and pick up a switch pattern at any convenient and available position. You have direct access to any place in RAM—both in and out.

We suggest that you think of RAM as "read and write." Your computer can store patterns there temporarily and within the system's mechanical limits while it moves other patterns around. ROM can only be read. ROM is where the "machine language" is stored so that it won't be lost.

We attach a little analysis now to remove the confusion from RAM and ROM. Confusion is assured by the fact that *both RAMs and ROMs are random access devices.*

The first "memories" were the read *and* write variety still known as RAMs. The label *random access* described the conceptual breakthrough for internal storage devices. Any of a large number of storage places could be used as long as each place had its own unique *address.* This meant you could store many different things in different places and get anyone of them back when needed just by knowing *where* it was stored. Things could be retrieved in any order, and this feature became the basis for the name: *random* access. You could select any piece of stored information at any time.

Then came nondestroyable storage and a dilemma. Now, the distinction was not *how* the information was used but whether you could write on it. This produced the name *read* only (ROM, or Read Only Memory) for the device you could not write over.

We think one of the computer industry's biggest blunders was to hide its mistakes behind a cloak of incoherent jargon. With the realization that even ROM was a random access device they should have changed the name of the writable memory to reflect its writability. (Perhaps RAW for read *and* write.)

Now, what do you really need to know about all of this stuff under the lid? What it does in a general way. While we're here, then, we're going to make a short side trip from the keyboard to the screen.

This is what happens when you hit a key and see the proper symbol displayed on your screen:

Hitting the key sends a signal to the controller. That signal is stored in RAM until the controller refers to a machine language instruction in ROM that tells it to test the switch and make sure that a key has actually been hit. If the answer is *no,* the controller may consult some other machine language instruction to see if perhaps something else has happened.

In any event, the controller will eventually come around full circle and test the switch again until it finds that *yes,* a key has indeed been hit. The controller then leaves the circle and copies into RAM (temporary storage) the switch positions identifying the key you hit. The controller then finds the location in STORAGE where the identities of the switch position are kept. The controller compares and identifies that pattern and then copies the identified pattern into another temporary storage position. Finally, the temporary positions are sent out to your screen's controller, which uses those patterns to place dots in a familiar shape on your screen.

Voila! You see the letter on the screen.

All of these activities take place in the tiniest fraction of a second. As far as your own observations are concerned, the machine's reaction is instantaneous—which should give you an insight into the concept of relativity.

As you can see, temporary storage is vital to what these chips do.

This may be more than you bargained for when you joined our safari under the lid, but we warned you that we would use this as an excuse to familiarize you with more of the jargon. There's still a way to go before we're out of the jungle.

Somewhere in here will be a block of plastic enclosing a crystal. It may only be identified by some code numbers, but it is in here. This is the heart of a system whose pulses synchronize all of your computer's operations. It is called a "clock," and the jargon beasts have done it again.

This "clock" is really a very fast metronome that operates at several million beats a second. Calling it a clock confuses it with a time clock or the kind of clock that could tell you the time of day. We think a real clock, the kind that records the time of day, should be incorporated in every computer, but we'll go into that later.

All of the chips are plugged into your computer's board by rows of pins that go all the way through the board, making contact on both sides. This makes for easier replacement and upgrading.

Somewhere near an edge of the board you may find a row of long plastic receptacles with slots of brass connectors down the center. These are INPUT/OUTPUT connectors, where you can plug in other boards for special jobs.

These are called "I/O ports."

I/O ports are described as being "on a common bus." That has nothing to do with rapid transit. *Bus* here means pathways for signals that have something in common. A bus is made up of conductors. (No! Not bus conductors! You see what happens with language?) These are *conductors* of electrical current. They are communications tracks between switch points, nothing more.

You will most commonly hear about three "buses" in computers— *data bus, address bus,* and *control bus.*

The data bus is where information flows.

The address bus leads to stored information *by the numbers.*

The control bus sends signals to different parts of the computer *according to your instructions.*

Here's another word the jargon beasts have inflicted us with: *interface.* You'll find computer interfaces under this lid.

Sociologists, psychologists, political "scientists"—almost every specialty in academe—have leaped onto this word with unholy glee. Ignore them. For your purposes, interface describes a device that matches one part of your computer with another part, however that match is managed. There can be a "TV interface" that lets you use your household TV as a computer screen. There can be a "tape interface" that lets you use a cassette recorder as an external storage device. There is a "keyboard interface" that lets your typewriter-style keyboard interact with the other parts of the computer. In computer usages alone, "interfaces" are already legion, and there's no end in sight.

Some of the chips under this lid contain transistors that are first cousins to those in your TV, your radio, and your stereo amplifier. Most of the transistors are just used in amplifiers to transmit trains of information through your computer. We tell you this to reassure you that all of the fauna under this lid are not alien.

By now you have noted that several parts on your computer's board have names printed on them. Take a closer look. You may see such labels as "Game IO," "Color Trim," or "Memory Select." Those names should not give you any trouble. What happens in there happens "at night."

For you electronics aficionados, the small resistors and capacitors you see attached to the computer board serve mostly to tie in the interfaces and match the timing circuits. (The rest of you did not hear us say that.) Exquisitely precise timing and tuning are an absolute requirement of computers.

Two more things under the lid are worth mentioning: a *character generator* and a *keyboard encoder chip*. They may be identified by name. The character generator translates computer signals into numbers, letters, and other readable (by you) symbols. The keyboard encoder chip takes the signals from your keyboard and translates them into patterns your computer can use.

Now close the lid. The truth is, everything under that lid "happens at night." However, we hope you understand a bit more of the jargon.

Review

Can you identify the following?
power supply
chip
ROM
RAM
machine language
random
clock
I/O port
bus
data bus
address bus
control bus
interface

7

History Without Hysteria

You should now have a beginning familiarity with the basic outline of how your computer works. That gives you the building blocks upon which we can add the other skills you will need. You should also have by now a pretty strong motivation to make this new tool a part of your life. As you now know, the principles of computer design are actually quite simple. Those simple elements can be mixed in a way that makes complex patterns, but no single step is beyond your understanding.

Reflect a moment on what your computer does:

1. It manipulates symbols according to preset rules.

2. It accepts and stores information, *and* it does the same thing with the rules.

3. It shows you its results.

4. It does all of this by flipping switches.

Nothing in that is overly difficult, and there is no need for us to increase the difficulty.

With that in mind, we are now going to digress for a brief history of computer evolution. If you already know that history, move on to the next chapter. Nothing in this historical excursion is absolutely essential to you. However, let us emphasize our reasons for introducing the history at this point:

If you know where you've been, it's easier to locate where you are now and where you can go.

History evokes an interesting insight into a pattern that people have repeated many times. We want to arm your intelligence with that raw material.

The Greeks had a combined calculator and astrolabe for navigation by at least 86 B.C. But artificial calculation is much older, as old as mankind's first awareness that we could count on our fingers and toes. In fact, there is an even more elemental bodily counting system called *Syriac,* which is based on 2s and 4s because we have two hands and two feet. Some South American tribes still give specific names to particular number groups in a Syriac system: 5 is "one hand," 10 is "two hands," 15 is "two hands and a foot," and 20 is "two hands and two feet." It has been suggested that this system is the origin of our own word "fourscore" for 80, 4 times 20 (a "score").

The Romans used counters made of pebbles or bits of glass, bone, or ivory. The Latin word for such counters is *calculi.* The Greeks employed a counting board or table with grooves or lines on it where the markers were put down according to place value. They called this an *abakion.* The Romans called such devices *abaci.*

This system is known to have been used in very ancient times all through the Middle East, India, and Africa. In fact, there are several "pebble games" still popular in Africa that can be traced back to this method of calculating.

In the New World the Mayans used a similar system with grains of corn strung on threads in rows of ten.

As you can see, all such devices are based on the ten fingers of the human hand. We know this device today as an *abacus.*

Of course the abacus is not properly a computer; it is a calculator, an ancestor of computers. The linguistic marker is there in our modern language, however, tied to our past by the same kinds of strings we can find in the word *computer* itself. That, too, comes from Latin—*com* and *putare,* meaning "to reckon with." (You had better believe that you will have to reckon with computers in your lifetime.)

The fact that *abacus* and *calculation* are still meaningful and important parts of our language points to another historical fact sometimes overlooked: The persistence of abacus calculating systems through the Dark Ages and Middle Ages. That persistence tells us how it was possible for our ancestors to perform quite involved mathematical operations while still using Roman numerals. We know that the Arabic notation with its zero and decimal-place rules was a relative latecomer. It is quite obvious that our ancestors did their actual calculations with "counting tables" or the equivalent. Roman numerals were used merely to note the results.

It's useful to understand this evolutionary trail because the calculating methods, the "mental tools," of those times persist today. Just as you can detect trial and error in those ancestral systems, with the survival of the most useful (or most commonly used) systems, the same sort of thing is happening today. Apparently, it has always been that way in the evolution of our tools.

The French philosopher and mathematician Blaise Pascal (1623–1662) built a gear-based machine for adding numbers. His machine, which he called *La Pascaline,* was interesting but impractical, too early for the mechanical abilities of 1642, when it was built.

However, interest in such devices cropped up frequently all through this period. Gottfried Willhelm von Leibniz (1646–1716), the German inventor of calculus, put his considerable talents to the problem in 1694. He built a machine that he called a "step reckoner," an improved version of Pascal's device. It could add, subtract, multiply, and divide. It also could extract square roots by repeated additions—which is exactly what modern computers do with such problems.

Leibniz's machine, too, was ahead of the mechanical abilities of his time. The "step reckoner" proved unreliable, although it demonstrated where the shortcomings were and it projected a time when a successful version of this machine could be made.

It wasn't until 1835 that Charles Babbage (1792–1871) solved the Pascal problem. Babbage, an English banker's son and self-taught mathematician, was a pioneer in what we call "operations research" today. With British government financing, Babbage built an "analytical engine." It not only performed the calculations of the Leibniz machine, but was a true programmable computer. It combined arithmetical and logical functions, and it was capable of storing partial answers for later use.

Babbage's "engine" could compare quantities and perform different instructions according to preset programs. It could execute very complex sequences of automatic operations, using punch cards, gears, levers and cams. Although its storage system was limited, the Babbage machine went a bit farther into esoteric functions than you might have expected from the available hardware of his age. Babbage did this by employing the punch-card system then in use for controlling the looms of textile mills. Punch cards controlled the sequence of numbers in his device.

Essentially, Babbage's technique is the same basic principle that has been carried over into today's high-speed computers. Babbage died before completing the machine to his own satisfaction. Still unfinished, it is preserved in a London museum—an instrument that anticipated today's computers.

In those parts of the world then in technological ferment, Babbage's work and its implications spread rapidly. Automatic tabulation of complex information was of particular interest to Hans Hollerith in the United States—particularly as it applied to the census. It was estimated that the information to be gathered by the 1890 U.S. census would require fourteen years to tabulate by hand.

Hollerith put together a census system in 1890 that scanned the data of that year through punch cards and electromechanical (electrical contacts) operations. His system cut tabulation time to less than half that required by the census just ten years earlier. On the basis of this success, Hollerith founded a company that eventually merged with others to become International Business Machines (IBM).

Developments in this field moved with relative slowness until 1939, when Harvard's Howard Aiken signed an agreement with IBM to build MARK I, the first automatic digital computer. It still operated electromechanically, and its noisy relay switches sounded like an auditorium full of tin crickets.

IBM failed to see the advantages of shifting to electronic switches and was not in on the development of ENIAC, the first fully electronic computer. ENIAC was the brainchild of John Mauchly and J. Presper Eckert at the University of Pennsylvania. It operated silently and thousands of times faster than MARK I. However, ENIAC was based on the vacuum tube, and this produced its own tremendous problems: heat and frequent breakdown, all adding to the high cost. ENIAC was also a complex monster; you had to rewire it for each new set of instructions.

The cost barrier was not broken until the 1960s, when transistors began to take over. Transistors and photoetching techniques also opened the door to miniaturization, and this brought on the rush of hand-held calculators. We'll deal with calculators in more detail in the next chapter, but there's an important historical fact worth noting here.

One of the reasons calculators came on the scene so rapidly and computers have been relatively slow gaining speed is that by the time calculators happened, all of the computer technology was already in hand. Even though the calculator in its hand-held version happened chronologically much after computers, the whole stage was ready for it. All that was really required was a set of standards.

At the beginning of the Computer Age there were no standards. However, automation was seen as desirable. Many different approaches to the computer/calculator automation problem were tried, and most fell by the wayside. At best, the early devices were large, clumsy, handmade, and mechanical. Early computers were hand-wired, disjointed patchworks of resistors, capacitors, and more or less continually failing vacuum tubes. Each new set of instructions required that the whole mess be rewired. Nobody would ever have made the mistake of calling those early devices "intelligent."

One of the first standards to evolve in the infant industry resulted from the decision to go for reliability: adoption of the binary system. We'll deal with this in a later chapter. All you need to know, really, is that this binary system uses numbers based on 2 instead of on the traditional 10.

The decision to go binary was made independently by many people and with the usual reluctance to choose any one method over the others in fear that you would throw out the baby with the bathwater. Most of the holdouts remained so deeply entangled in the mechanics of trying to keep their systems reliable that they never got down to solving other problems.

The binary system, with its natural affinity for the two-state switch, gave us a basic building block. From that designers could dream up an infinite variety. No matter the immediate problem, it was now known that if the digital computer were to evolve into a useful tool, anything connected to it (including you) had to be capable of handling binary information in some way. Anything transferred to or from the computer had to be converted to binary form. (For those of you who insist on sticking to the decimal system, most computers can do the binary translation internally.)

Certain physical things began to happen in computer design as a result of this landmark decision. Key functions became standardized. The number 2 and its successive multiples became the starting point for determining the number and length of storage places.

Among other things, this means you can find off-the-shelf hardware and programs to do an enormous variety of jobs. You do not have to originate unique programs unless you have truly far-out needs. You can shop for existing systems and programs to meet your demands. Two important things are happening as a result of this: The number of things your computer can do is undergoing wild growth, and the cost of systems and components is plummeting.

(An offshoot of this situation is that much of the industry is in a state of chronic obsolescence. This leads us to give you some cautious advice: Don't buy last year's model unless it fits your needs *and* the price is irresistible. You may not be buying just last year's model but a model that is several *generations* old. Shop and compare with your own needs and budget as your primary concerns. Above all else, don't buy before you consult the Buyer's Guide section of this book and use its guidelines.)

After the shift to binary, computer designers homed in on transistors.

The move to transistors made mass production possible and increased reliability. The smaller size allowed the design of components that were easily replaced if they failed. It was possible then to locate the general area of a malfunction and replace an entire unit. The computer could be restored to working order quickly while the actual faulty component could be repaired at leisure.

This development dictated a functional approach to design. It was necessary to minimize the number of wires that tied together the different parts of the computer. And that approach blended smoothly into the next breakthrough: the shift to integrated circuits (ICs). The IC puts many transistors into one piece of semiconductor material and lets you make standard circuits capable of being combined in many different ways. It also permits another dramatic reduction in size.

The industry had new building blocks.

What originally took thousands of square feet of floor space and vacuum tubes from floor to ceiling was reduced to a small roomful of transistors and then to a box scarcely larger than a desk filled with ICs. Connections which originally took miles of careful handwiring were exchanged for conductive pathways sealed in tiny semiconductor crystals. Logic units that once required fifty pounds of hardware were reduced to a few grams of semiconductor and plastic.

The stage was set for an evolution in miniaturization that has not yet bottomed out. We are fast approaching the point where the electronic elements of a computer can be compressed into a package about the size of the tip of your thumb, perhaps even smaller. In fact, the miniaturization of some computers and calculators is now limited only by the size of your finger. You still have to punch keys and buttons.

One parallel improvement was critical to today's miniaturization and increase in power for computers. In current computers your instruction codes can be stored in the machine the same way as data. To modify instructions or even change them dramatically you merely manipulate the trains in the switchyard. In effect, your computer flips its own control switches internally, following your commands.

Earlier, we explained the "stuck switch" type of storage and compared it with its opposite number, the kind of switch that can be manipulated either by you or by the machine. You will recall that it is a common, although not universal, feature of the *un*stuck storage to self-destruct when you shut off the power, thus giving your computer amnesia.

Before the days of stuck switches and fixed storage, whenever the computer was turned on, it had to be reprogrammed from scratch. Part of that procedure involved flipping bunches of switches by hand and copying their patterns into storage until there were enough machine language instructions for the processor (SWITCHING) to copy other switch patterns from one of the higher-speed input attachments.

Such instructions circled back upon themselves in a way that allowed you to push a button that caused SWITCHING to do the things you asked of it. SWITCHING would do these things over and over until you pushed a button that stopped everything.

Assuming you got all the initial switch positions right, you could shift to the high-speed input device and put more machine language switch positions into the machine. SWITCHING would faithfully copy each pattern into storage until you decided you had reprogrammed it to the point where it would perform as desired. At this stage, you could stop everything, flip some switches, and push another button to set the processor on the correct instruction to get things started. You then pushed the *start* button. If each individual step had been done correctly, you were rewarded with a bell or the thunk of a teletype machine and you were ready to use the computer for something worthwhile—such as playing chess or space war or even figuring the interest on next year's mortgage payments.

As you have probably guessed, a lot of things could go wrong. Any one of these things was almost certain to be a disaster. The name of that game was frustration, and the answer involved plenty of coffee and late hours.

The major solution was the stuck switch, not exactly a new invention, but it has only come into its own in the past decade. And one of the handiest things about this solution is that your computer doesn't lose all of its marbles when the power fails.

What the designers did was to incorporate a great many stuck switches into just the right positions and patterns. All you do is turn on the power. Before you pull your hand away from the power switch, the machine has gone "ding" or "beep" or done something else to tell you it's ready to work.

This is today's technology: semiconductors and individual transistors, integrated circuits and the combining of tens of thousands of individual parts into a thin crystal wafer. The extreme precision of machine etching in these crystals requires computer-controlled manufacture. This is leading into an obvious evolutionary path—computers that design and build more and more effective computers. Once we get this going and produce machines that pass along the preset improvement pattern to more and more effective computers, we will be into a brand new ball game.

This has given rise to the story that computers themselves are really out of our control and are building themselves. That myth ignores the fact that it required millions of man-hours in planning and design plus billions of dollars to make it happen. Even more importantly, it passes over the fact that the improvement pattern must be preset and revised and that it must be measured against our requirements.

As we've shown, none of these things would have happened without standardized design—and that brings us face to face with economic reality.

Back in the early days when you wanted to remake a circuit, it could be tedious, but you really were only cutting wires and perhaps adding some transistors and more wires. However, with the advent of large-scale integration—more and more complex things in smaller and smaller packages—when the manufacturing machinery was set in motion, economics dictated that millions of components had to be built just in order to break even. You had to be right when you tooled up for a design change.

Of course the designs had been around long enough for the designers to know pretty much which things did what. But the designers do not know *everything,* and it's unlikely they ever will. This is one of the reasons that the whole computer industry is still in such a wild evolutionary state: Electronic experimenting is in the hands of a great many resourceful people who owe no allegiance whatsoever to existing companies. A product emerging from someone's basement workshop could make a multimillion-dollar investment obsolete overnight. It has happened before and it will happen again.

Intel, the first company to put a computer on an IC chip, is a case in point. The IC is a rectangular (and probably soon to be square) bit of plastic with protruding metal connectors much like the legs of a science fiction spider. The IC's functions are identified by serial numbers that you can look up in the manufacturer's manual. The manual will tell you what pulses or charges of electrical current you can send into one leg and what you will get out of another leg when you do this.

Intel's computer chip, the 8080, created its own industrial revolution. It was really a computer of impressive power and wide versatility, how wide was not at first appreciated. It was not until Ed Roberts of Micro Instrumentation and Telemetry Systems (MITS) in Albuquerque, New Mexico, brought out his Altair computer, a kit based on the 8080, that the rocket took off. That was in 1974, and the price was a ridiculous $420 for a computer whose competition, in terms of computing power, was still thinking of "$100,000 cheapies."

Roberts advertised in *Popular Electronics* and *Scientific American*. Those ads mark the beginning of the first stage in the personal computer explosion. But the ads were only a small part in the wildfire spread of the personal computer. Word of mouth gave Altair an even bigger push. This graduated almost overnight into computer clubs and other exchange networks where you could find out anything from how to hook up accessories to sources for specialized programs to fit your machine.

There was and still is just south of San Francisco, California, the heaviest concentration of companies making chips, computers, and accessories. It is called "Silicon Valley" and extends from near San Francisco International Airport south through San Jose. It is an area of extremely competitive business with industrial spying and sabotage more common than the industry would like to admit.

The area around Silicon Valley was one of two hotspots in the spread of personal computers. The other was in the shadow of Massachusetts Institute of Technology at Cambridge. Special magazines and other localized publications copied on duplicators sprouted all over those landscapes. They were circulated by hand or distributed at club meetings, and they set the pattern for what is happening today.

Twenty-twenty hindsight is the only thing you can trust completely in the computer industry, and it takes a great deal of courage to invest in a major design change. Keep that in mind when you turn to the Buyer's Guide section of this book (Chapters 13 and 15). Don't let it stop you from buying your own computer—you really can't afford to stay out of this revolution. Just be cautious.

All of this is why we turn your attention to something you can rely on—the thrust of standardization. There is no paradox here. A great many machines are being manufactured. They are very powerful, and because of standardization, they are increasingly interrelated. This is doing valuable things, especially where computer languages are concerned.

The same high-level commands have been made to work in the same way for many machines. Standards have been developed for how the letters and numbers may be represented in intermachine communication. Languages have evolved in which many operations follow a standard grammatical structure. They have the same internal rules.

One result of this is that your computer can now talk to a wide variety of other machines. Information and highly complex programs stored in other computers are available to you . . . and the prices are dropping.

Standard machines, standard languages, standard programs—these mean we share a base of useful knowledge available to everyone.

Which is what this book is all about.

8

The Gadget World

Those of you who have been wandering around complaining that 1984 is already here and that computers are going to be everywhere pretty soon make us wonder where you've been the past decade. Have you been so interested in your doomsaying that you missed the invasion?

We've already been "wiped out."

Look at what has been happening to automobiles. Today's cars talk back to you, telling you such important matters as "You forgot your keys." Or "It's time to change the oil filter."

Gadgets which do these things are correctly called computers. They are stripped-down, fixed-purpose computers.

These devices take many forms—TV recorders, traffic light controllers, video games, elevator controllers, teletypewriters, furnace thermostat mechanisms, automobile cruise controls and fuel metering systems, oven timers, airline flight booking systems, foreign language phrase reminders, digital control centers for multiphonic music systems, automatic telephone dialers, home security sensors, weather monitors (to close windows, turn on lights, turn off irrigation systems, and the like), and, of course, programmable calculators. The list goes on and on, a book in itself.

All of these things have in them a device with a built-in program that reacts in a preset way.

Most electrical devices are fast becoming or incorporating computers. There is compelling economic motivation behind this rapid shift.

First, it avoids the cost of more complex wiring.

Second, it frequently makes the device more versatile and adaptable to your needs.

Third, because they often are easier to use, the computer-based device is more attractive in the marketplace. It really is the "latest model."

One of the most universally accepted computers is the element at the core of the hand-held calculator. It is also one of the most advanced computers technologically because of its impressive miniaturization. It is also considerably more straightforward from a functional viewpoint because it has a single input source (the buttons) and a single output (the numerical display). Although it contains fewer elements than the massive systems found in the Pentagon, its general structure and the types of things it does are almost identical.

We're going to take a closer look at these calculators now because what they do gives you a powerful leverage in understanding what other computers do. Since you probably have already used a calculator, we will approach our explanation from the process of adding two numbers and seeing the displayed answer. We start with a single-digit number, add a two-digit number, and make the answer a three digit number. Here's how it goes:

1. You turn on the calculator and push the button that clears everything. This starts you at zero.

2. You push one button for a single-digit number. That number appears on the display.

3. You press the "+" button.

4. You press the first (tens) digit of your two-digit number. This causes the original number to disappear and the new digit to appear in display.

5. You press the second (units) digit of your two-digit number. The first (tens) digit moves one space to the left and the second (units) digit takes its place beside the first digit.

6. You push the button with the "=" on it and read the sum on display.

Internally, this is what happens:

1. When you press a key with a number on it, that number is translated into the unique switch pattern (binary) that the manufacturer uses to represent the decimal digit.

2. That switch pattern is copied into a place where many switches have been reserved for keeping track of numbers you are putting into the calculator.

3. When you push the "+" button, the first number is copied into another group of switches reserved for this purpose.

4. When you push the "=" button, the machine pulls out the stored numbers and performs the indicated operation—displaying the result.

Keep in mind that the only things in the storage system of computer *or* calculator are bunches of two-position switches. Any significance associated with the positions of those switches is the result of our own preparations—the programming.

For example, all the manufacturers we have studied chose the four-switch pattern in which all switches are off to represent the digit 0. This is translated to activate lights that make the closed oval shape on the screen we associate with the digit 0.

The machine is programmed to translate one switch pattern into another switch pattern that activates the proper display of lights, creating the symbols we have learned to recognize.

The most common optional feature on calculators is the "memory." You may already have reasoned that this is just another group of switches that get used whenever you want to copy what is being displayed. Sometimes, you find arithmetic functions associated with such storage systems, in which case the switch positions are first copied into a place where they are treated as operands before the arithmetic function is carried out and the answer is then copied into the storage switches. (In case you've forgotten, an *operand* is just a quantity upon which a mathematical operation is performed—convenient mathematical shorthand, no more.)

You can get the same effect by flipping a control switch that makes the storage switches one of the operands, then performing your operation, and, finally, flipping the control switch back to its original position. The next operation you perform will then refer back to the switches for the required arithmetic function. In one instance, you store the numbers; in the other, you store the operation. The end result is the same.

Another optional feature on calculators is the "parenthesis." This allows you to perform intermediate operations on operands before using a result with other operands. You do this with the control switch.

The optional feature that makes a hand-held calculator most like a full-size computer is the "programmable" model. This lets you save a particular sequence of operations for future use. An example would be in figuring how much you're spending on interest for a loan over a period of many payments. Such a model will display the payments easily and quickly.

One thing you'll notice about the programmable calculator is the extra buttons that do nothing unless you're in the "learn" or "program" mode. The buttons have such labels as "GOTO," "STO," "RCL," "WAIT," "START," and "END."

STO and RCL stand for "store" and "recall." If you have a calculator with memory option, you already know about these buttons. They allow you to put things into storage and recover them.

The other buttons tell the calculator's processor where to GOTO next or they stop it, permitting you to do something without trying to catch the problem on the fly.

Everything it does is preprogrammed, waiting only for the problem you give it. This is a conceptual background that you will find useful all through your use of your own computer.

It would be difficult to overemphasize the importance of that most basic capability your computer needs for automation: the ability to locate and copy a number that has been previously saved somewhere so that when it comes time to use the number, it is available.

What you have in your machine is a gadget that, in effect, can examine binary digits. You'll recall that we call such digits bits. The gadget can examine the bits and compare them. Are they the same or are they different? Reading this, it can store the answer in a "carry" column just the way you do when you're adding a column of figures in the decimal system.

Believe it or not, the gadget that does this is called an *adder*. Computer users have been known to make terrible puns around this, such as "Its byte is worse than an adder's."

The adder is the basic element from which all other calculations in your computer originate—not only addition, but subtraction, multiplication, and division (not to mention hyperbolic sines, square roots, and elliptic integrals . . . from the simplest to the most esoteric).

Because you can store special symbolic patterns in your computer, the machine itself can automatically display the decimal equivalents *after it does all of its mathematical operations in binary*.

From these few simple facts, it is easy to see that we are at the barest beginning of the computer-driven gadget revolution. You had better learn how to use these gadgets before they are turned to using you.

9

The Logical Crutch

Your computer is limited to what is called a "Boolean logic" system. This is named for an English mathematician, George Boole (1815–1864), who devised the deductive system upon which modern computers are based. It uses only three operations—"AND," "OR," and "NOT." This confines your computer's comparison abilities to the "is . . . is not" rules that its switches can handle:

"This and not that."

The rules of this logic include the rules of syllogisms, a further limit on what these machines can do because your problem has to be based on only two premises.

A typical form of this argument goes: "All *A* is *B*; all *B* is *C*; therefore all *A* is *C*."

This says that if your premises are correct, your answer will be correct. But that is an extremely blurred argument outside of mathematics. And we are here to keep reminding you that your thinking processes operate mostly outside the rules of mathematics.

The concept "logic" has entered our mythology as a kind of ultimate answering system, a Delphic oracle that cannot fail. People believe it is a source of absolute truth. One of the reasons the "computer brain" myth has taken such strong hold on popular fancy is the fact that your computer will not question what you feed it unless you have introduced a logical or mechanical error.

Let's face it. This is a constraint on the machine that does not apply to you. Your computer is a moron. It calculates as an idiot savant might calculate. It cannot judge. Computers do not choose between *opinions*. It has no inherent sense of values. It is logic-based, and this is condemning the machine to a secondary place in the human scheme of things without even faint praise.

LOGIC IS A LIMITED AND LIMITING WAY OF THINKING.

Don't get the idea from this that we want to throw out all logic. We merely want to put it in perspective as one more tool available to us when we need it. Most people don't realize how tight are the restrictions on this tool. Like any other tool, it has its strengths. We found out long ago that if you state your limits carefully, you can address unknowns by logic. What your computer does is speed up this process.

It is our argument that logic has become too much the hoary eminence of science. This has reached such a stage that many scientists engage in a conspiracy of silence about how they use the tool. Many very famous men have admitted that they made their scientific breakthroughs by intuition, by a "dream" or a sudden insight "like awakening." It was only after the fact that they assembled the logical steps of a process by which the discovery *could have been made*. This was done for scientific publication.

Overdependence upon logic can weaken our abilities; it can even block one of the ways we achieve our insights. It diminishes your appreciation for your own native abilities.

Your digital computer works under another limitation: It can handle only one kind of time, the second hand of a clock and all the fractions thereof. You manipulate and function within another kind of time, which we choose to call *continuum time* or "CT."

Continuum describes an unending, infinitely expandable movement and place for such movement. It is the unbroken smoothness of this expansion that is important. There are no discrete steps or separations. It is the difference between what you can do and what a movie does that is the key to understanding the continuum. A movie simulates unbroken movement by the very fast display of many individual frames. We have not been able to identify such *frames* for people. If we do operate in discrete steps, the display must be many orders of magnitude faster than that of a movie, and—what is even more important—we can control the display speed across an awesome range.

Many of you will recall personal experiences with CT. The most memorable of such experiences occur at moments of extreme stress. You are required to make an immediate survival decision in seconds or less. Suddenly, you experience a sensation as though time had stopped or slowed to a crawl, but your thought processes accelerate to a dizzying speed. You are able to compare long strings of options, choosing just one decision upon which to act. You do this in a fraction of a second.

Both authors of this book had such an experience while driving an automobile. A review of the experiences showed that each of us chose the one survival decision from a large number of options. Each automobile, moving at about sixty miles an hour, could not have covered more than ten feet while those life-and-death options were being compared.

Many people have reported similar experiences.

Such CT events are usually written off as "purely subjective" and therefore not amenable to scientific proof. What that really means is that these very real experiences cannot be confined within the logical limits we have described. They occur in a dimension computers cannot use.

People who argue for the "electronic brain" are refusing to admit those limits of logic. If this were not tied up with such deadly consequences, it would be laughable. Logic is always calling something a "law" that is not a law at all. What you must recognize when you use computer logic is that you govern the machine. It will follow your program; it will conform to your scheme of things. It is a blank page that will sit there and do nothing until you give it your purpose, and your purpose has roots in dimensions and experiences the computer cannot use.

Computers may be superb for logic and accuracy within described and describable limits, but don't ever depend on one for creative work. The machine will not go outside its limits. It has no imagination. In fact, people of limited imagination, people who don't understand what you mean by "creative brainstorming," tend to lead the argument for the "electronic brain" myth. They impose limits on themselves and they want to apply similar limits to the universe because that makes them feel safer. Despite the mask of logic on this argument, it is an emotional matter.

We must keep reminding such people that our brains work in dimensions other than logic. When those who would limit us say that the occasional sparks of brilliance can be explained by your brain's multichannel capabilities, we must correct them by saying that it is just as accurate to describe your thinking as multidimensional. Always remember that you can deal with the continuum; a computer cannot.

You are not a mechanical toy. That's the essence of it. The patterns in a computer's circuits are not alive. You evolved to confront infinity. Computers work within mechanical limits.

One of the best things to come out of the home computer revolution could be the general and widespread understanding of how severely limited logic really is—that plus a new appreciation of our own capabilities.

We have really known this for a long time. Scientists express it when they say: "By the time you have the question properly formulated, you already know the answer." Folk wisdom says: "Ask a stupid question, get a stupid answer."

People who deny these things apparently don't trust their own abilities very much. They also assume that every aspect of your thought processes is based on rules that can be determined and converted into computer programs. The best evidence now available says such rules do not exist in an absolute and unchanging form. The basic concept of communication (including, of course, nonverbal forms) appears open-ended, infinitely expandable, and without any boundaries. Given no limits, we do not have a system that can be enclosed in absolutes; we do not have a system that can be reduced to a works-every-time program or any other rules.

We are saying that it's about time the philosophical implications of Einstein and Heisenberg entered the mainstream of our technological inventions. We do not agree that philosophy is "just one more science with a more important theme but a clumsier method" than that of the other sciences. We find it impossible to separate philosophy from anything we do, and we believe this is a good thing. We have an *opinion* about it. There ought to be an underlying philosophy to anything we attempt. That's what binds our substance together. We don't understand things when we take them out of their working environment. You cannot understand "mind" by separating it from "body." You cannot understand "politics" by separating it from "economics," and you cannot understand either of these artificial concepts without accepting all of their extensions—including the possibility of war.

No auto mechanic worth his salary would think he could tune up an internal combustion engine every time by adjusting only one part. Getting an engine to run properly is often a balancing act. Philosophy is the balancing act we chose to use while we walk the tightrope of this book. We think that if there is any single underlying conceptual approach to our universe, an approach that allows for infinite variation in everything, that will be a philosophical approach, not a scientific rule.

To play fair with you, then, here is our philosophy:

In any logical system there can be different steps of "truth" such that you cannot prove the truth in one step by taking that truth out of its context. Every truth requires a context and, in fact, can be proved false outside that context.

This is a clear implication from Einstein's special theory of relativity and Heisenberg's demonstration of the limits to observation and measurement.

Before this understanding entered our awareness, countless logic-limited people devoted their lives to attempts at unraveling paradoxes such as the famous Epimenides paradox. This is usually seen today as a small card on one side of which is printed: "The statement on the other side of this card is true." And on the other side, the message reads: "The statement on the other side of this card is false."

The card itself clearly demonstrates the two completely separated contexts. They are incompatible. They must be looked at spatially—separate and forever divorced.

The real problem here is the servile dependence upon a one-context universe within which you seek absolute rules. (For "context" you can substitute "dimension" or "system.")

The multicontext universe of *relativity* gives us a more dependable ability to predict the workings of our "natural universe."

The implications of this insight are enormous.

First, it says that the number of possible contexts (dimensions or systems) is infinite.

Second, it says that the truth of one religion (government, philosophy, etc.) cannot be proved by an artificial comparison with the truth of another religion (government, philosophy, etc.). Such matters can only be tested in the crucible of survival, not in the play of symbols.

Symbol jugglings that ignore this (including those in computers) are exercises in futility.

Folk wisdom has recognized this for centuries: "One man's truth is another man's lie."

This is also one of the things we are saying to you with our philosophy: Limited systems are often seen as better systems because their performance is easier to predict. It's a simple step from this observation into the belief that you have found the Rosetta stone that will open up the universe. That idea has great current attraction because it has helped us produce powerful technical devices—including the computer. However, the end results of such technical prowess are growing more and more sour. It did not take the Three Mile Island charade to tell us that systems are failing. It is observable that people are being destroyed by the *uses* of our technology. More and more outright lies are being told to shore up the facade around potentially catastrophic failures.

We are saying that it is not our tools that are at fault, it's how we use those tools and the beliefs we invest in them. We say also that the personal computer is potentially the most powerful instrument of individual freedom ever conceived. You are called upon to juggle more and more survival information every day—to recall it, compare it, and revise it. The mental abilities with which you were born, *enhanced and amplified* by your own computer, give you the capacity to meet that challenge. An interactive network of such computers widely distributed throughout a free society is, if used openly and wisely, a bulwark against all attempts at enslavement.

We are questioning more than the philosophy behind our dependence upon limited and limiting systems. We question the power structures that have grown up around such systems. We question the multinational monopolies that deepen our dependence and usurp the functions of representative government.

The tool is at hand to meet that challenge. We will not escape, however, unless we have a well-grounded understanding of computers and their limits. Computers operate within the narrow boundaries of logic, one step at a time with discrete information and a limited time frame. You have greater abilities.

Take this as a challenge. Computers are challenging us to use more of our abilities. All animal forms, and we're no exception, can be shown to profit from such a challenge. We are throwing down the gauntlet in front of those defending a particular current idea about computers, people who say: "Computers are much too complicated for the average person to understand."

Nuts! That's just job insurance, a defense mechanism to protect their own positions. What the *bigdomes* don't tell you is that computers are actually such simpletons they are relatively easy to understand.

The nature of the lie is easy to penetrate. Larger computers have been defined to suit marketing schemes, to maintain dominance in those particular markets. This requires a premeditated and built-in complexity plus a high level of difficulty before the machines can be understood. If you are in the business of selling complicated devices and their accessories, which are advertised as being not only profitable but necessary, then it's obviously not in your economic interest to make a computer that is easy for people to use.

That is defining computers according to monopolist interests, according to the needs of certain computer manufacturers, not according to your needs. Many computer companies have followed this lead like processional caterpillars. We recommend to the directors of such companies the poignant lesson reported by J. Henri Fabre, the great French naturalist. This is an insect drama, but we pray that its lesson will not be lost on the world's leaders nor on any of you who define yourselves as followers.

Fabre discovered by close observation of processional caterpillars that they would follow the slime trail of a leader without deviation. To test this, he places a long row of processional caterpillars on the lip of a large pot. Dutifully, the caterpillars humped and crawled around the pot. Then an interesting thing happened. The leader came upon the slime trail of his own procession and became a follower. Around and around the procession went without food or any other relief. Even when members of the procession began to die and fall off the pot, the caterpillars closed ranks and maintained their mad circling. They kept it up until all were dead.

Let this be a warning. The computer monopoly cannot be maintained. Too many people are busily engaged in redefining this machine according to your requirements, simplifying the hardware, simplifying computer languages and the programming. The home computer business soon will have machines and programs to equal or surpass the best built by the big companies—and priced at less than you would pay for a used car.

Because the computer monopoly has been punctured, many other monopolies will fall.

(It's worth noting that IBM rejected the opportunity to take the lead in development of electronic computers back when there were no such computers. Apparently, IBM was too committed to mechanical computers and calculators.)

Many of you no doubt have noticed that we, too, are busy redefining computers in your terms. And by this time you should be focusing on an operational definition of computers—what the machine can do, as opposed to what you can do. The two are far apart.

Always remember that computers are machines. They are tools, mechanical devices. And just as you can drive an automobile without knowing how to build one, you can use your own computer without knowing how to assemble it. Your computer is a moron or less. We assume that you are not that limited.

But computers are going to happen to your world. Make no mistake about that. They give an enormous time and information storage advantage to the people who can use them. It is inevitable that computers will permeate almost every aspect of our lives. The positive rewards make this a certainty. They will kick in a dramatic speedup to the changes and evolution of our world. If you have your own computer, you will be able to adapt to those changes with relative ease. You will have your own "time machine."

10

Let's Get Organized

Now that you know quite a bit about computers and how they evolved, we're ready to explore more of their functions. In the process we'll increase your familiarity with more jargon.

Every speciality shields itself behind jargon, which is another kind of job insurance. Computer programming and design carried this tendency to some ridiculous extremes, but, with your help, we'll get them back into the main channel. Just remember that computer mythology arises out of and is fueled by the same emotions that gave rise to Utopian dreams. It is the dream of Walden II and Oneida. In each instance, the authors are saying: "Please, let us have a world like this because that's the kind of world where I feel safest." Symphathize, but be careful how you follow.

One of the most useful things your computer does is to shift things around according to plan. That's one of the reasons they're such great organizers.

This essentially uncomplicated action is basic to such jobs as sorting meaningless jumbles of information into neat, orderly, and coherent bundles of information that have been organized precisely according to your needs—all done in the twinkle of an electron and without any backtalk.

If you're one of those people who are always "getting organized," you're going to find the investment of time and effort spent learning to do this with your computer the wisest such investment you've ever made.

If you tend more toward *wanting* to get organized but never quite achieving this, you're going to discover that your computer is a necessity.

For those of you groping around in a paper fog of information that is essential to earning your daily bread, the computer-as-organizer will mean survival.

Understand that you probably won't save much if any time putting your information into the machine. Getting it out according to your exact specifications is another matter. That's why you're likely to be happiest with your computer's ability to organize and store large blocks of information for ready access.

When we say your computer will become your favorite tool for keeping track of things, that is the voice of experience. Computers are the organizer's dream machine. They do it by the numbers, but you don't have to know anything about those numbers except that they are addresses in the machine. If you tend to forget addresses, your computer will save them for you and list them at your command.

Just remember that in spite of the fact computers have been made to do a lot of fast and tricky things with numbers, they don't *know* what a number is. We're here to keep reminding you that the only thing your computer "understands" is a switch, and it really doesn't understand a switch the way you do. But you can make the machine respond depending on whether a switch is *on* or *off*. It will react with its preset electronic reflexes whenever you touch one of its triggers. (Yes, we warned you we would join the anthropomorphic game, but only in fun.)

We can assure you that the first time you see your computer doing exactly what you wanted without any mistakes and faster than Superman, the experience will fill you with an elation hard to describe. You may find yourself overcome by a severe case of the smiles and you will probably want to demonstrate your triumph to someone—explaining quite carefully that this computer had to be directed by you (or by a program that you initiated) through every step of this marvelous problem. You not only gave it the information but told it what it had to do with that information.

We will never forget the fully matured and highly respected department chairman at Stanford actually giggling with glee when he saw his new toy not only doing what he had ordered it to do but responding more efficiently and effectively than he had expected.

In effect, your computer is a specially organized office—organized just to fit your needs.

Not only can you put things into the machine and save them there for later reference, you can also print those things on paper if you add a printing accessory. A printer is optional equipment and not cheap at this writing, but you may find it a necessary addition. Be alert to the fact that extremely fast and sophisticated printers are coming on the market; this is making some very good secondhand printers available.

With a printer you can have a neatly typed shopping list ready for you while you put on your coat before going to the market.

You can print out the telephone numbers to leave with your baby-sitter.

When a neighbor comes over asking for your lemon pie recipe, you can put the pastry recipe cassette in the recorder and type a command which prints the recipe for him. No need to look up the cookbook.

The more alert among you already have noted that the printed paper is another form of STORAGE. Very handy under many circumstances. When we describe our ideal "Rolls Royce of computers" in the next chapter, you will observe that it would print out any program the machine has developed. That should alert you to our belief that a printer is quickly becoming essential.

What we're dealing with here is your *interaction* with the machine, computer-people interfaces. Several devices fall into this category—punch cards (fast becoming obsolete because of their bulk), paper tapes, magnetic tapes, magnetic cards, and telephone cradles. None of these things can be interpreted easily and immediately by human senses.

Two other classes of interaction devices are on the market—optical scanners and light wands (or light pens). The optical scanner reads printed characters from a page. The light wand lets you choose different sections of the screen for preset messages.

Your screen can be divided into sections, each section displaying a different activity, in a number of ways. Such sections are called *windows* or *panels*. Windows and panels are always defined by lines around them. When you set aside a place on your screen without a border, that's called simply an *area*. You've seen similar things done on your TV when a close-up of sports action is shown simultaneously with a general view of the game.

Don't let this TV-CRT comparison fool you, though. The CRT may appear so much like your TV screen that you assume it is exactly the same. In a hardware sense, that has some truth to it, but that's where the comparison stops. In the first place, it's likely that the present form of CRT will be replaced soon by something similar to the display system on a hand-held calculator—larger but using the same electronic techniques. In the second place, your CRT carries its different messages in different ways. Here are some of the terms that will help you understand the differences:

CURSOR

This is a marker that you (or the computer) can move around to indicate a starting point on the screen. It takes several forms on different computers and is sometimes confused with a PROMPT symbol. The word CURSOR is rooted in the Latin for "runner" and stands for control of movement in the computer. When the computer moves the cursor, that's to tell you where you should be looking or where the next symbols will appear. The cursor points to a particular place. It's like a bookmark, showing you your place on the screen.

PROMPT

This tells you what the computer is doing. It *prompts* you to do something, and the small flashing marker may be accompanied by words telling you what it is you should do. When your computer displays something for you to do, that's a *PROMPT*. When there is a particular place on the screen for such a display, that's a PROMPT AREA.

There are quite a number of other performance signals that can appear on your screen, things it can do or conditions for your interaction. People are still inventing them and the possibilities appear infinite.

There is, for example, the *light pen*. You can use a light pen and its program to draw on your screen. The light pen is really receiving light from the CRT. Those signals flip switches in your computer very rapidly. Some combination of light pen and graphic symbols appears to promise a new leverage on your interaction with a computer. This is being built into some exciting new languages, which, at this writing, have not been perfected.

When a computer is set up to display things on a screen, that is always a two-way street. Even without a light pencil, you can respond to the display and shift those internal switches by other devices—the keyboard, knobs that turn, a thing like an aircraft's control stick (called appropriately a *joystick*), also by waving your hand across or through a sensitive electrical (or magnetic) field, by changing your brain-wave patterns (we'll go into this in more detail later when we talk about the "biomachine"), by talking to a speech-activated interface . . . and so on and on.

When the computer reacts to a choice you have made or to a choice directed by a program you have initiated, that reaction is called a *branching*. It is comparable to the branch-line switching in our railroad switchyard example, but with this important difference: Every track intersection leads to every other intersection *and* you create new tracks every time you make a new program.

Computer branching appears to be limitless. The possibilities are compounded as the branching systems interact with more and more of your senses and response abilities. If you can see a picture on a screen and change that picture to fit your choices, the interaction grows tight. If you only have to think about the changes you want on the screen, or the changes in sound patterns, or in the lines of a new design, the interaction is very tight.

When you order your computer to shift things around, the *controller* swings into action. It goes to an address that you give it or that it receives because of a switch pattern you have set in motion. At that address it writes a pattern into temporary storage. It then opens up a place where you want to use the essential information carried in the temporary pattern, and it puts that information into the new position. Both positions can be temporary, and temporary can stand for a millionth of a second.

A small section of your computer keeps track of where to find the next instruction in your program. This is called the *program counter*. It contains program instruction addresses only. It keeps your program steps separated from the information that is also kept in the same internal storage areas. The only way a program step can be performed is if the address of that step is first put into the program counter. Once located, the instruction is put into another device called an *instruction decoder*. Here, the appropriate switches are flipped. And *they* direct the trains of switch positions that are juggled to solve your problem.

Now, don't let all this business about addresses put you off. The things a particular program can do are always shown on a MENU, which you can list on your screen. Each menu item is flagged by a number preceding it. That number is an address. It's like shouting back to the short-order kitchen: "I'll have a number 10 and hold the mayo!" When you tell your computer to give you a "number 10," it will do that thing which is listed on the menu after the number 10 in your program.

Earlier, we mentioned another device essential to this performance, a device called a "clock," which is usually designated in computer manuals as a "CLK." This device provides the synchronous beat for the operations we've just been describing. It is similar to the quartz crystal in electronic watches, but it doesn't tell time. All it does is tick electronically very fast. Each tick starts one of a series of operations involved in something you've told the computer to do. If you want a clock that tells time, you will require another device that counts the ticks.

It may seem overly complicated to do things this way, but there is a reason: economics.

Back when computer designers made the decision to go with the far more expensive two-position switches, they knew that if anybody was going to afford the finished machine, they had to keep everything else as simple and inexpensive as possible. One of the economic limits arising from this decision was that, if it was possible to get along with just one of an essential part in the computer, they would find a way to use only that one part, they would do this even if it would be more convenient to hook up additional parts.

We hope you realize we are not yet talking about expensive deluxe versions that contradict this guideline. Believe us, a very small percentage of computers have more than one or two deluxe features that set them apart from the rest of the herd.

That's why there is in most computers only one device to find a particular address in STORAGE. And that is why you find the seeming complexity of operation, which, as far as the computer is concerned, is not complex at all. Remember that computers work very fast and have no opinions about such things as complexity.

Review

Describe the following in your own words:

printer
STORAGE
interface
optical scanner
light wand
light pen
window
panel
area
CRT
CURSOR
PROMPT
PROMPT AREA
branching
controller
program counter
CLK
instruction decoder
MENU

11

The Rolls Royce

On the international automotive scene, there exists some argument as to whether the Mercedes or the Rolls is the better engineered general-purpose car. Some people argue that the Rolls leads the pack only because of its high price. Others say the Mercedes prestige can be attributed to the myth that Germans make better mechanical devices.

We don't intend to get into that argument except to warn you that you should avoid thinking a high price necessarily means a better machine. We did, however, choose the Rolls Royce as the symbol of our dream computer partly because the machine we have in mind would probably cost a very large bundle of money.

And just as we would be the first to admit that there probably are a lot of things about the Rolls that could be improved, we have not included every imaginable improvement on our "Rolls Royce of computers." We have confined ourselves to what we consider are essential improvements, and we should advise you that some of these things are already available or are just over the horizon.

One reason we've taken this approach is that when you come to purchase your own computer, there are many things other than price to consider—and prices are coming down dramatically for highly sophisticated systems.

In this respect, buying a computer is a lot like buying a stereo music center. You expect your stereo to work for a reasonable period without breaking down. Whether the cabinet goes with the rest of your furniture could be far less important than the quality of performance. After all, it has been demonstrated clearly in stereos that bad sound reproduction can tire you rather quickly. Just so, you don't want a computer that is tiresome to use.

Here then is our Rolls Royce:

It has its own program-writing feature. The machine will compose its own programs and print them out for your examination.

One of the least desirable things about today's computers is the difficulty you have in making them perform automatically at your whim. The right kind of program is basic to automatic operation. Even though important strides have been made recently toward easier programming, this still takes a lot of your time and concentration.

Buying your programs from a specialist is useful in many applications but not a complete answer. To be truly effective, programmers should not only be specialists in computers but also in the field where they are using a computer to solve problems. There can be little doubt that an MD who is also a computer expert would write better medical programs.

The present system requires a great deal of compromising. This has the effect of producing programs that are all too often designed with a poor understanding of either the machine or the problem—or both.

Program languages have become easier to understand, and BASIC, the language we recommend you learn, is really quite simple. But all presently available computer languages suffer from at least one serious flaw: They are designed from the viewpoint of the machine's internal construction. This implies that the programmer must first know everything about the technology behind the machine—how it flips its switches, what the easiest flow channels are, and so on and on.

Don't let this implication frighten you. It does not hold true for you unless you want to graduate into extremely sophisticated programs. But we do believe that the language and the machine ought to be designed primarily from the viewpoint of your needs and not from the needs of the computer.

A far better approach than what you find today would be to set up the computer to generate the relevant questions that need answering when you write any program. That way, when the machine has enough information to solve the problem, it also should have the *program* to solve the problem. You would not have to be concerned, then, with the mechanics of the solution. You could concentrate on typing in accurately all of the limits and elements of your problem.

Most of the drudgery in programming is of a bookkeeping nature. It could reasonably be turned over to the computer. The machine would be programmed (with stuck switches) to ask such questions as:

"What sort of program do you need?"

"What accessory equipment will be used?"

"How many accessories?"

"What performance demands will you place on the accessories? Speed? Capacity? Form of output?"

"What name?"

"Where will the input originate?"

"Do you require a permanent record?"

"Where do you want the information stored?"

"How do you want the information retrieved?"

"What options would you like?"

And so on until enough questions are asked and the whole program can be composed by your computer. We know this is not a simple problem, but our Rolls Royce would have it.

Our dream machine has all plug-in components.

To some extent this already is a feature of many personal computers. The most common problems with them can be solved by removing a chip and plugging in a replacement. This is only slightly more difficult than inserting a conventional electrical plug into a wall socket. Guarantees being what they are today, the replacement should cost you no more than the waiting time for the new component.

For example, we had a problem with the personal computer we used as a demonstration unit and a reminder while writing this book. Any key you hit would repeat itself ad infinitum. A telephone call to the manufacturer pinpointed the glitch as a faulty encoder chip. That is the chip that translates keyboard signals into signals the computer can use.

The mails had a new chip in our hands three days later. It was obvious that an amateur could have made the repair without even knowing what an encoder chip did.

If we had lived closer to a major urban center, we could have had the chip in one day. The price we paid for enjoying a more primitive rural environment was two additional days for the shipment.

We think plug-in components are such a desirable feature that every part of our Rolls Royce would be exchangable this way—everything from keyboard to CRT—simple multiple-pin plugs.

Two components are of critical importance in your ideal computer system: the keyboard and the CRT.

Unless you have one of the new "speech lab" units, by which you actually can vocalize your commands to the machine, the keyboard will be your only means of "talking" to the computer. Even with a vocal-response system, your keyboard is likely to get more frequent use.

The keyboard, then, should have a decent "feel." The keys should move smoothly and positively. The keys should, of course, transmit accurately what you type into the system. These are typical keyboard problems the Rolls Royce should never have:

1. Pressing one key gets you two or more characters. (The thing has an electronic stutter.)

2. You get a different character from the one you typed.

3. You get no response at all.

With these problems in mind, you should inquire about the performance record of any keyboard before you buy it.

Unless you buy a printer, the screen will be the only way your computer can display its answers and keep you posted on your progress. Your screen should have these characteristics:

1. A steady image—no bouncing or jumping around or other distortions.

2. Good contrast. You should not have to burn out your eyes reading it. The symbols should be clear even in a well-lighted room.

3. Easily read character symbols.

In printing and computer jargon, the symbols of one style and size are called a *font*. Most computer fonts are built up out of patterns of dots that are five dots wide and seven dots high. That's enough if you only want capitals (referred to as upper-case letters) and numbers of the same dimension. If you want both capitals and small letters (upper and lower case), you need at least six dots by eight, but seven by nine is better.

Our Rolls Royce has a seven-by-eleven matrix and not only can display in black and white but in color. The colors each come in four shades for further differentiation.

It might interest you to know that these color shades are available today as an option on some personal computers. The cost depends largely on the required internal storage capacity.

We come now to the manuals that accompany each machine and are supposed to tell you how to run it. Many people have complained that computer manuals generally appear to have been written only for experts. We have seen some manuals that may not have been written by people—or at least not by people who speak English. There is a suspicion that they were written by computers to be read only by computers.

There can be no denying that some jargon is required for computers.

We are, after all, entering an area of new experiences and need new words. But jargon for the sake of jargon is ridiculous.

Our Rolls Royce meets this problem head-on. It has a special program that is an explanatory dictionary and graphic demonstration to be shown on your own screen. The demonstration will be in cartoon form and will display the operation of each of the computer's parts. It will be written at a level a child could understand.

We're reasonably sure this Rolls Royce feature will appear on the market before long, and we hope it will be at a Model-T price. Until it does appear, make sure the store where you buy your computer has someone standing by to translate for you when the confusions arise. Either that or find a friend who already knows computer jargon. Have the friend sit down beside you when you first open your manufacturer's manual. We have provided a glossary that should be of considerable help, but new jargon keeps being invented.

If our short course in jargon plus your friendly expert still do not make the manual understandable, call the manufacturer and lay it on him. It may alert him to make his manuals more understandable, and it may produce an answer to your puzzlement.

A word of caution: If you buy from a department store or from an ordinary electronics store that is not familiar with computer problems, don't waste your time going back to that store for help. Chances are very good that the salesman will not know as much about computers as you will after you read this book.

Our Rolls Royce will have no ordinary printer; it will have a photo-typesetter. This is a marvelous device for reproducing symbols on paper. When you want something on paper—even extraordinary shapes and graphic symbols of your own invention—you program those shapes through your computer onto your screen. The symbols on your screen can then be edited, reshaped, put into any type font you desire. When you are satisfied that the screen shows what you want, you tell the computer, "Put it on paper." The computer copies the dot patterns of the screen to the phototypesetter, giving you on paper an exact match of what you had on the screen.

Phototypesetters are already in use in the reproduction of Chinese and Japanese ideographs, Arabic script, and Cyrillic. People using them say they have barely scratched the surface potential of this versatile accessory.

The Rolls Royce will have its own microwave transmit/receive system. When you want access to any large information center around the world, you say, "HEY, YOU! Give me the straight quill on the mating habits of North African sand fleas. Try the Library of Congress first. If it's not there, try the Little America Free Library. I'm sure one of them will have it." Your computer then makes contact with the various information centers via microwave and satellite.

ROM (the stuck switches, remember?) in our Rolls will be very high powered. There will be enough for the most enhanced version of every high-level language plus the most versatile operating system.

There will be enough RAM (the changeable storage) that everything you have tied to your computer can run at the same time, quickly and independently.

Each accessory will have its own CPU, RAM, and ROM. There will be a central CPU that controls the sequence of operations for each peripheral CPU and the intercommunications.

MASS STORAGE in the Rolls will be more than enough for information and programs to be taken from any source and used immediately. There will be file systems that automatically switch to a larger-capacity mass-storage device when they outgrow their existing storage.

SOFTWARE in the Rolls will provide translators from every programming language to every other programming language, including machine languages.

There will be a CPU from every model of every manufacturer which can be used at will with any part of the Rolls system.

Furthermore, this computer will control kitchen appliances, sprinkling system, burglar alarm, fire extinguishing, heating and air-conditioning system, power generation and distribution and storage, window shades, lighting, and fireplace dampers. It will read mail, pay bills, answer the door and the telephone, and record selected TV programs *sans* commercials. It will call computers that send incorrect bills and read them the riot act, causing their fuses to blow. It will rock you to sleep when you're suffering from insomnia, and it will throw you out of bed when you have to get up.

That's science fiction?

It will be fact quicker than you think. Which is one reason we have projected our idealized computer. Knowledge of a hypothetical Rolls Royce will alert you to extremely valuable features, which, because of the rapid rate of development in this industry, may be on the market at a price you can afford by the time you read these words. At the very least, you should ask about the possibility of adding such features. How open-ended is the system you are considering?

These things we have visualized and even more are going to happen. If you're prepared for them, you can help to make them useful tools. You see, what separates the professional from the amateur in many fields is attention to detail. Your computer can look after almost infinite detail without ever a complaint. Whatever it is that bores or annoys you, think of how you can turn that detail over to your computer. That's what we did in the mental assembly of our Rolls Royce. While we were doing it, we well knew that the eventual reality will go far beyond our initial projection.

12

The Computer Two-Step

This chapter is about binary arithmetic. You do not need to know about binary before operating a computer. Your computer can handle these matters for you. Even if all things mathematical turn you off, though, you might like to dip into this chapter. If you've never before heard about binary, that's good. If you have heard about it, there's a good chance that you have been confused. If you will give us your unprejudiced attention, we will attempt to succeed where the public schools defaulted to "old math."

As we've told you earlier, there is no complex mathematical ability in your computer. It cannot do anything except add. Presumably, you can add, subtract, multiply, divide, and perhaps much more. Your computer only simulates the functions other than addition. It does them by laborious, but very fast, addition. It does all of this in binary and for a very good reason.

It requires a ten-position switch to represent a decimal digit. A binary digit can be represented by that far simpler two-position switch, upon which modern computers are based.

But most of us are used to the decimal or "base-10" numbering system. One of the first things we learned about it was how to count. This is really a complex procedure. It involves starting with the number 1, then adding 1 to it which gives us the number 2, then adding 1 again and so on. One of the things most of us were not told was that you can only count as high as the biggest digit before you have to add another digit to get the next number. This is perfectly obvious when you think about it because everybody knows that the biggest digit is 9 and when you add a 1 to 9 you get 10, a two-digit number. However, what you may not have been told is that 9 is merely the biggest digit in the decimal (or base-10) system. There are larger numbering systems where, when you get to 9, the next number is still only one digit. And there are smaller-based systems where 9 of the base-10 system is already represented by two or more digits.

As you know, your computer operates with on-off switches. If one of those switches is on, you are looking at the binary number "1." If the switch is off, your binary number is "0."

Having learned that, you now know as much about elementary binary switching as the most accomplished computer expert.

You can make your computer react one way or another depending on whether a switch is on or off. The dumb machine doesn't know or understand anything about this operation. It just reacts with its electronic reflexes whenever you touch its triggers. As we have told you, to say that it knows when to add A to B and store the answer in C is about like saying when you're drunk that you car knows the way home. Both thoughts are dangerous.

In its infancy, the computer industry tried many different kinds of electronic switches. One early model used a ten-position switch. There was even a system using a one-hundred-position switch on the theory that the more positions per switch, the fewer switches were required to represent larger numbers. The main hope was that this electronic marvel would enable its designers to calculate at the breakneck speed of several additions per second. And there was the fact that a switch was a *part* and the fewer parts the cheaper the machine.

However, it did not take long to discover that the more positions you gave a switch, the less certain you were about its position at any given moment.

Just consider a multiposition switch with which you probably are familiar: your TV channel selector. This is a thirteen-position switch. Each position gives you one channel turned on and the other twelve turned off. Now, consider the problem if the channel indicator light fails and all of this happens in total darkness.

We probably do not have to remind you that electronic gadgets sometimes fail. That fact spelled the death of ENIAC (Electronic Numerical Integrator and Computer), the first fully electronic switching computer. It used eighteen thousand vacuum tubes. On average, a tube blew out every seven and one-half minutes. The best they ever achieved after design improvements was a breakdown every two days.

It finally was recognized by the computer industry that, since accuracy and reliability were so important, the best switch was the two-osition model. (For the trivia-minded, the two-position switch is fully wice as accurate as the next most reliable one, the three-position.)

And thus we come to binary arithmetic.

The highest number your computer can represent with a single digit is the number 1. The highest digit of any numbering system is 1 less than its base. And for very elemental reasons, base-2 is the smallest numbering ystem possible. When you have just started counting in binary, you are lready as high as you can get with only one digit. The smallest two-digit umber in this system is "binary 10." Don't confuse that with your old amiliar "decimal 10." The thing to keep in mind is that a binary 10 counts n entirely different quantity than a decimal 10. They are two distinctly ifferent numbers. The quantity you count with binary 10 is the same uantity as decimal 2. We get each of them the same way—by adding 1 nd 1.

It may be helpful at this point to follow the train of discovery by which one of the world's greatest mathematicians came upon the base-2 ystem. The mathematician was Gottfried Wilhelm von Leibniz (1646–716). In his day the peasants used the binary system for a simple nultiplication method called "peasant multiplication." With this system, ae peasants did not need to know their multiplication tables beyond the s.

A simple problem will show you how they did it. We'll multiply 36 mes 47 using the peasant method.

To begin, place 36 and 47 at the top of two columns you are about to nake. Then divide 36 by 2 and divide that number by 2 and so on until you each 1. You then *multiply* 47 by 2 successively, as shown below:

36	47		
18	94		
9	188	. . . .	188
4	376		
2	752		
1	1,504	. . . .	1,504
			1,692

Right away, you observe that 9 cannot be divided evenly by 2. But ince we are peasants and not expected to be very good at arithmetic, we throw away all extra 1s. Next, we cross out every number in the secon‹ column that is opposite an even number in the first column. After that, w‹ only have to add the remaining numbers in the second column.

The answer, as indicated, is 1,692.

Try it yourself. You will find that it works every time. Leibniz mad‹ the same discovery. He saw this as a way to build an adding machine tha‹ would multiply. This is exactly how your computer multiplies. It is ho¼ most modern adding machines multiply.

Peasant multiplication can be explained quite simply by the binar² system. Expressed in binary, the number 36 is binary 100100. To chang‹ a number from decimal to binary, all you have to do is divide it by successively, just as we did with 36 in the foregoing problem. You the‹ put a 1 opposite all odd results and a 0 opposite all even results. Th‹ binary number 100100 is then read from bottom to top. Here's how thi‹ conversion looks:

36	0
18	0
9	1
4	0
2	0
1	1

In peasant multiplication we eliminated every number opposite a‹ even number, which means in binary the numbers opposite the zeros. T‹ multiple 36 (binary 100100) by 47 like a computer, we multiply each dig‹ of the second column by successive powers of 2 and again by 47, then w‹ add the products. Here's how it goes:

$$0 \times 2^0 \times 47 = 0 \times 47 = 0$$
$$0 \times 2^1 \times 47 = 0 \times 94 = 0$$
$$1 \times 2^2 \times 47 = 1 \times 188 = 188$$
$$0 \times 2^3 \times 47 = 0 \times 376 = 0$$
$$0 \times 2^4 \times 47 = 0 \times 752 = 0$$
$$1 \times 2^5 \times 47 = 1 \times 1,504 = 1,504$$

$$188 + 1,504 = 1,692$$

That's identical to the system in peasant multiplication. All we di‹ was to convert 36 into binary and multiply it by 47. This is precisely wha‹ your computer does, converting the 47 into binary form as well. Even th‹

exponents in these equations would have to be binary, but your computer solves that problem by more repetitive additions.

You see—your computer is a peasant.

Generally, when computer people talk to one another they prevent confusion about the number system by calling each digit separately or by preceding their number with the word *binary* The binary for decimal 2 would be called out as either "one, zero" or "binary ten."

As you can see, binary racks up a lot of digits without counting very high. For example, decimal 8, a single digit, is four digits in binary—one thousand (1000). Decimal 64 in binary comes out one million (1000000). Decimal 600 in binary is more than a billion.

Conventionally, four digits are often used for any binary number up to decimal 15. (Another binary digit must be used when you count higher than decimal 15.) This is done by placing zeros in the empty columns. This doesn't change the value because, as you will recall, we're still in *peasant multiplication*. By this convention, decimal 3 becomes binary 0011. Decimal 4 is binary 0100 and so on. The following decimal-binary table shows the basic notation. Zeros would be added to the left.

Decimal Notation	Binary Notation
0	0
1	1
2	10
3	11
4	100
5	101
6	110
7	111
8	1000
9	1001
10	1010
11	1011
12	1100
13	1101
14	1110
15	1111

You can convert from binary to decimal by starting with the right-hand digit and adding values. The rule is that you add a value when the binary digit is a 1 and don't when it is a 0.

You get the value of a digit by doubling the value of the digit to the right, starting with 1 for the rightmost digit. The value of the right-hand digit is 1. The value of the second digit from the right is twice that of the rightmost digit, or 2. The value of the third is twice that of the second digit, or 4, the value of the fourth is 2 times 4, or 8, and so on. With binary 1111, you get $8 + 4 + 2 + 1$, or 15. With more binary digits you would carry this out that many more steps. Binary 11101 becomes $16 + 8 + 4 + 0 + 1$, or 29. Binary 111001 becomes $32 + 16 + 8 + 0 + 0 + 1$, or 57 . . . and so on.

These conversions become awkward when you reach very large numbers, and various conversion codes have been developed in attempts to simplify the process. Any computer can be rigged to make the conversions automatically. All of them should display binary results in decimal. No computer will get bored doing this.

If you now go back over what we've said about binary numbers and work a few problems on your own, you should have a sufficient grasp of the system and how you translate either way between binary and decimal. This facility will come in handy if you really get hooked by the intricacies of computer programming.

We hope you understand that binary is important because you can add a pair of such numbers together electronically if you look at each switch position of each binary place of both numbers at the same time, starting with the units position and going sequentially on up through the largest binary digit of the longer number. *Then* if you have one extra switch, you can keep track of the "carry." Look back at the multiplication of 36 times 47 and you will see that this is exactly what we have illustrated.

Your computer can do this because it can store part of its information in its microminiaturized circuits. Those circuits are laid out in stacks of gridiron patterns. The pattern forms a series of intersections, each of which can have a switch position. One way the intersection records an "on," or a "1." The opposite way records an "off," or "0."

You now have all the clues you need to understand how your computer can deal with symbols other than numbers. Depending on the pattern it *recognizes* and upon which the designers have agreed, the machine can light up tiny spots on your CRT. Those lights can be arranged to form any symbols you may need. They also can select the keys of a special typewriter or of another printer.

It was observed in the early stages of computer development that if a fixed number of bits and a unique pattern were always used for each specific symbol, then you not only could identify the symbol (repeat it accurately every time) but you could also know where each symbol started and stopped just by how many switches had been used since the start of the message. By including letters, numbers, and punctuation symbols along with a few basic typewriter functions such as tab, backspace, and so on, you could write anything you would normally want. It takes 7 two-position switches to provide a different on-off code for each of 128 different symbols.

We now can explain why 8 bits equal a byte. A bit, you will recall, is the smallest unit of information to which computers can respond. It is a binary digit.

While 128 symbols seemed enough for most purposes, the designers decided to allow for an eventual 256 symbols, thus making the basic symbol length equal to 8 binary digits. Such "overengineering" has invariably proved valuable in the past and there was no reason to doubt it would be equally valuable with computers.

Some computers use the extra symbol patterns for special symbols—graphics, the Greek alphabet, Chinese or Japanese characters. Most employ the eighth digit for an extra degree of reliability. It was decided that since any symbol will always have either an odd or even number of "on" switches, the eighth digit is either on or off to make the total agree with a verification code—an identifying odd or even. By counting the number of "on" switches, you can make sure that a particular eight-binary-digit sequence is a legitimate symbol.

13

Buyer's Guide I

If you think you're now ready to buy your own computer, read this section before you go to the store. We hope you now accept the reasons for getting your computer and know that you have been misled about how difficult it is to gain the necessary skills.

We are urging you to buy this valuable tool as soon as you are able to do it. Not only are the reasons urgent, but the economic timing is excellent. It's a buyer's market and will be for some time. There's another important reason you should buy as soon as possible: You will learn how to operate it faster and more skillfully if you use it while you study about it.

Just as in learning to drive a car, a book is useful but never enough. You have to get your own hands on a car before you can be called a driver.

First, we owe you some precautionary advice based on experience and investigation of many computers. In giving you this advice, we want to emphasize that in no way do we imply there are a large number of problems with personal computers. We are telling you something anyone should realize on a moment's reflection, but it is something which needs emphasis:

These machines are made by people and are subject to some human failings.

Reliability, however, is on an obvious and dramatic increase. Standardization plus automated (computer-controlled) manufacture of many parts make most repairs relatively simple. Considering the complexities to which the various hardware combinations can be put, problems are astonishingly rare.

Unless you are a qualified expert, confine your own repair efforts to those plug-in replacements. Don't get in there with your soldering iron. Seek out a specialist who is familiar with any glitch you may encounter. In most cases your problem will turn out to be something simple; a faulty connection, a short in a chip—seldom anything more complicated. It may even be that you have misread the manufacturer's instructions.

The store where you buy your computer should be able to put you in touch with other people using the same machine. Insist on this before you buy. Find out how those other users like that model. Ask about problems and be specific. We'll get to some specific questions presently. Feel free to copy those questions and take them with you when you go shopping.

Keep in mind that there will be varying degrees of expertise in the computer-user population. However, *they will know the real experts*. Find one of those real experts if you need help. We guarantee you'll meet some interesting people.

Whatever your problem, help is at hand somewhere. More and more specialized computer stores are opening every month. The ones that endure will be run by people who understand computer problems. Word gets around among the users of personal computers. Ask how long the store has been in business. Ask about the specialized experience of the people who are running the store. Don't be bashful. With any given store, they need you; you don't need them. The same goes for any given manufacturer. There's another store (factory) "just around the corner."

If you do encounter problems, consider returning a machine to the manufacturer as a last resort—*only when all else fails*. But keep your machine's special packing box just in case. Failure to protect the computer in shipment can void the guarantee.

Finding a computer to fit your budget is much easier today than it was, say, in the early 1960s. For only a few hundred dollars you can get a computer with greater capacity and versatility than one with a price tag in the hundreds of thousands of dollars in those earlier days. It's really bargain times.

But "Buyer Beware!"

There are good reasons for so many bargains—competition and the rapid progress in computer development. This is generating a chronic obsolescence in the industry, and it represents a possible pitfall for the unwary first-time buyer.

You want a tool, not a toy.

There are some "cheapie" models around with a limited higher-level language in them. They will not copy information into an external storage system such as a cassette recorder. They will copy programs but not information. These are toys, not tools. They will play games with you but very little else. You cannot, for example, save your checking account records on a tape with one of these toys. They are little more than calculators, as far as computer power is concerned. A hand-held calculator would be cheaper and more accurate.

If you already have one of these toys or feel that the price is too attractive to resist, you have a couple of options. You can convert this toy into a tool by biting the bullet and paying the extra amount of money to expand the system according to the manufacturer's specifications. This will probably cost you more than twice what you paid for the original toy. The other option: Find a local expert who can convert the thing for you. The price of having your own conversion done should be a fraction of what the manufacturer usually wants. But it will probably void your guarantee.

The terrible part of all this is that there is no technical reason why the cheaper machines could not be built correctly in the first place—to copy and store your information. We suspect that this is a marketing gimmick; they lure you into the toy and then stick you for the expansion price later. After all, you already have their machine.

We strongly recommend against the purchase of such toys. The question you ask is: "Will it copy *my information* into an external storage device and then accept the playback of that information into the machine?" You want a machine that takes *your information,* not one that just takes programs.

Obsolescence creates other problems. You don't want a machine for which there will be no new attachments or more powerful programs in the near future. But an older computer may exactly fit your needs, even though it uses more parts. If the price of such a machine is attractive, you should consider it. You are interested in performance, not necessarily in the number of parts. If those parts are standardized, easily replaced, and readily available, they should not impose serious limitations on your computer.

The first question you should ask yourself is: "What do I want to do with a computer?" If you know in advance exactly what you will want your computer to do for all of your life, your job in selecting the right hardware is easy. All you do is find one that does what you want in the way you want that done.

It is not quite as simple as selecting a console entertainment center, however. When you have decided whether you want a tape recorder, TV, radio, record player, or such, all that remains is to find a system with the required features in a pleasing package and with the desired sound quality.

Not so with a computer.

More often, a home computer is bought in a stripped-down version. This basic model will probably be enough while you learn how to use it and decide what you will want to do with it. As time goes on, though, you will probably increase its accessories.

To do that, choose a model with a wide range of accessories which are supported by the manufacturer.

Even though you are buying the bare-bones model, you will want to see the deluxe version in action. That was one reason we ran the Rolls Royce past you. Stay aware of new accessories. As these new accessories come out, make a point to see them in action. That will provide you with information on what is possible with your computer. It is important that you stay abreast of the possibilities—the potential. For that, your machine has to *have* a potential. Don't paint yourself into a corner with your first machine.

You should enter this list with operational questions of the most specific type, the questions that are most directly involved with what your computer will do and what you will have to pay for it.

Recall the box labeled STORAGE in our basic diagram? The versatility of your machine is a direct function of its storage capacity, of such problems as whether it handles color or a more advanced higher-level language.

With storage systems you pay for speed and size. Small and slow usually means less expensive, but that, too, is relative. Each new generation of computers gets bigger in capacity and faster. Because last year's model might give you just what you need, knowledge of changes in storage capacity could give you some useful economic leverage. Ask whether there is a newer, faster, more powerful model of the machine that attracts you. Ask whether an improved version is about to come on the market. Then ask yourself whether you really need all of that upcoming power and storage.

Also ask yourself whether you need a disk driver or a cassette recorder. Disks are faster and cost more than cassettes. Both function as external storage, but you can find information faster in a disk and you can revise that information more quickly. Disks also will interact with a computer's internal storage in a much more responsive way.

If speed and fast interactive capacity are what you need, then by all means go to disk. For most users, though, cassettes are more than adequate.

As you might expect, the simpler the computer you choose, the more likely that you will be able to walk into the store and buy it off the shelf. If you get into a larger and more complex machine, however, you may be asked to wait a suggestive nine months for delivery. Don't let this ignite any fantasies about how the machines are actually reproduced. If you are asked to wait for your particular model, keep track of what's happening in the industry during the interval. Put a clause in your purchase contract that will allow you to withdraw with grace and not too much expense if the machine for which you are waiting is superseded by a far better model before you even get the thing in your hands.

We recommend that you go to a computer specialty store for your first machine, but don't even set foot in the door without going completely through this Buyer's Guide section, which is designed to give you specific operational questions. Better yet: Finish the book; the book as a whole should allow you to generate your own questions—a far more valuable asset.

Gut Questions

Believe it or not, one of the most difficult problems for a first-time computer buyer is to define what it is he wants his computer to do. We have a way to approach this problem that we believe you will find helpful.

Take pen and paper and list the demands you expect to make on the machine. Put each demand into as clear a statement as you can—language not easily misunderstood. Avoid strange technicalese. What you are defining is what you intend to do with your computer. You want a direct way of describing those things, and that's a very powerful leverage on both your language and your understanding. Your first statement may be something like this:

"I want it to do all of my household bookkeeping, my savings account, my checking account, and all of the balancing. I want it to contain my budget and to have as complete a breakdown as possible of where my money goes."

A relatively simple computer can do this provided it can copy and put your information into external storage (cassette or disk).

Now, that sample statement appears to contain all the necessary requirements, but this is not the case. The following questions will make this clearer:

How do I use this computer?

Where do I control it?

What else does it do?

Is there a model that would be easier for me to use?

How do I feed (activate, renew, supply, repair, maintain) it and the accessories?

Where do I install it?

How do I connect it to a power source?

How do I shut it down when it's not in use? (You want one switch for start-up and shutdown, no more.)

How big should it be (and still meet my needs)?

How small can it be?

Is portability necessary?

How do I connect attachments?

Am I limited in the kinds of attachments that can be fitted to this computer? If so, how?

Is there a less expensive way to do what I want?

Is there a more reliable way to meet my requirements?

What is the history of this machine?

How often does it break down?

On the average breakdown, how long is it out of service?

Can I fix most problems myself or does everything require a specialist?

How vulnerable is it to damage by my mistakes?

Is it soon to be superseded by a better or less expensive model?

Will it soon go so far out of style (common usage, and so on) that repair parts and attachments will not be available? (Many people still own early-model Polaroid cameras, very good cameras with excellent lenses but for which film is no longer generally available.)

And don't forget to ask how long the computer store has been in business, or how long it has been selling computers.

As you can see, some of these questions focus on the same or on similar elements of your problem. This is good practice: Ask your questions several ways. All should relate to your original demand: What do I want my computer to do?

It's not enough to say that you want your computer to do all of your bookkeeping, even if you define what will go into this chore.

This is the operational approach. This list of questions has far wider application than just to computers. Almost everything we use would be better understood if subjected to such a test.

Our questions are all built around the idea that the machine must be made to adapt to you, not the other way around.

It should be clear by now that finding a computer to fit your needs presents some problems. You'll want to avoid the dogs and lemons, the quick-profit toys. But there are ways to meet this challenge, ways to arm yourself with knowledge and, especially, knowledgeable questions. Here are more well-tested questions and some of the reasons they should be asked:

Does the manufacturer make only computers and/or their accessories? Or is the manufacturer a subsidiary of a noncomputer corporation?

If computers are only part of a corporation's business, you may have problems. Generally, management of big corporations will only invest in strong market trends. They are prone to mount expensive advertising campaigns and dump their mistakes. You don't want to be their "dumping ground." You want some sign that the manufacturer's research, development, *and production* are committed to your needs.

Does this manufacturer sell worldwide and have they sold more than a couple of thousand computers?

If the answer is yes, you are buying experience. This is generally safer, but no guarantee. If the answer is no, bring in some really expert opinions *of your own choosing.*

Does this manufacturer have a local service center?

The most important service center is the one in your community. It's worth paying something extra for a machine that provides this.

What manufacturer-supported accessories are available with this computer?

There is a great deal to be said for matched equipment that is tested by and guaranteed by the one manufacturer. If they also have a local service center and can provide you with the software (programs) you need, you'll always know where to go if you have problems.

You may have to deal with more than one manufacturer to get just the system you want, but understand the problems raised by your decision. The manufacturer of your disk driver may not want to be responsible for the connection with your computer . . . or vice versa. Whatever you do, you want to insure ongoing advice and help.

How flexible is this computer?

This is another way of getting at the machine's potential. It gets into things you may not know you will want to do with your computer. You want to know how much additional storage, both internal and external, this machine can handle. Can it take on several jobs at the same time? If it can, you will pay less to expand your system. Take it for granted that you will discover new things you will want your computer to do.

What are the electrical power requirements of this computer and its accessories?

Some computers will lose everything stored in RAM if there is a power failure. Some will even lose what's being stored on a disk when a failure occurs. If you live in an area subject to frequent power outages, you may have to consider taking protective measures—batteries or an information storage system not vulnerable to power failures.

Do you have a grounded power line into which you can plug your computer?

The machine should always be grounded to protect the internal circuits. If you don't have a grounded power system, adding one will be a hidden cost.

Does this computer require its own power line, without any other electrical equipment on that line?

Some of them do and this could be another hidden expense. Find out. Discovering hidden costs after you have bought your computer can really destroy your budget. While we're on that subject, get the store to put all of the costs in writing—*including installation.*

Is a maintenance contract available?

If you are going to put a lot of hours on your computer, this could be cheap insurance. It is comparable to buying the same kind of contract on a refrigerator or a freezer. For a fixed sum the store guarantees to maintain and keep your computer in operation.

How fast is this computer?

You want to know how long it will take you to do the various things you contemplate. This involves such things as how long it takes to store information in an external system? How big a display can you put on your CRT at one time? You may want to put an entire page of a letter on the screen—much faster than scanning the letter a few lines at a time. Remember that if you're going to use this computer every day and a slow interaction adds fifteen minutes a day, that's more than a week every year. The right computer is a magnificent time cruncher, but it's possible to build in tedious delays. When you know what you want to do with your computer, ask how long the machine will take with these jobs.

Does the manufacturer spell out installation requirements?

This is another way of uncovering possible hidden costs. You want someone to be responsible for the machine being installed in your house *and working.* With home computers, this most often will fall on your shoulders, but the backup from the seller is crucial. If your machine does not work, will they send someone to help you solve the problem?

Will the store guarantee that what it is demonstrating is what you will have when you get the computer in your home?

Special demonstrations can lead you to believe a particular computer is just what you need. Computer demonstrations can be made to look as though they are doing exactly what you want when in fact they will not perform that way at all. Always ask this question:

Will you guarantee in writing that when I get this computer in my home, it will do exactly what you are now demonstrating?

If you can buy a maintenance contract, find out if there are maintenance requirements for your computer that are not included in the contract. Get specific answers about the maintenance history of excluded items.

Don't get the idea from any of this that you're walking into a den of thieves when you enter a computer store. We just want you to know that there are a few "sharpies" around. Our questions will smoke them out.

Getting to Know You

Buying your own computer is sure to create another "entity"—you *and* the computer. Every such relationship has a break-in period. This is true of a lot of consumer products, including cars and major household appliances. It is especially true of computers. Here's the basic rule we would like you to apply before buying a computer:

You should be able to understand the elementary operating procedures in no more than a half hour of use and instruction.

A half hour, no more.

This brings us back to a central theme of our book: There should be an easily measurable pathway through these computer skills, starting from that introductory half hour.

No matter how clumsy you are at the start, using a computer is still the best way to learn.

What about computer courses offered at various colleges and night schools? Some of those courses are still being taught by faculty who insist on high complexity. Investigate this carefully. Reject complexity. Such courses will be phased out by the obvious evolution of computers going on all around us.

Many courses, even in the best schools, use antiquated equipment. It doesn't take long for very expensive hardware (especially stuff based on the complexity myth) to lag behind by at least a generation. Consider for a moment how education is financed and how school budgets are administered.

"You want a *new* computer, Dr. Johnson? You already have a computer and it's only four years old!"

Proceed with caution.

And understand that you are not likely to be satisfied with waiting for your turn at the computer in the natural rotation of a class. These machines are fun to use. So you pay $150 for a computer course at the local night school. Big deal! You get to use the computer twenty minutes on Tuesdays and Thursdays—but only after you've plowed through their complex textbooks.

The $150 would have been better applied to the purchase of your own computer. You'll get more for your money, especially in education. And after you've learned to use it, you will still have the computer. That computer may very well be all you will ever need—unless of course you branch out into spaceship design.

Get your own machine. It's the best way. And follow our two basic guidelines:

1. Spend as little money as possible for a computer that will do what you want.

2. Make sure the computer not only does what you want now but can be expanded or modified to match your growing skills and your increased demands.

Designed for Each Other

Many products in the marketplace (not just computers) are obviously manufactured more for show than for performance. We call this the "chrome-trim and flashy dial syndrome." While such things are not conclusive, they should make you immediately suspicious.

Don't rush in and buy the first computer that blinks its pretty lights at you. Take your time. Shop around. Make it clear from the first that this is what you are doing—to yourself as well as to the salespeople. And even after you find a computer you believe suits your needs and your budget, don't whip out your checkbook. Seek out another computer that fits your requirements. Compare.

Many consumer items, especially those based on electronics, can be divided into two distinct categories: (1) "ritzy taste," and (2) "designed for people."

There was, you will recall, no "ritz" in our Rolls Royce. Even the most expensive additions were included only because they were functionally valuable.

But taste is a controlling motivator in the marketplace, and manufacturers have known for a long time that taste can be manipulated. We all know this. A market can be built to follow manipulated taste. The sheer size of the U.S. advertising industry should be sufficient evidence that this is true. Fashions in automobiles and clothing demonstrate the fact.

This involves those things we classify as "chic" and all of those other status symbols by which our society marks its niches.

In spite of this, we all recognize that for any product there must be a "best design" that is strongly determined by how the thing is used—by what you use it for, where you control it, how you keep it in functional condition, where it has to be housed, any possible dangers in using the thing—all of this and more. For that "optimal design," the thing must fit not just some abstract called "environment," it must fit you.

Designers have long been aware that people come in various sizes and shapes, and with a variety of physical conditions, attributes, abilities. Somehow, the designers have to listen to you, and the machine has to be modified by what you do with it. But the dialog between human and machine has been a latecomer to the design board. Popular jokes reveal a common awareness of this. There is, for example, Finagle's Law:

"With any given mechanical device, that part which requires the most frequent repair, adjustment, maintenance, and replacement will be the most difficult to reach."

We all sense that the key to better design is to be found in simplification, a return to the Model A Ford while keeping all of the comfortable luxury features to which we have become accustomed. This involves an interplay between designer and buyer, an interaction modified and sometimes distorted by manufacturer decisions not really based on improving the product.

Here's where the intense competition works for you. There already have been many significant redesignings of computers. There are strong clues telling us that this will continue until the product more closely fits you. The Dartmouth group that redesigned the computer languages FOR-

TRAN and COBOL into BASIC had the right idea. The proof is that BASIC has taken over the personal computer field. BASIC will be replaced only when a more easily used *and learned* programming language is fitted to the hardware.

We have taken you on this tour of "ritz and design" for two reasons: to warn you against being dazzled and to alert you to pressures that may be brought to bear on you, aimed at getting you to "throw out the old and buy the new."

It could very well happen that a sufficiently useful improvement will come along at such an attractive price that we all will want to "throw out the old." But this takes careful thinking. Does the improvement mean we all have to be completely retrained? Some of the big manufacturers have counted on resistance to retraining as a means of keeping a share of the market.

These are seldom easy questions to answer. We introduce them because they are a help in understanding some design changes. We emphasize that computer design must follow your demands. What you buy ultimately controls the marketplace. Why you buy is subject to both internal and external influences—all subject to modification.

As more and more computers come into private use, simplicity and clarity should exercise an increasing control of the market. Hardware and programs of greater simplicity and power are increasing in numbers. When you buy, remember that "simple" does not have to mean "weaker" or "less useful."

The first limit on a wider acceptance and use of computers was the failure of most people to understand the enormous personal advantages gained by using them.

Then there was the failure to realize how simple and clear the things could be made.

That is changing. Response to a market is a wonderful thing to see—like a gold rush or a land rush—and never more exciting than what you see in the computer industry right now. Recognize that this has advantages and dangers. Armed with enough knowledge, you can make the times work for you.

Small Investment—Big Return

Are you a "joiner," or do you resent the very idea?

Even if you have a deep-seated prejudice against "clubmanship," we advise you to put it aside and join a computer club as part of your initial education. All of them are young and fermenting, full of exciting new ideas. The first such club probably was the Southern California Computer Society, started in 1975. There now are chapters of SCCS scattered all over the North American continent.

The value of such a group as a source of advice and exchange of programs cannot be overemphasized. They also publish informative newsletters and magazines, often on mimeograph. The SCCS newsletter, *INTERFACE,* is one of the most useful sources of specialized information about personal computers available. You must be a member to receive it, but we agree with those who say *INTERFACE* is worth the price of admission.

INTERFACE has a commercial spinoff called *Interface Age,* but first-time computer users frequently complain that it is too technical. You may graduate into a subscriber, but it cannot be recommended for the neophyte.

Our appendix lists names and addresses of computer publications available at this writing. Getting subscriptions has to be your problem. We will make a few comments, but publications have been known to change rapidly—for the better as well as for the worse. Look before you buy.

A number of slick publications are trying to cash in on the personal computer bonanza. They range from highly technical periodicals to strictly hobby magazines. You would be advised not to subscribe to any of them in a burst of new-found enthusiasm. Browse at the magazine stand and the library first. Shop for one you can understand, one whose articles (as demonstrated by several months of publication) clearly fit your needs.

One of the most popular commercial magazines in this field is *BYTE,* founded in 1975. At last report it had more than a hundred thousand subscribers. *BYTE* is sometimes technical if not obscure, sometimes beautifully simple for the newcomer. "Creative Computing," a "users' programs" feature in *BYTE,* has attracted a large following.

Electronics hobby magazines such as *Radio Electronics* and *Popular Electronics* are now running computer articles in almost every issue. Unless you already subscribe for other reasons, we don't recommend these magazines for the beginner. If they are easily available at a magazine stand, scan them for what interests you. Watch the announcements on their covers. They are sometimes very good, but they're not consistent.

Look into the sales-oriented books published by computer manufacturers, such as those sold by Radio Shack. If you have bought Tandy's tool instead of its toy, the Radio Shack publications could be useful. However, at this writing, they are not sufficiently broad gauge for us to recommend them as "generally useful."

Our best advice is for you to browse, pick, and choose. Be selective according to your own needs. No one knows those needs better than you. The range of interests in computer magazines is large and expanding. Look for new magazines and look for changes in old ones.

Program for the Players

"You can't tell the players without a program" is just as true of the computer industry as it is of baseball. It'll help you decide on your own machine if you know how the industry sees itself. There are several categories:

Kits
Ready-made systems
Standard systems
The PDP-11 family
"Loners"
Others

KITS

Before you decide to assemble your own kit, ask yourself whether you want the immediate use of a computer or if you would rather be entertained by a long preliminary trip through the hardware?

Unless you are really into electronics, we urge you not to begin at the assembly level. It's not as simple as the kit promoters would have you believe. A certain amount of skill with a soldering gun and the ability to follow schematics is required.

And please don't believe that this is the way to learn computer programming. Any programming you learn by building your own computer from a kit will have very little scope. It is bit-level programming, the setting of switches one by one. The whole procedure of learning by assembly is comparable to learning how to drive a car by building your own from roughly shaped and unfinished pieces of metal.

There's a better way to learn programming, and we'll get to it presently.

READY-MADE SYSTEMS

Ready-made systems can be attractive. More than twenty-five manufacturers are already on the market or about to enter it with ready-mades. There are some questions you should ask yourself before choosing one.

What language does it use?

The language must match the system. That system is all of the hardware plus the preset of the internal switches. We recommend that you learn the language called BASIC. It is simple, easy to acquire, very similar to English in its meanings.

Is the machine aimed only at a limited specialty market?

Right now there is heavy promotion of machines that do little more than play video games. Be warned that you will probably want a computer to do much more than that. The tool can be used as a toy, but often the toy cannot be converted into a tool.

Can this machine interact with the wide range of new accessories that are coming on the market so fast?

Some ready-mades are limited in the accessories they can use without expensive modification.

Are a great many people using this computer and its language?

This does not mean that you should buy only the most popular ready-made or any other category of computer. But the number of people using a particular machine can be a measure of several important things.

1. Is there widespread experience upon which you can draw in learning how to use your new computer?

2. Are there likely to be a wide variety of programs to do the things you want?

3. Will it be easy to get parts and repairs?

Ready-mades represent one of the strong arguments for standardized parts in the computer industry. Not all of the ready-made manufacturers have heard this message. Many of them, however, use the S-100 bus.

Buses, as you will recall from Chapter 6, fall into three categories:

Data bus
Address bus
Control bus

The three together are referred to as your computer's "system bus."
At least part, and often all, of the lines in the system bus go to each

part of your computer. Many of the accessories you may wish to add to your basic system will have to connect to these lines. That is the reason for the I/O ports. Not all I/O ports are standard.

The I/O ports allow you to add accessories. The connector on the accessory must match the I/O port—that is, each line on the accessory's connector must be in the same position as the corresponding line of your I/O port. Think of the port as a complex wall socket. The plug must match that socket, or the things you connect to it won't work.

As a standard system for I/O ports and accessories, many manufacturers have adopted the S-100 bus. An older version of this standard is the S-50 bus, with a fifty-line connector. The S-100 has one hundred lines. In both cases, each line has been assigned its own position and function.

Whether your computer has one of these standards or its own special port, it is imperative that any accessory you are considering match the I/O port of your machine. Ask before you buy.

The S-50 and S-100 ports are for "parallel" accessories. That is, they accept accessories that transfer information to the computer a byte or more at a time. Some devices transfer information "serially," or a bit at a time, and they use a different type of I/O port. The RS-232 port has long been a standard for serial communication. Most computers matching serial accessories use it.

STANDARD SYSTEMS

We define standard computers as "those machines whose manufacturers have chosen to compete in the same marketplace with a large number of interactive parts, accessories, and computers."

You should consider a standard if you will want a wide range of accessories. This is an important question.

Is it likely that you will want to buy some special accessories now or in the future?

Not everyone will want graphics or interactive graphic screens. Nor will everyone want automatic telephoning systems, specialty printers, heating control to balance temperatures in every room of a house or office, a music synthesizer, interactive architectural drawing and printing systems . . .

Specialty devices make up a long, open-ended list. But if that is the way you intend to go, you will want a wide choice of specialty devices. *You will want to buy in a competitive market.*

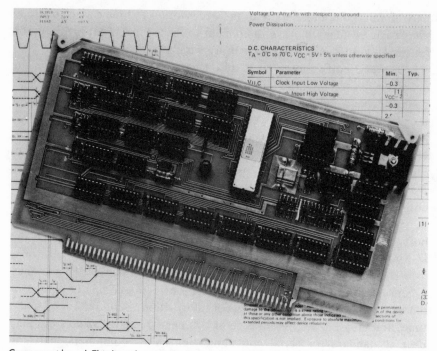

Component board. This board was manufactured by a photoetching process that left the metallic "wires" intact. The chips were then plugged into it. The board is coated to protect its conductive pathways. The connectors (offset bottom) plug into an I/O port that is compatible with an S-100 bus system. *Photo courtesy Vector Graphic, Inc.*

You should ask about availability and matching problems of the various standards and their accessories. Go back to our "gut questions" and be demanding in your search for answers.

If you buy a standard, you should give strong consideration to a maintenance contract. With standard systems all repair and maintenance may be your personal responsibility. Ask about "interface maintenance." Find out if the seller will help.

Don't make this the only issue controlling which computer you buy. Remember that you should not have to fit your life to the computer; it must fit you. And there's another possible solution to maintenance. There is a growing population of computer professionals who are branching into repair and maintenance at a community level. They are into personalized instruction, program writing, and related fields.

They make house calls.

Your supplier may be able to connect you with just such a person. If not, then go to a computer club. Tap into the population using the kind of computer you want.

THE PDP-11 FAMILY

We have separated the PDP-11 family from the others for sound reasons. Many computer designers and users swear that the PDP-11 from Digital Equipment Corporation (DEC to the aficionados) is the world's finest. While it is not our Rolls Royce, we agree that it is a superb machine. The beauties of DEC's PDP-11 are more than skin deep. It probably offers more languages and more powerful languages than any other readily available computer.

But understand that this is an expensive way to go—and not just on the first purchase plus installation. Programs and accessories can also have high price tags because they are designed for the PDP-11. There often is very little competition.

DEC offers a small and less expensive version called the LSI-11 with all electronics on a single card about a foot square. However, the LSI-11 is incomplete and certainly not something for your novice hobbyist kit assembler. When you buy the card, that's a bare-bones beginning. You will still need a housing, a power supply, and much more. DEC will sell it to you complete as the "11-03," but by the time you get it installed and working, you should be well over the five-thousand-dollar mark.

Heathkit, through an agreement with DEC, has offered a cheaper version, but all accessories must come from DEC at the full markup. You won't save much on the total system if you start buying accessories—and you will be buying accessories.

You may be told that an advantage of the PDP-11 and its cousins is to be found in the large library of programs available from DECUS, DEC's software library.

Be warned that most of this library is highly specialized stuff that is not likely to meet a neophyte's needs. Check out that library's ability to do what *you* want before you commit your cash to the system.

We're not trying to downplay the many advantages of the PDP-11. We just want you to know what you might be getting into. If money is no object, by all means consider the PDP-11.

As an alternative to buying DEC's own accessories for its system, you can buy a hookup from General Robotics that permits connections to the regular PDP-11. This lets you shop for compatible accessories in a much larger marketplace and at much lower prices.

Here's the place to tell you that the whole problem of compatible hookups is also in a wild state of change. Some highly ingenious modifications and programs are coming on the market. These will permit some very exotic cross-couplings, not only of computer-to-computer but of computer-to-accessories.

The situation is in such a state of flux, however, that we can provide little advice except to tell you that you should look into the possibilities. If, for example, you find an older and limited computer at an extremely attractive price, there may be a way to modify it into a more versatile tool.

Should you decide on the PDP-11, you will want to know about UNIX, the PDP-11 operating system from Bell Laboratories. UNIX uses a "structured language," meaning it is tied very tightly to the system hardware and is, therefore, extremely powerful. If you are really serious about developing your computer skills, find out if the machine you want can be or will be improved to take such a "structured language." Don't worry about learning such a language right now; just know that such languages exist and that they are valuable.

UNIX is expensive and the price is expected to rise, but if you can afford a fully operating PDP-11 system, you can probably afford the "structured" operating system.

"LONERS"

"Loners" takes in the volatile hobby market. Here are a number of companies that offer hobby computers that will not match any standard system of interconnections. What you see is what you get. Walk very cautiously into this area, but don't necessarily avoid it. If you want a tool and not a toy, make that clear to the seller. Understand that it is not necessarily a bad thing to buy a "loner." It is also not necessarily true that you are confined to what this manufacturer makes if you buy his computer. For some manufacturers, what "loner" describes is more a state of mind than an actuality. Modification systems are coming along, and it is possible to get a tailor-made modification for some computers.

OTHERS

Under "others," we lump all the computer manufacturers whose machines are somewhat less than loners but not really standards. They impose some limits on the accessories you can hook to the computer. Sometimes, those limits are severe. You can identify them immediately because they will spell out "recommended accessories" for which they will be responsible. Those "recommended accessories" will be rather small in number and often extremely specialized.

Even when such systems are based on very fine engineering—and some of them clearly qualify—make a careful comparison with a system from one of the other categories before you buy. You may very well find here a model that does precisely what you want and at a far more attractive price than that asked for any other system. Just be aware that you may be getting into a dead end. Go to our section on computer uses in this Buyer's Guide and take a long, hard look at things you may want to add to your system.

With loners and others more than with any other category, you must consider the popularity of the particular computer. Find out how many of them have been sold, especially in your area. Discover if there is an organization or a club that concentrates on the computer that has caught your eye.

Finding It a Home

Before you buy your own computer, decide where you are going to put it in your home or office. This requires that you be able to answer a few questions on how you will use the machine.

What accessories and attachments will you hook to it? There has to be room for them.

Is there a nearby electrical outlet? Make all the necessary electrical connections as short as possible.

Will there be easy access to the computer? Ease of access for the kind of work you will be doing will determine whether you really use it.

The computer should be close to the things you will be using with it—your desk, the source material for household bookkeeping, and the like.

Think of as many uses as you can, uses to which you *may* put your computer—filing menus and recipes for the kitchen, educational programs for your children, electronic games (and how many will play them at one time), sorting information for your job or business. Go to the section on computer uses and let it stimulate your imagination.

How much remote wiring will you attach to your computer? You may want to link your computer with remote CRTs and keyboards.

Do you want your computer to be compatible with the furniture around it? You may have to get a special cabinet built just for you. Make sure the cabinet has proper ventilation. Don't enclose your computer in a "hot box." In fact, check out your chosen installation site for its general ventilation. Don't put it in the presence of too much dust and moisture.

Will it be easy to protect the computer from contamination? Let everyone who has anything to do with the machine (even those who merely stand and admire your skills) know about a simple precaution:

Get no foreign matter, liquid or solid, into the machine. Don't park your coffee cup on it. Don't put an ashtray there. Don't work with your computer while you have a cigarette dangling from your lips. A talk with any computer repairman will tell you why. A surprisingly high percentage of computer repairs involve "accidents" with coffee, water, wine, food, or ashes spilled into the keyboard or into the cassette recorder or disk driver.

Why invite problems?

When you understand these things, remember that your computer is your MASTER CONTROL CENTER. Put it in the control room. Provide it with a table of its own. Hang up a "no smoking" sign. Give it room to breathe. Dust it. Don't water it. Ordinary room light is sufficient.

Uses

The more you think about it, the more things occur to you that computers can do. The possibilities that we list here will be incomplete. Any such list will be at least partly out of date before it can be printed.

Just review these things that a computer can do with information:

Compare and select.

Correct and rearrange.

Adjust on a screen or paper anything from a sequence to the position of a line or a diagram.

Magnify or reduce the whole or any part.

Keep in mind that a computer will give you instant feedback on results, then change the material according to new instructions. It allows you to work with little pieces or big ones.

Computers can be made to direct the performance of any machine. They will type a novel (which a person has written) or they will guide a jet to a distant city. A major advantage of these machines is in automation, where they can relieve us of both monotony and peril.

Despite the direct implications of automated factories, it is highly unlikely that any alert person will be made obsolete by a computer. Don't think of yourself as being replaced by a machine.

The age of leisure predicted by so many science-fiction writers as an absolute outgrowth of computer automation does not appear very probable. There is always that area of things that you can do that a computer cannot do. There has to be the constant assertion of personal worth.

How much do you value yourself?

Computers can already be applied to almost any routine machine-oriented job that takes the tedious presence of a person. What they can do is free us to focus on other things, but that does not necessarily mean leisure.

When we talk about uses of computers, we are talking about where we direct our design emphasis. Design has to start first with what you want a device to do. Functional performance is the key to most products, not just to computers. Pinning down what you want the device to do and *how you want to control that function* become crucial first considerations. You do not start from the technical end—what the hardware is capable of doing—you start from the performance end: what you require from the product. With computers, this assumes enormous importance. These are, indeed, "universal machines." Feedback from computer use into the society that uses them is already very great and will be even larger. We must be careful in deciding what we want them to do.

Before listing some uses of computers, we are directing your attention to one of their more dangerous pitfalls.

Getting into computers will influence the ways you think. That involves us directly with something called "futurism." Futurism is the art of trying to plan a course without knowing exactly where you are going. Under those circumstances, if you are not ready at every turn to change your course, you are acting stupidly.

14

Computers Are Not Oracles

A few years ago, a friend asked one of us how computers differed from programmable calculators. The friend received a mumbled answer about peripherals and storage space, but the real difference lies in the stuff being handled. With calculators, it's numbers; with computers, it's information. The information may be numeric, verbal, graphic, or any of a host of things that can be represented by an electrical signal and subsequently quantified by a computer.

Information is the raw material with which intelligence works. Computers are usually nothing more than information rearranging devices. There is no such thing as an intelligent machine, and the label "machine intelligence" is one of those devious oversimplifications that sound true but are dangerous nonsense.

Your computer must use logic. All that is called logic is not necessarily logic. Cold calculation is often called logic. Cold calculation is *usually* a form of emotion, often no more than ambition. The effort to make logic shoulder every job in our world is the effort to create a world that can be totally controlled. That is done for emotional reasons. It is a power trip. Carried to its illogical extremes, it will fail. Computers can accelerate that failure.

We think you are now sufficiently well armed that you can consider some present and potential uses for computers. Remember that you already have a whole bag of things you like to do. A computer can amplify your enjoyment of those things.

Any clerical work falls into the province of computers. Certainly, this includes all bookkeeping, balancing your checkbook, doing your taxes.

At-home banking and bill paying by phone can be monitored and controlled by your computer.

A computer can adjust your furnace automatically according to a preset mix of inside and outside temperatures—balancing various heat sources such as solar and electric, adjusting temperatures according to whether any people are on the premises, or even whether you are still in bed or are up and around *and* in a particular room.

A computer can call the police if a burglar enters your home, giving the police all the necessary information—your address, how many burglars, whether they are carrying metal objects that could be weapons. You can even key such a system to respond to your voice; if you say, "Burglar emergency!" your computer calls the police.

A computer can *listen* for particular voices and alert you when those voices are nearby.

Keep in mind that you can attach accessories called *peripherals,* which respond in ways similar to your senses and muscles. Accessories can mediate between your computer and the outside world. A computer can be rigged to *read* printed pages and abstract information according to your requirements. It can respond to outside messages by phone or keyboard.

A service called "News-Share," which can provide electronic delivery of local newspaper stories to any home computer, has already been demonstrated. Computer-edited news sheets printed in your home or announced for your ears on your demand will not be far behind. You will even be able to have such a service tailored to select only news items that fit your particular interests.

Don't get the idea that these uses of computers are off in some far distant future. In Washington, D.C., an assistant secretary of transportation for the U.S. Government is already using a computer to keep track of his daily calendar, transmit notes to his staff, log his telephone calls, file (and dial) his telephone numbers—and his system is portable. Any telephone line links him with his office.

It is possible to have a remote display system, each CRT with its own limited keyboard, at every telephone in your house. These remote units will be linked to your index, providing every number you may want to call. The computer itself will do all of the dialing.

Information retrieval from a remote or central storage system such as a library is well within present computer capabilities. Using such sources, your computer can tell you where to find equipment or information you may need.

With remote sensors, a computer can tell you when to fertilize your garden or water your lawn, even when fruit is ripe. It also can frighten away pests such as birds.

A computer can alert you when to call for repair of equipment. It can even make appropriate repair calls automatically.

Don't underestimate what is happening with optical scanners, which can read the printed page, nor such vocal interfaces as "Speech Lab," now being marketed for home computers.

There are people walking around happily alive today who would be dead were it not for computers. In the medical and social fields computers can accumulate enormous amounts of information and compare this information in ways that would take centuries for the plodding human senses. Never forget that computers are time crunchers.

Computers have already provided information that has changed ways of dealing with such diseases as cancer and some congenital defects. Projected medical uses of computers are even more exciting. You will see holograph images of the human body, the sections enormously enlarged and coupled with microminiaturized instruments for extremely fine operations—all in a real-time relationship. The surgeon will see what is happening as it happens. This forecasts awesome improvements in such fields as brain surgery and dentistry.

The ability of computers to reproduce any symbol, plus the fact that we can tailor electronic sensors and analog-to-digital interfaces (circuits that translate voltage changes into encoded signals, for example) have profound implications. They will, for instance, catalog anything and summon up the whole or pieces according to your precise needs. This means that once you get the computer adjusted to your needs, it will act like an extension of your abilities.

Architects will be able to do everything from sketches to finished plans in the computer and according to a very sophisticated system. They will be able to do the drafting and the design with a light pencil that draws directly on the screen. The computer will make the materials comparisons, the engineering, and reveal which materials can be used where. The finished design can be projected in its natural setting, tested for its relationship to sunlight, to a view, to other features of the landscape. When the architect is satisfied, he can direct his computer to produce the blueprints and all of the necessary construction details.

The savings should be obvious. You will not have to erect the building and *then* discover it should have been turned at a slightly different angle to the sunlight, the prevailing wind . . . whatever. You will not get four-fifths of the way through construction and then find out that the foundation is inadequate. The computer will have stored the geological and engineering information and will have inserted it at your command.

A key to the computer's extreme value when coupled to various display systems is found in its ability to store and recall extremely fine detail. The computer doesn't worry about working overtime while sorting through the characteristics of different building materials. Just as long as the information has been stored correctly, the computer will go through that information in any way you ask.

The entertainment industry is only now beginning to see the possibilities in computers. *Star Wars* barely scratched the surface of computer-directed special effects. Computer direction of much more sophisticated "reality simulations" will be a personal toy available before long in your home. This can do little else than ignite a renaissance in creative imagination.

Right now, this is an expensive process, but several research projects to make this facility available to personal computer users at a much lower price are already underway. Two of the research directors swear they will be successful, that the difficult work has already been done and all that remains is refinement and cost cutting.

Computers are now being used to print newspapers and books. Soon, they will monitor all distribution and marketing of printed matter. That probably spells the end for most regional distributors of books from the major publishing houses. The publishers will be able to fill orders directly on the basis of information supplied daily by bookstore computers.

The linkage of control diagrams to various mechanical operations will open up even more computer uses. With control diagrams you create a picture of a desired effect on your screen. At your signal the computer performs the indicated action in the external world.

Oil refineries and distilleries are already using this process. Instead of having someone manually turn valves and route the flow of liquids in the system, an operator projects a map of the flow system onto a screen. Wherever he wants a valve adjusted he touches that point on his screen with a light pencil. The selected area is then enlarged automatically on the screen. The operator can keep on enlarging the selected area until the needed detail comes up to sufficient size. He then touches the selected valve symbol in the enlargement. Numbers in a panel on the screen change to indicate that the fluid has been routed properly and is flowing at the correct rate. When the flow reaches a predetermined rate, the operator can change other valves in the system to conform to the new pattern. All of this can be done in a few seconds.

Economic advantages make it a foregone conclusion that the entire refining and processing world will be forced to convert to this kind of computer-assisted central control. Steel mills will be run this way. And auto factories. Every consumer product that can be carried on an automated assembly track will be produced under this kind of manufacturing management. Reliability alone would make it certain this will happen.

Any flow procedure can be improved by control diagrams.

In the not far distant future, the instructions for many new products will be built into them through a fixed program and some way of playing that program on a screen—perhaps through your TV. This will be a reactive system that will tell you how well you are performing as you learn to use the product. It will be a teaching device, part of the package you buy when you get a new car, a freezer, a home music center. . . . You get the picture.

Someday, the only way you will learn to drive a car or its equivalent will be through a computer. Computers will also teach you to play tennis, Ping-Pong, and many other games and skills. You will do this electronically. If there is danger in the real thing you are learning, that danger will only be simulated while you are learning, but with a high degree of "reality sense." The Link Trainer, for teaching "blind flying," and the more sophisticated current descendants of the Link Trainer will be looked back on as primitive.

Electronic games have to be one of the biggest spin-off businesses to come from the personal computer revolution. Such games are certain to become increasingly complex and sophisticated, teaching many new skills. Educators will pick up on the use of such gaming procedures in many academic areas. If learning becomes fun, the problem of motivation vanishes.

No study of the various uses to which computers can be put is complete without at least a brief review of some different kinds of computers presently available. We divide them into *digitals, analogs, direct analogs, hybrids,* and *fixed-purpose.*

The digitals are what we have been describing thus far all through this book. They are based on Boolean algebra and the binary switching system, with which you should be pretty familiar by now. If you have the need, they will do numerical computations of almost any complexity with both speed and accuracy. That numerical accuracy has been translated into symbols, where you encounter an inherent weakness of symbol systems: They cannot be made to describe all aspects of everything.

Within its limits, however, a digital computer can perform as a "truth machine." Wherever the computer has sufficient information to provide an answer, it can tell you "true" or "false." To explain this, we will introduce two symbols: ">" meaning "is greater than," and "<" meaning "is less than." You then can ask your computer whether one quantity ">" another. If you tell the computer to print a statement saying that the one quantity is greater than another, the computer will respond with a symbol for "true" or a symbol for "false." This becomes useful when you pose problems that include long strings of variables. With this, you can set up your own syllogisms. Just remember that "true-or-false" questions and syllogisms are extremely limited in our "real world."

Analog computers operate in quite a different way. They set up mathematical analogies to whatever problem you wish to pose. The speedometer on your car contains elements that are analog computers. The speedometer clocks the rotational rate of a shaft and converts this into speed and the distance travelled.

While analog computers are not as accurate as their digital relatives, they are usually lower in cost and simpler to program. Analogs also work continuously. Digitals are discrete. Analogs can represent a physical problem that may have many ongoing elements to which you require answers. They are valuable in the design of such complex devices as cars and airplanes and in attempts to understand such complex systems as the weather and human societies. They will operate under a wide variety of theoretical conditions. The best way to understand analog computers is probably to think of them as models that simulate a physical system under actual use.

Direct-analog computers have a fixed purpose and can be broken into three general types—mechanical, electrical, and fluid. Scale models are the most common example of the mechanical type. Tests of a model will tell a designer many (but not all) things he needs to know about the full-scale device. The scaling problems, both up and down scale, can be extremely complex and can involve subtle differences that are deliberately introduced to preserve accuracy.

Many modern electrical and electronic meters used in the design and building of electrical and/or electronic devices employ analog circuitry that simulates equivalent circuits. There are special alternating-current and direct-current analyzers that use relatively simple networks to "stand in" for giant electrical distribution systems.

Fluid types are represented by models of rivers, dams, harbors, and estuaries that tell engineers what they need to know about proposed construction projects. Another fluid type is used to test models of ships. A wind tunnel is a relatively crude gas/fluid type in this group.

One of the most common examples of the fixed-purpose type is the Link Trainer, a flight-training simulator that provides a student with aircraft responses while never leaving the ground.

Hybrid computers use both analog and digital elements and methods. Some automobile speedometers are beginning to use digital components and may be thought of as hybrids. Any computer that takes analog information, analyzes that information through programs in a digital system, and then displays the results on some form of screen or paper printout is a hybrid.

Many present uses or currently *possible* uses of computers predict their increasing involvement in our lives. Right now they switch telephone lines and are employed in editing TV tapes and film, collecting and grading college entrance exams, credit card monitoring, airline flight booking, commercial billing, the delivery of goods, and psychological testing. They are beginning to keep tabs on our federal budget. Many businessmen are using computers to set up their forms and to keep up with the mounting volume of information demanded by the bureaucracy. In fact, businesses are turning to computers in response to an interesting phenomenon in our society—the spread of the so-called "computer freaks."

The youths who "breadboarded" their own computers and began nibbling away at the big computer manufacturers' business are either big themselves now or fast on their way to that status. When a young computer expert goes to a local businessman and says:

"I can handle your inventory for you at a fraction of what you've been paying."

. . . that's a revolution.

Businessmen have a way of listening to such statements. When the truth is demonstrated, they may hope to keep this pleasant knowledge from the competition, but there is no way to keep something this big a permanent secret.

Per-capita spending on data processors, including home computers, is expected to top $2,000 by 1985. If present trends continue and are adjusted for such variables as inflation, that could well be a low figure. Computer business at that time could account for more than 15 percent of our gross national income. Many areas of our economy are coming to understand that computers are cost-effective when you figure in the time they save and the errors they prevent. It is clear that right now computers prevent far more errors than they cause. This is a ratio that is sure to become even more attractive.

The question is not "What's it all mean, Alfie?" but "Do you really know what your time is worth?"

What are some of the other computer-use implications?

We probably will see the custom manufacture of many consumer products—clothing, shoes, furniture, and even various kinds of vehicles—all on a mass-market basis. The entire process from ordering to delivery will be computer controlled.

Voice activation with computers suggests that we may return to the oral tradition of our earliest ancestors: fewer and fewer written records, more and more records on tape for immediate replay at your individual command. In its turn, this calls for a greater dependence upon your memory as we become increasingly interactive with computers.

The reduction in our use of paper could save entire forests.

15

Buyer's Guide II

Wares

Before tackling the problem of separating one ware from another, we had to make decisions about categories. How you break down a problem always includes some arbitrary choices. We tried to follow a logical pattern that would make it easier for you to understand programming. (We will go into more detail in Chapter 18. Consider this an introduction.)

First, there are the language levels. By language we mean the agreed-upon *words* that flip appropriate switches and make the machine do what you want. We broke the language levels down this way:

1. machine level
2. higher level

Machine level happens completely within the computer and is not generally readable by a human being without some computer aid. A higher-level language is one you can be taught to read. The words bring about a specified performance.

We then broke down the programming categories into three levels:

1. compilers
2. interpreters
3. assemblers

A *compiler* is a program that converts a language you can read into machine instructions. The language you can read is called a *source language,* and a program written in it is a *source program.*

An *interpreter* is a special kind of translating program. It takes each of your statements and translates them one by one, causing each translated statement to be executed before the next one is translated.

An *assembler* is a machine-language program. It has *words* that are abbreviated descriptions corresponding to machine-language switch patterns. Attempts have been made to have these words be easily remembered, but they don't necessarily make sense outside of their machine applications.

We had then the problem of the relationship between the physical devices for internal storage of programs. This, we divided into two categories:

1. RAMs—software
2. ROMs—firmware

Because RAMs can be changed by your program, they relate easily to the software concept. ROMs, on the other hand, are usually fixed firmly into the machine. Their switches are stuck. ROMs relate easily to the concept of firmware.

Two more program categories were then introduced:

1. service
2. applications

Service programs are operating systems. They put the machine and its accessories through their paces. Applications programs go to a specific problem, adapting the machine to particular jobs that you require—such as keeping track of your checking account.

Now, we can tackle the problem of "wares."

Wares has an archaic meaning of *being aware, conscious, watchful,* or even *cautious.* We want you to be at least watchful and aware while we explore the various computer wares.

In common usage, these wares come in three forms. There used to be only two, hard- and soft-, but the hard was too difficult to change and the soft was always slipping around and surprising people.

Firm- filled the gap.

Hardware refers to the actual equipment—the keyboard, the circuits, and all the physical devices attached to your computer. Hardware is solidly in place. The only way to change it is with screwdrivers, soldering irons, and an in-depth understanding of digital electronics.

Software refers to programs. It originally meant all programs including the ones that make the hardware work. Now, it's evolving into a word for programs that meet special requirements. These "applications programs" must be adapted easily to changing needs.

The advent of ROMs made it possible to put standardized machine language software into stuck switches. The result cannot be changed unless the ROM is replaced. This type of program with hardware permanence became known as firmware.

Firmware is evolving to include all types of programs that are not meant to change, whether they are in ROMs or not. These are the programs that make things happen "at night." They are tools of the applications programmer.

A great deal of programming goes into making your computer work. There are programs called *device handlers,* which cause pieces of equipment to function properly. Without them nothing happens.

There is a *master control program* called a *monitor.* It keeps the rest of the programs in their proper places and makes sure your commands are followed.

There are higher-level language translators that convert your BASIC (or other higher-level language) to a machine's corresponding switch patterns. Without these translators, the only way to write your programs would be to use the "1" and "0" bits at the single-switch level.

The program you will use most is called the *editor.* It lets you write what you want. You use it to write program statements and to issue commands.

If you have a mass storage device such as a disk, you will need special file maintenance programs to keep track of where things are stored.

These programs and others like them are called collectively the *operating system.* Your machine's operating system must match the hardware.

You can enter the wonderful new world of computer programming in several ways. If you're really inventive, you can make up your own rules, invent your own symbols and your own language. You just have to remember that the computer responds to electrical signals according to a very tight logical system. To program a computer you must be just as logical and just as regular no matter what symbol system you use.

Programming is nothing less than the skill of making your computer do what you want. You have some choices. You can learn it. You can buy it "prepackaged." Or you can buy some of it and modify this to create your own personal programs.

Here again, you have several choices on how to get your operating system. You can make it yourself. You can buy it as firmware—those stuck-switch ROMs. Or you can buy the software in one of several forms and install it yourself. You can also combine these methods for your own tailor-made system.

If you are a true do-it-yourselfer, you may want to write your own machine-language programs. You would start with your own assembler—the program that lets you write machine-language instructions with *words* instead of with "1s" and "0s." Perhaps you'd rather start with a cassette handler, again using "1s" and "0s" but giving you a way to save your assembler when you've finished it. Then you could write the keyboard interpreter loader and the handlers for the other devices, making them all work the way you want. Your own high-level language would be next on the list, after which you could start writing applications programs. The whole process could take several years.

Unless you want to work with computers themselves as a career, don't choose this route. Get a system that's already working.

Firmware operating systems are relatively new, relatively transparent (most things happen in the dark), and always there when you turn on your machine.

The disadvantage of firmware operating systems is that they cannot be changed without replacing ROMs. When you want to add a new piece of hardware to your computer, you either have to replace firmware or add appropriate software. If you try to combine software and firmware in a single operating system, don't blame us if you can't get it working.

Software operating systems are flexible. They have to be loaded somehow every time you turn on your computer, but this can be made automatic with a ROM loader. Later, if you decide to add a new piece of gear, you can modify software or add new and integrate this with the rest of the operating system. That is exacting work, not recommended for an amateur. You would be better off most times hiring an expert to do it for you.

Whatever operating system you choose, it should be tested thoroughly before you buy. Make sure the documentation is accurate and easy to read.

However you go about it, remember the levels of entry:

machine language
firmware
software

To the hardware, the only programming code is machine language. This uses the internal wiring system of the computer. Every elemental instruction your computer obeys has to be built into it with machine language. As we've indicated, that's a long and complicated process, which we do not recommend for beginners.

Sending one symbol from the keyboard to your screen may take twenty machine-language steps. You do not have to operate at that level; just know that it occurs. Because those steps are built into your computer, you can use a higher-level language, which combines them into longer steps each time you type an instruction.

The other type of language you may encounter, *assembly language,* was originally intended as a three-letter code that would correspond exactly to machine-language bits.

As you might guess, there is some confusion and overlapping in the use of the labels for the various languages.

What you need to remember is that firmware is the programming package that makes your computer work. It is often referred to as *system software.* Make sure it doesn't cramp your style. You address the firmware with a higher-level language. Think of firmware as intermediary between software and hardware. In the hardware, basic circuits are built into long trains of logic, the *instruction set.* These are coupled to even longer strings, the firmware. This steps up into much longer strings of logic, the software.

Firmware is written by specialists to help applications programmers perform their jobs. An applications program performs a specific task, such as making up a payroll. Firmware takes some of the tedium out of programming and helps eliminate errors. Just remember that you can buy it.

If you want to get into your own programming, almost any computer system will provide you with enough capability to learn the fundamentals of a higher-level language, one you can use to do your own programming. In fact, purchasing your own computer could be a much better investment for a would-be professional programmer than many of the classes being offered. At today's prices for specialized education you could even save money. Keep in mind that there's an art to programming that can only be mastered by practice.

Where do you buy programs?

At a computer store, from a manufacturer of computers, from a computer users' society, by mail order (look in the computer magazines), or from a professional programmer you hire for the job.

What do you do before buying an operating system?

You try to reject it.

You ask hard questions. Does it really do what you want? Does it work on your computer? (You'd be surprised at how many people mess up on that: wrong program for the computer.) Does it come with documentation?

Documentation should give you the name of the person responsible for the program. It should contain a short outline of the system with some comparative notes that detail benefits from using it. There should be a "handbook" section explaining essential things you need to know before using the system: output file instructions, the coding, any possible shortcuts and problems that are known from experience with the system.

The documentation also should contain some other historical notes on what users have encountered: special applications and possible modifications.

The whole thing should be in orderly form with an index and any reasons for changes in the variables.

Before you buy any system, you also should ask if it allows for the correction of typing mistakes. With some systems you have to start over every time you make a typing error.

And don't buy before you test the system yourself. This is the really critical question: Does it work for you? If it needs modification, are you sufficiently familiar with the programming language that you can modify it yourself?

You've decided you're going to buy the system?

Don't. See if you can find another one that does the same thing. Compare.

Welcome Home

Okay, you finally did it; you bought your own computer. NOW, don't do anything until you've read this short section.

First, exercise special care when you unpack the machine from its plastic cocoon. There may be small parts and manuals in there concealed between layers of protective Styrofoam.

You found the manual? Good.

Take your time setting up the computer and *follow the directions exactly.* You would be astonished at how many "machine errors" occur at this point—through faulty connection of elements by the buyer, a misreading of how you start up the computer, and such like.

Match the connectors carefully. Make the hookup to the CRT (which could be your home TV) only according to instructions.

Before you turn on the power, check to see if you have conformed to the grounding requirements for your new machine. Using a grounded socket makes good sense with any electronic equipment, but especially with computers. Some of them, if plugged into an ungrounded socket, are vulnerable to damage from a short circuit. If you don't have grounded sockets and they are a requirement, rig your own or call in an electrician. Grounding does not need to be a complicated nor a costly precaution. It can consist of nothing more than a wire from your plug clamped to a convenient cold waterpipe.

Make sure that every accessory you intend to use with your computer is matched to it. You should do this before buying, but there have been mistakes in shipments. Check it and be sure. If you have a problem with a mismatched accessory, the manufacturer of the computer and/or the accessory may have no solution to your problem. Everything must match—disk driver, cassette recorder, game controls, printer—anything that attaches to the computer.

These are all simple and ordinary precautions. Some are listed here only as reminders. We do not intend to indicate a serious *number* of problems. We want to emphasize that manufacturing flaws are remarkably rare with computers. One of the most common problems is the failure of a first-time user to follow installation and start-up instructions.

Get that manual and read it first.

16

Soloing

Put on your flying hat and goggles. Tie your Red Baron scarf around your neck. It's time for "switch on!"

The keyboard actually does look much like that of an electric typewriter, doesn't it? But notice the extra keys. Luckily, they are few and easy to learn. There should be one labeled RETURN or ENTER. That will be the most commonly used key on the board. It's a signal that you're finished with an INPUT and it's time for the computer to do its thing.

Okay, flip the switch to turn on your machine. The screen may show some random dots or lines or even other symbols. Whatever happens first, it should shift at once into a uniform background with nothing on it except perhaps something to indicate that your computer is standing by for your first commands. This may take the form of a small blinking square or rectangle, or an arrowhead—a *cursor* or a *prompt*.

Remember that a *cursor* merely marks your place on the screen. A *prompt* is a suggestion that you do something.

Some computers don't blink unless you make a mistake. There's nothing complicated about these signals from the machine. They just tell you what's happening.

There should have been a manual with your computer. If not, turn the machine off right now and go get a manual. The manual should describe the type of cursor/prompt and what the symbols indicate. The manual also should tell you what signal will be displayed on your screen to indicate that a higher-level language is in there and ready to use. Whatever that signal, it should flash onto your screen when you have done the right things at the keyboard. Just follow the instructions in your manual.

Some computers require you to enter BASIC from a storage device, such as a cassette. This will require you to type certain words and letters on your keyboard in a prescribed sequence, then punch the ENTER or RETURN key. A message indicating that the language is being loaded into the computer will appear on your screen. You may then see a rapid display of numbers. The thing is merely flipping its switches, not flipping out. The numbers and other symbols indicate switching sequences that are being programmed into the machine automatically.

If you have a friend who already knows BASIC, it would be helpful to have that friend sitting beside you right now. If not, refer to our chapter on BASIC, and remember that your new machine may use a *dialect* of BASIC slightly different from the one we used.

When the language is fully loaded in your machine, the screen should clear and the cursor should reappear. Depending on the computer you have bought, there may also be a list on your screen showing how much internal storage is still open for you to use.

Even without learning a language such as BASIC you can use quite sophisticated programs simply by loading them into the machine from an external source, using a cassette or disk driver. For this, you will need no more knowledge of the higher-level language than how to type the words LOAD and RUN.

LOAD means you want your machine to accept a program. When you type LOAD and hit the RETURN key, your computer is ready to accept a program.

While it is LOADing, your screen should display some sign that the system is doing what you told it to do. The cursor may blink, or there may be an audible *beep* and a play of numbers on your screen, or there may be just a *beep* and a steady cursor. Different computers respond differently. The manufacturer's manual will tell you what to expect.

When the program is loaded, there will be a distinct signal of some kind—a *beep,* an indicator on the screen, or simply the stopping of your tape deck or disk driver.

If something went wrong in the loading, your computer should also let you know this. The most common signal is the appearance of the word ERROR on the screen. It may also tell you what kind of error, whether you set the volume and tone controls wrong on your cassette recorder, for example.

ERROR signals that flash on your screen can take many forms. They include some of the following:

SYNTAX: You broke one or more of the rules that the computer's language structure must follow. (Worth noting: *Syntax,* meaning the grammatical rules of a language, is generally interpreted as meaning that the rules are finite. We assume that such rules have no absolute limits.)

NO END ERR: You forgot to tell the machine where the program ends.

RANGE ERR: You have gone beyond the numerical limits built into your computer.

STR OVFL ERR (string overflow error): Your computer cannot handle that long a train. Some computers will accompany STR OVFL ERR with a message such as STOPPED AT 20. That tells you at which statement number (20) the program stopped. You then can ask the machine to LIST 20. This puts the statement at 20 on your screen, where you can examine it and locate what you did wrong.

MEM FULL ERR (memory full error): You tried to put too much in a STORAGE system. Such systems have their limits, too, and your computer's manual will tell you the capacity of the system.

As you can see, the messages are direct and simple. Remember that you're dealing with a stupid machine, and such messages often define the limits of the machine's performance. It tells you how long a train you can assemble, how big a number you can use, the STORAGE limits, and the sequential strictures of the syntax. If you understand these messages, you have learned something about the machine's limits: which command signals you can send through it, how you pace your statements, and which orders *you* must follow to get the thing to *behave.*

Observe that just in using English to lay out the elements of these computer limits, we have employed a far more complex system than a computer can use.

However, once you've loaded the program correctly, all you have to do is type RUN and hit the RETURN or ENTER key. Remember that RETURN or ENTER signals the computer that you're done and now it's the computer's turn.

When you've typed RUN and hit RETURN, your screen should light up with a display telling you what this particular program does. This is your MENU. If the program deals with your bank balance, the MENU will tell you how to enter your new information, how to examine and perhaps change previous entries, or how to strike a new balance. You just follow the instructions and type the things that are spelled out in the MENU.

As we hope we have made clear to you, the computer can do such things as balancing your checking account when you hit a few keys on your keyboard. The computer will do the boring and tedious stuff automatically and very rapidly.

After you've examined the MENU and selected something for your computer to do, the screen may display instructions for the next step—how to strike a balance, how to enter new checks, how to examine the old checks, how to find a particular check (SORTING). . . . All you do is follow the simple instructions.

One of the nifty things such a program can do is to sort your checks according to your demand. You may remember only that you wrote a check to the hardware store sometime last year. Your computer will find the information on that check in a few seconds—amount, date, what it bought. You may remember only the amount. Your computer will display every check of that amount—with dates, who got them, and what they bought. You can go in by date, knowing only that you wrote such and such a check last year on December 23. All of the information on that check will come up on your screen. The computer will even display this information with no more INPUT from you than what it was you bought.

All of this can be done in your own simple code, a code you originate—TPHON for telephone, DEP for deposit, GASL for gas and oil, and so on. You can store the code itself in case you forget what meaning you assigned to what group of letters. You may forget, for instance, that you assigned STTX to state tax. Your computer will remind you when you LIST your code.

Presumably, you will remember without prompting that IRS stands for a common yearly problem shared by all of us. Please believe us, your computer can make such a profitable snap out of figuring your income tax that you'll wonder why you went so long without one.

Remember that every payment, every deposit you've made for the entire year is coded and identified and is in STORAGE only seconds away from your nimble fingers.

At your command the computer will display how much you spent during the year on your telephone, how much of that was business or long distance, what your food costs were, how much for entertainment, your gasoline taxes, the interest you paid on loans, what your savings earned, how much of anything in there was a business-related expense—all of it or any part of it available in just a few seconds, and shown as itemized displays or as totals or subtotals.

From all of this information sorted at your command and according to your own code, your computer will figure your taxes for you in only a fraction of the time it once took you. A half hour should be more than enough for the average householder. In that time you can try your tax computation in any of the ways legally available. Should you use the short form or the long form? Joint or separate returns? Itemized deductions or allowable averages?

Another feature is worth note: You can print out this tax information for visual inspection or audit. If you can't afford a printer, the printing can be purchased. You just take your cassette or disk to a computer store or similar establishment with a printer. Such facilities are becoming increasingly common and are sure to become even more common. We can even see the day when the IRS will provide this service. You're called in for an audit? You take in your receipts and your cassette. Your computer *talks* to their computer, and it's all over in a few minutes.

(A tax consultant of our acquaintance believes that the wide use of computers by householders to figure their taxes will force some fundamental changes in the law. Computers tend to show up illogical and confusing conflicts in rules. He also expects the members of his profession to get more and more into consulting and less and less into the actual figuring of your taxes; they will really be advisers rather than simply accountants. He estimates from his own experience that many householders could save the cost of a small personal computer in only a few years by wisely employing one to figure taxes.)

Keep in mind that you don't save much if any time feeding the necessary information into your machine. When you need the information, though, the time saving can be startling—seconds as compared with hours, a couple of hours as compared with weeks.

But you say: "I'm the world's worst typist! I make mistakes all the time!"

Simple. Most systems permit you to backspace to a mistake and correct it. Select only a system that does this easily. Even if it's a mistake you don't discover for months, there should be a relatively easy way to get back and reenter the corrected information. Insist on this capability. To make the correction, you may have to LOAD an entire program over again, but remember that your computer does this in seconds via tape or disk. Most computers have a CONTROL (CTRL), BREAK (BRK), or ESCAPE (ESC) key, which stops the program. To restart it, you just type RUN and hit RETURN. You're right back to square one and can repair any error just by following the instructions on the MENU.

Part of the *system monitor* lets you make such changes. This is the part called the *editor*.

When you type a statement, the editor puts it in the correct place in your program. It finds where the statement number belongs in the program and makes room for it by copying any larger-numbered statements into the unused portions of internal storage.

If the statement number has already been used, it copies the new statement in the same place while adjusting the storage size to fit the new entry. This obliterates the old statement—the one you have now corrected.

We told you that *soloing* could be fun. And we hope that the high-flying finance really was enjoyable. When you're finished with it, you can erase the program from temporary internal storage. It will be saved for you on the external storage device. Your own high finance—the checks and other information—can also be saved in external storage. You record it from the computer onto the tape or disk. Do this before you shut down your machine and lose all of that INPUT.

Erasure of internal storage is easy, sometimes too easy. Learn the procedure carefully and how to avoid it when you don't want it. Check the manual. It will describe the procedure. In erasing a program, you'll want to be sure that you don't also erase BASIC. For most computers, erasing temporary programs is simply a matter of typing NEW and hitting the RETURN key.

It's time to end your first solo flight now. Before you shut off the machine, make sure you're not about to cause a crash. That is the word, by the way, for a loss of information through a power failure or other shut-down error. Save your information, then turn off the machine.

That's how it works. Simpler than you expected, wasn't it?

17

Review Time

In the beginning there were just 1s and 0s.

Different two-state switch patterns of a program made different things happen. The things that happened received names that roughly corresponded to what was happening and where it happened.

It was all very technical.

As time went on, the names were shortened to groups of letters called *mnemonics*. These were like the alphabetical names of government agencies. They often stood for several words—like ISZ for "increment and skip on zero" or IOC for "INPUT-OUTPUT command."

Still very technical but much easier to read than a column of 1s and 0s. Programs called assemblers were made to translate the mnemonics to their corresponding switch patterns in the machine.

One day, a "data processing chief" was ordering another filing cabinet. He was checking sizes and uses of the ones he already had when he saw an overloaded cabinet with a tag on it: "INPUT." He asked his file clerk what the heck that meant.

The file clerk said:

"We've had two thousand programmers through here in the past six years, and they all had one thing in common: They liked to figure things out for themselves. We used to keep files according to author, but nobody could remember who'd written what, and last year you sent out that memo telling us to arrange this stuff by subject."

"So what did you do?"

"Well, I didn't know quite what to do because most of this stuff is beyond me, but I talked to Dennis in Programming about it. He said he'd have a look at it, and it turned out that all two thousand programmers had these complicated and somewhat different ways of doing what Dennis calls 'setting the switches.' "

To make a long story short, the data processsing chief had a look in the filing cabinet called INPUT and found out that every programmer was using a slightly different assembly language program.

"I'm building a Tower of Babel!" he said.

The answer was obvious. There had to be some standardization of languages at a higher level. But his programmers objected, crying out for "flexibility," meaning each wanted to do his own thing. This flexibility is great, but flexible languages are harder to use and certainly harder to learn. Easier languages are rather rigid. BASIC, the higher-level language we are recommending, is really quite rigid, but it is very easy to learn and a beginner can use it.

Standardization, then, required a compromise between flexibility and ease of use and learning. The compromise resulted in what are called *operating systems,* and this brings in a whole new vocabulary. We'll get to that presently.

As we have said, programming is nothing less than the skill of making your computer do what you want. You have some choices. You can learn it. You can buy it "pre-packaged." Or you can buy some of it and modify this to create personal programs.

If you're really inventive, you can make up your own rules. You can invent your own symbols and your own language. You just have to remember that the computer responds to electrical signals according to its very tight logical system. To program a computer you must be just as logical and just as regular no matter what symbol system you use.

Even if you buy and use only the prepackaged variety, remember the levels of entry and the labels:

Machine language and assembly language. These are firmly attached to the hardware, built into the preset switching systems.

Higher-level language—firmware. As the *firm-* implies, these also are solidly fixed, not to be changed.

Applications programs—software. These are the things you can change if you know the language. The code has a certain flexibility.

Machine language uses the wiring system internal to the machine itself. Every elemental instruction your computer follows has to be built into it with machine language. Sending one symbol from the keyboard to your screen may take twenty machine-language steps.

Because such steps are built into your computer, you can use a higher-level language, which takes longer steps each time you issue an instruction.

Assembly language was originally intended as a code that would correspond exactly to machine language *words* rather than to numbers.

Assemblers have advantages and disadvantages. Both are to be found in the language itself. To understand the mnemonics, a programmer needs a background in digital electronics. The advantage, also found in the language, rests in dealing directly with machine language. This yields faster and more efficient programs.

Compilers are often frustrating. If there's anything wrong with any statement anywhere in the program, nothing happens except an incomprehensible list of error messages. It takes a long time to translate the entire program, and all the programmer can do meantime is hope against hope that this time the thing will actually get translated. But there's usually something wrong somewhere, and you have to "debug" it. However, once it's working, the translation is pretty efficient. Any programmer worth his salt will guard a working compiler translation with his life.

With any program you buy or adapt keep in mind the facility of the language in which the program is written. The program should be compatible with you as well as with your computer. If you choose to write programs in an easily learned language, you will sacrifice some flexibility for the ease. The limits of your computer's storage, given a rigid language for programming, can limit the kinds of programs available to you. Rigid languages use up a lot of storage very fast.

It boils down to what you want to do with your computer. Presumably, you already have gone into that decision. Just make sure the program language and the system will work for you.

All of this is preparation for your next step. You now should be ready to go on into more advanced Computertalk.

18

Computertalk
Spoken Here

As is probably clear to you now, the past three decades have seen the age-old tradition of trial and error run wild in the computer world. Language evolution followed much the same pattern in computer programming that it did in human languages—starting with pictographic switch patterns and running through brief phrases that embodied extensive accumulations of human experience.

That's right: *human* experience.

Remember that it was human experience that made computer languages happen. The experiences of thousands of people directly involved in making computers useful were combined over the years. Sections of programs that were used repeatedly in many different applications were converted into single units that could be used by name.

Gradually, the list of names grew. These, in turn, were combined into single groups of higher-level languages.

It should not surprise you that one computer language can say things others cannot say. After all, you can say things in Spanish which you cannot say in English—and vice versa. Some languages have difficulty separating yesterday and tomorrow. The operative word means "not today." It is common to hear speakers insert brief bursts of English to meet this problem.

With computers, a lot of different machines were built by different people to solve a wide variety of problems. The major categories involved business, scientific, information handling, word processing, simulation, graphics, and process control. In time, the list grew to include such things as medical diagnosis, aircraft navigation, and, of course, computer games.

Each general application had its own specific set of requirements. For instance, the major requiremert of the scientific and engineering crowd was to find quick answers to complex calculations. The business community wanted a device to print the many forms they needed to keep their books up to date, a way to keep up on inventory and sales. Governments, large corporations, and libraries needed to keep track of enormous quantities of information. Industry needed computers to control the operation of complex machines. Research and development centers needed ways to simulate designs, make changes, and explore consequences of their changes. Architects and designers needed ways to make drawings that could be changed easily.

Most of these problems were solved from the ground up, independently. Each specialty struck off on its own. Machines were built that could calculate efficiently, print, store information, and control other machines.

Languages evolved to make these different machines do their different jobs. And some of these languages were formalized by the American National Standards Institute (ANSI).

Early languages suffered from a common malady: They were difficult to master. Although attempts were made to relate names of operations to conventional languages, the parallels were often obscure, and limits were imposed by such things as storage size and accessories. These varied widely from machine to machine. Complicated formats had to be followed exactly. Even then, errors in manufacturers' manuals were frustratingly common. Machines broke down often, and there was a shortage of people who could repair them.

On top of all this, the machines were so expensive that only a small percentage of time could be allowed for program development. Programmers often had to wait weeks to find out whether a particular program worked properly. If the program did not perform as expected (the case more often than not), it took more time for the programmer to get back into the original train of thought before he could resolve the problem.

A great deal of time and effort went into finding a reasonable solution to these problems. This led to the development of new types of languages. Before we get into these new languages, you need to know some of the things that made it difficult to use the old ones—even after they had been mastered.

Briefly, the names used were translated by the machine into groups of machine-language instructions that enabled the computer to do its work. This translation was done by a special program known as a *compiler*.

The compiler process involved putting a complete higher-level language program into a computer's internal storage *along with the compiler*. The compiler program itself was a long and complex thing. And you had to make sure that the higher-level program was complete and that all the limits had been observed. It was tedium amplified.

This was only a beginning.

You then had to go through the laborious process of translation. The resulting machine-language program had to be placed step by step into internal storage. Often there wasn't enough room for this in internal storage. When that problem showed up, it was necessary to do the job piecemeal, placing sections of the programs into some external storage and copying back into internal storage when needed. When you did *that*, you first had to move another section of program out into another external storage system to make room.

This was not only time consuming, it led to monumental bookkeeping problems.

Today, we have a new type of language with which it's easier to make changes. It's called an *interpretive language* and it differs from compiled languages in fundamental ways. Instead of translating the whole higher-level program all at once into machine language, the translator program (in this case called the *interpreter*) is in permanent internal storage at all times. It interprets only one higher-level instruction at a time. It then performs the machine-language steps of that instruction and goes on to the next instruction.

That procedure saves a considerable amount of time and space.

There's another new type of language, even more important in potential, about which you should have more than a nodding acquaintance. It is similar to the older higher-level languages in that it must be compiled. But it is much easier to learn than the old languages because it has been successfully unified. The basic programming concepts have been reduced to a short list of building blocks similar to an alphabet. With this language you no longer need to treat each peripheral machine attached to your computer as different from any other machine you have attached. As far as the computer is concerned, there is no difference between switching information to an external storage device or to a telephone line. Switching to a CRT, to another place in internal storage, or to a printer—it's all the same to this language.

That uniformity makes it easy to simplify the programming operation into the necessary juggling of information. It lets the operating system take care of all the mundane details and the information ends up where it is supposed to go.

This is the *structured language* to which we have referred (see page 114).UNIX uses a structured language.

What the structured-language concept has done is to open the door to an enormously increased variety of applications. It lets you concentrate on putting information into the system and getting out what you need. A structured language consists of a short list of carefully thought-out operations that go directly to the essence of SWITCHING. Special routines are called into action just by naming them. Once the structure is learned, structured languages are the easiest with which to write programs.

The bad news? The structure is complex and somewhat difficult to learn, making it less suitable for a beginner.

Let's go through the vocabulary once more and get it firmly in your mind.

Assembler

This translates assembly language into corresponding switch patterns of machine language.

Compiler

This translates Englishlike higher-level languages into switch patterns. The entire program is translated each time.

Interpreter

This also translates Englishlike higher-level languages into switch patterns, but each statement is translated by itself during execution. Interpreters speed up programming. If a statement is set up correctly according to the rules, it gets translated and executed. If something is wrong with it, it stops and prints an incomprehensible error message, but at least you know where the culprit is. The same thing that makes an interpreter nice for programming makes it lousy for efficiency. Every time it is run, the program has to be translated statement by statement before it can be executed.

Handler

A machine-language program that makes a specific accessory work. It is said to be *dedicated* to that accessory. It is also called a device handler and is not to be confused with "device management," which will be explained shortly.

Monitor

A master control program. It accepts commands and invokes various routines needed to carry out those routines. It usually includes an editor.

Operating system

All of the firmware. It includes handlers, monitor, language support, and device management. In the operating system, device management divides up the system so that many devices can share it.

What you should understand from all of this is that each language has its limits—its range of performance. The language handles details for you automatically, commanding sometimes hundreds or even thousands of the tiny machine-language switching patterns.

The higher-level languages are already legion and growing. They sometimes have strange names such as BLISS, MUMPS, SNOBOL, FORTH, LOGO, and GRASS. Sometimes they go simply by initials—such as APL.

APL stands for "a programming language." It was devised by Kenneth Iverson and is a powerful system for expressing mathematical concepts. That makes it very useful in programming. Because mathematical-scientific notation just "growed like Topsy," it has many chaotic features. Iverson undertook to take the chaos out of such notation by creating a new system that follows some orderly general rules. APL may survive as the one lasting achievement to come out of the complex computer mystique that fostered it. If you're interested, Microsoft markets a version of APL.

Earlier, we mentioned FORTRAN and COBOL as the parent languages from which BASIC was derived.

FORTRAN simplifies the programming of algebraic formulas. It stands for "formula translation." Many programmers now consider FORTRAN to be a "period piece" that has been supplanted by languages better at what it was supposed to do.

COBOL stands for "common business oriented language." As with FORTRAN, it is decidedly inflexible for certain applications and is rapidly being superseded.

BASIC is the standard language of hobby and amateur computing and, because of the ease in learning it, will very likely be the basis for all home-computer systems for some time. As a beginner's language, it may never be superseded, although it is sure to incorporate some changes.

If you're looking for a structured language, try PASCAL.

Here are a few others:

ALGOL—a language expressing mathematical procedures in a relatively pure form. As such, it is widely used to compile computer procedures in a way that other programmers will understand.

PL/I (programming language 1)—a product of IBM and, as such, has a strong bias toward maintaining the salability of IBM computers. It combines elements of FORTRAN, ALGOL, and COBOL, picking up many of their strengths and also some of their limits.

SMALLTALK—a language created by Alan C. Kay and associates at the Xerox Palo Alto Research Center. The development of SMALLTALK was guided by ideas in SIMULA, a programming language developed in the mid-1960s by Ole-Johan Dahl and Kristen Nygaard at the Norwegian Computing Center in Oslo. SMALLTALK leans heavily on graphic symbol techniques and for this reason is readily understood by beginners and children. The concepts being developed in SMALLTALK may very well sweep the computer language field.

Before leaving this short overview of the various higher-level languages, we should mention the LAMBDA languages, all based on Lambda calculus (which you do not need to know even if you want to use them). A key strength of these languages lies in the fact that the results of any operation can be made the basis for any new operation. The original LAMBDA language is called LISP, and one of its most identifying features is its frequent use of parenthesis. LISP stands for "List Processing" and it is an interpretive language. It provides a powerful handle on symbolic lists and on arithmetic logic.

If you want a language with such features, you have some choices: These include LOGO (developed at MIT) or TRAC. TRAC was invented by Calvin Mooers and is a trademark of Rockford Research, Inc., 140½ Mount Auburn Street, Cambridge, Mass. 02138. Both are suited to small computers. TRAC can be run with only 8K storage.

You should emerge from this chapter with an understanding that hardware development is far ahead of software development. Software is much more tedious and difficult to create than the beginner suspects, but this is changing rapidly. Someday, your computer will create your software for you.

19

Let's Talk About Programming

Things we've demonstrated and described have probably given you the correct notion that it requires time and concentration to program a computer in a way that will make it perform to your satisfaction. Before you start using that as an excuse to avoid everything about programming, you should be reminded that these machines have been around long enough that there are a large number of people who have spent much of their lives putting many little computer pieces together, and one result is that what once had to be done in a tedious way by machine language can be done today in big chunks. What once took months can be done now in a matter of days or even hours. This process of putting greater and greater detail into more and more powerful (but less cumbersome) statements has not stopped.

In common with other interpreters and undercover agents, programmers not only must second-guess the king but keep from rousing the rabble, that is, they must speak both the hard and soft languages. That's why we began by introducing you to the moronic hardware, the simple switches first, and are now graduating by easy steps into the more complex switch patterns of higher-level languages.

Take heart from the fact we mentioned in the first paragraph of this chapter. Because so many people have recognized the need to understand programming before these machines can be made to perform, there are an increasing number of programmers around. What this means is that the novice has a far greater chance today of finding a program to suit a particular need—or very nearly suit that need. It also has become easier to buy programs that can be changed, and it's easier to change those programs to fit your needs.

It is misleading, though, to suggest that your computer will *only* do what you program it to do. That sounds true, but it assumes you can predict everything a particular computer and its programs will do. Sorry, but there's always an edge of indeterminate reaction even in simple computers. That's a product of many things, but they all boil down to human error and ignorance.

Ignorance has a special meaning here. It touches that barrier between consciousness and unconsciousness through which bursts of insight sometimes cascade, that reservoir of "the unknown." Being aware of this, all you can say about a computer is that no matter what it does, the performance can be traced back into how it was manufactured and into the logical limits imposed by its hardware and programs.

When you doubt your computer's results, go back to what went into the thing. "Back to the drawing board!" is often the best rule in many human enterprises.

DON'T DEPEND ON OUTPUT UNTIL YOU'VE TESTED THE ASSUMPTIONS.

Untested assumptions are tricky, but the trickiest of all are those assumptions we do not even recognize as being assumptions.

Programming involves many assumptions about the various wares. These are generally rooted in the assumption that the hardware *works*. Reliability of machine. Generally, you should make that assumption the object of a quick test when you have problems. Switches on? CRT plugged in correctly? Just remember that you have a more powerful thinking system than the computer has.

Check the logic.

As we told you earlier, your computer builds all of its activities around Boolean logic—three concepts: AND, OR, and NOT—plus STORAGE. These produce your computer's instructions—the elements of programming. The system operates only one step at a time. It requires an internal "yardmaster" to switch between trains of operations and trains of information. (Anyone who believes that this defines human thinking has to be pretty simpleminded.)

To program, you will be dealing with a hierarchy of logical steps— from the king, who can give grand orders, right on down to the peasants, who must carry out every tedious detail.

There are laws of the land that even the king must obey. Syntax is one of those laws. This refers to the grammatical rules of the programming language. The rules for BASIC are few, simple, easy to learn.

To program your computer, you will divide the program into necessary steps. This will break down what you want to do into its most elemental parts. You will have to make a list of those parts, one statement at a time. We'll get to that presently.

We've taken this short excursion because we think you should at least get into the rudiments of programming, but we want you to understand some of the restrictions.

When you play a computer game, use a one-purpose control system such as an automatic telephone dialer, or even set a preprogrammed thermostat, you are using someone else's program. You are not learning how to program, you are learning how to set the cruise control. This can be useful and even fun, but it doesn't provide real insights into the scope of your new machine.

What you really need to know about this programming hierarchy is that it's in there performing in a stepped fashion—from the simple to the more complex. Each key you touch on your keyboard executes a number of switching responses in the machine. Your handle on the system is the programming language. We're recommending you learn the language called BASIC.

20

Telling It Who's Boss

Many people who dive directly into the use of computers discover quite early that the hardware is so stupid you have to know something about programming if you ever hope to make the machine do anything.

We hope we've made it plain that you can get a great deal of valuable use out of your computer without knowing very much about programming. Many of you may decide never to enter this area of computer use, and for a variety of understandable reasons:

It just doesn't interest you.

You don't have time.

You think it's too difficult. (That ain't necessarily so.)

You think it's too tedious. (It *can* be tedious, but it also can be fun.)

We urge you to ignore all of those *rational* arguments and get into programming at least on an elementary level, and for important reasons:

It can make your machine more versatile.

It gives you another powerful lever on a world fast becoming profoundly computerized.

It makes you less dependent upon specialists.

Even if you lean heavily on prewritten programs, your own ability to program will let you modify those "store-boughts" to suit your individual needs.

Learning to program keeps the machine in its proper place—your tool. The thing is a dumb machine. To program it you have to tell it every step to take and when to take that step. Omit one step and it flunks out. A three-year-old child requires less "programming" to perform complicated tasks.

151

We have an axiom that states the case:

ENGAGE LOGIC BEFORE PUTTING PROGRAM IN GEAR.

There is a relatively recent approach to the required skill called "top-down programming." This means that the entire purpose of the program is written down in plain English before any attempt to translate the problem into computer language. Storage sizes are specified, sequences of operations are laid out—everything the program will do is clearly identified.

A tool of this plain English version is the flowchart. We'll give you an introduction to flowcharts presently. There's a more detailed treatment in Appendixes C, F, and H. For now, you only have to understand that a flowchart serves mainly as a picture of the order in which your program *flows*. It is a rough sketch of information movement and program functions.

In programming, you are translating *down,* stepping down from the general to the specific. You are working out consequences, arranging the logical placement of decision points. Your goal is a kind of deceptive precision, where the answer will be no better than the information through which you got that answer. By now you should understand without any hesitation that your computer responds only to electrical signals in a very tight logical system that can be handled by two-state switches. The switches are set in on-off patterns, which can stand for a great many different things and *which can be recognized.* To program such a device, you must be every bit as logical and regular. You must follow a stepped sequence—by the numbers. The computer does nothing more than process what you give it. Remember GIGO—garbage in, garbage out. Like a goat, your computer will "eat" almost anything. When you doubt the results, you have to go back to the front end. What went in?

Programming is good training for you. Never doubt that your computer is a superb educational tool. Programming teaches you orderly thinking, another piece of armament in your mental arsenal. A computer is absolutely unforgiving in its demand for order.

There's a right way, a wrong way, and the computer way.

The right way is the way people think without computer limits—in the round, multichannel, recognizing grand patterns and intuitively grasping totalities, with thoughts smoothly flowing in a continuum.

The wrong way is the way that gets you into the blind alley described by the old Down East joke: "There ain't no way to get there from here, mister."

The computer way is stolid, one step at a time, rigorously logical, reduced to clear and elemental order. In a real sense, you are shifting into a "low gear" and therefore into a very powerful system that will haul heavy loads.

As we've let slip on several occasions, we recommend that you write your programs in BASIC. This is one of those "higher-level languages" we've mentioned from time to time.

BASIC stands for "Beginners All-purpose Symbolic Instruction Code." It originated with a group working at Dartmouth in the 1960s. They set out to make a computer easier to understand and to use. In part, BASIC is a simplified version of FORTRAN (formula translation), but it also reveals a relationship with COBOL (common business oriented language).

Do not confuse BASIC with basic English. They have aspects in common, aspects you will find useful, but it would be misleading to confuse them. Basic English is still "plain English." Your computer's BASIC is a kind of easy shorthand that is derived from English and from the design requirement of the machine. It unites a large number of elementary instructions in each statement and, what is highly important, makes most of those statements with common words that signal to you as well as to the machine what is to be done. Rooted in English, BASIC is a very powerful tool for operating your computer, and because of that affinity to English, it is relatively easy to learn.

While BASIC is one of the easiest of all computer languages to learn, complex problems require complex programs when you are confined to this language. Be assured, though, that the way it echoes English plus its similarity to other higher-level languages more than make up for its limitations. It will probably endure for many years as a first language for beginners.

Computers that employ BASIC all use a similar syntax. In case you have forgotten, syntax refers to the rules and patterns that control the meanings in sentences and phrases. It is made up of agreed-upon signals that tell you the meaning (if any) in any group of words. We all know, for example, that "The man ate the cow" has quite a different meaning from "The cow ate the man."

Computers with similar syntax in their BASIC may differ in size of vocabulary and the definitions of some words, but you can consider all such variations as minor differences in dialect. One BASIC will let you understand another quite easily. Substitution lists are available for translating from one BASIC to another. Such lists are very small. It's as though you were translating from British English to the American version. "Lift" would become "elevator." "Bonnet" would become "hood of a car." Your own experience with the two versions of English probably already tells you what limits to expect. We presume you don't have too much difficulty understanding a British-made "flic" when it's played on your "telly."

Capacity limits also influence the language. If you bought a computer with a small but highly efficient version of BASIC, say one taking up only 4K of storage, then it probably would break down if you tried to write your program in an 8K BASIC. (K = thousand, remember? In computerese, *K* stands for a "thousand bytes." For technical reasons, this is actually 1,024 bytes, but you can ignore this in most applications.)

As you've probably guessed, there's another side to this capacity coin. An *Extended* BASIC, requiring 12K or 16K of storage, would be able to override the limits of the simpler form. Extended can also perform more complex operations.

All programming languages have rules. Some of the rules are so fundamental you must know them before you can do anything. Others let you do more things or make it easier to do certain types of things. We are taking you on a tour of BASIC and *its* syntax. Those rules involve the order in which you must *say* things. We all know it's unlikely a cow will eat a man, but we certainly understand the meaning carried in the sequential order of the words. We know who did what to which simply because of the order.

In BASIC the most elemental syntax of typing things on the keyboard requires that you type the thing and then hit the RETURN key. This key signals the computer that you're done typing something. Anything you type has to end with it.

BASIC has two modes of operation: command mode and program mode. When your computer is turned on, it is in one mode or the other. When it is in command mode, you can type a *command instruction* (*command* for short) or a *program statement* (*statement* for short). When it is in program mode, whatever you type is taken as INPUT information to the program. Whether it is a command or a statement or a program INPUT, the last key you type is the RETURN key. Here is the most elemental BASIC syntax:

```
SOMETHING
RETURN
```

Hitting the RETURN key when you have completed a line of instruction, a command or an input, should become second nature. Do it enough times and you won't even think about it.

When you first turn on your computer, it is in the *command mode*. It is ready for you to type a command or a statement. The syntax of a command is

COMMAND

then

RETURN

This causes something to happen immediately. You type it, the computer does what it's supposed to right away, and then the command signals are gone. Commands are not saved anywhere in the computer.

Statements are different. The first thing you type in a statement is a number. This is called the statement number. It signals your computer that the line is a statement instead of a command. The syntax of a statement is

STATEMENT NUMBER
INSTRUCTION
RETURN

The only thing that happens when you follow this statement sequence is that the things you type get saved in your program.

When you hit the RETURN key, that signals the computer that you're through with what you're doing and now the computer must do what it does. Every separate command or statement has to end with you hitting this key.

The shortest program you can have in BASIC is one statement long:

32000 END

You turn on your computer and make sure it's in the command mode. (Refer to your manufacturer's manual for this procedure.)

Now, type the word NEW.

This is a special command that removes any BASIC program from internal storage and allows the input of a new program. Other special commands that let you do things "around" your program will be introduced as we proceed. They are different from statements that are the actual program steps.

END is a statement. Even if your computer lets you RUN a program without this statement, you should get into the habit of using it. Many computers with limited BASIC require END as the final statement of a program. If you fail to put this statement in the program on such a machine, the program won't RUN.

Each line of a BASIC program has to start with a statement number, sometimes called a line number. Normally, the statement in a particular line will be executed when its line number is the smallest of the remaining numbers in the program. This orderly sequence (from lower numbers to higher) can be modified by the program with a special type of statement called a *control statement,* which we will explain presently.

Since the END statement must have the largest line number in the program, you can anticipate this by writing it at the beginning with the largest allowable number, 32767—usually rounded down to 32000. That puts it at the END where it belongs.

Now, we can type our shortest program:

32000 END

That's it. The program is finished.

To execute it, we use a special command: RUN. Commands don't require line numbers. Just type RUN and hit the RETURN key.

When you hit RETURN, the cursor moves over to the left and another prompt is printed. It would appear that nothing has happened, since just hitting RETURN when you're in command mode *always* makes the cursor move over to the left and print another prompt.

However, there is a difference.

The word RUN does execute whatever BASIC program is in the internal storage. If there's no program stored, an ERROR message is printed. If something's wrong with one of the program statements, an ERROR message is printed. Under these circumstances, the only way to prevent an ERROR message is to have a valid BASIC program in the machine.

Here's what happens:

The program is first checked to see if there's an END statement. Since there is, the program is executed. But the first statement is END, which signals that the program is finished. The prompt is then displayed and the machine is ready for your next command.

Let's go on to something more important now.

If you were to ask for the most important statement in BASIC, the answer would have to be PRINT. Without it, your program has no way to get your attention. Everything going on inside the machine would be invisible.

There are several versions of the PRINT statement, but we'll just go into one of them at this point. This is the use of PRINT to display any symbols enclosed by double quotes. Put this in your machine:

```
1000 PRINT "ANYTHING"
32000 END
```

When you run this, your computer will display

```
ANYTHING
```

PRINTING things in quotes is useful for requesting specific information. When your program is at a point where it needs input, for instance, you can insert this sort of thing:

```
PRINT "TYPE NAME"
```

If you put that just before the INPUT statement, the person using the program will see on the screen exactly what is needed.

This sort of PRINTing is limited to "constant" information. It's something you already know when you're writing the program. A "variable" however, is something that can change. Since this variable *something* often happens "in the dark," if you want to know what it is, you can PRINT it.

There are two types of variables: *integer* and *string*. Integer variables represent numbers between -32767 and $+32767$. String variables represent groups of characters (letters, marks, or special symbols).

Integer variables are named with a letter. (Some computers allow a name with more than one letter—see your manual.) The letter is followed by a number in parentheses. The number indicates how many integers use that variable name.

String variables are named with a letter followed by a dollar sign ($) and a number in parentheses. The number indicates how many symbols can be in the string.

The dollar sign is what differentiates a string variable from an integer variable. Your manual will tell you the maximum number of symbols you can have in one string and the maximum number of integers that can use one integer variable name.

Don't be confused by our use of *name* in this context. If you have a dog named George and you call his name, George is supposed to show up. If you have a string variable named *G$* and you call that name (on your computer), that string variable is supposed to show up. The difference between George and *G$* is that *G$* may give you a more reliable response. The dog George we had tended to ignore all calls except those for dinner.

Now, back to BASIC:

With most machines, should you want to see how the BASIC program is inserted in the machine, you simply type LIST and hit the RETURN key (or its equivalent). Your screen now will list lines of letters, numbers, and other symbols. Each line will be preceded by a number in increasing order, the statement number of the program.

The personal computer we used as a model and reminder for preparing this book employs Extended BASIC. There are some easily remembered things you do when you work with such a machine syntax. For instance, quotation marks have a special significance. And one of the most common BASIC instructions is PRINT. If you tell your machine:

PRINT 15 + 5

and then hit the RETURN key, it will display

20

It has added 15 and 5, which is what you commanded it to do. But if you put quotation marks on your command this way:

PRINT "15 + 5"

it will produce this display:

15 + 5

It will simply display whatever you put between quotes. Similarly, if you type

"15 + 5 ="; 15 + 5

and *now* hit the RETURN key, your screen will display:

15 + 5 = 20

Anyone unfamiliar with the things we already have revealed to you and seeing such a display might assume the computer had done something intelligent. We leave it to you to explain to such a rank amateur that the machine merely displayed the results of *your* intelligence. Anything your computer does, no matter how advanced, sophisticated, or complex, is just an extension of that kind of intelligence. You do it; the machine obeys.

You may have noticed the semicolon in the line we told you to type. The semicolon controls the number of spaces inserted after the equals sign. Commas, semicolons, or TABS merely position the symbols on your screen. These can help you set up columns, tables, and the like as well as space your information for easier reading.

You already have learned some important elements of BASIC programming. Quotation marks in the PRINT command cause your computer to display whatever you type between them. If you type:

PRINT "MY NAME IS JOHN HENRY"

your computer displays

MY NAME IS JOHN HENRY

The train of symbols between the quotes is called a *string*. Your computer has limits on the length of such trains it can handle. No big deal. Whatever that limit, when you reach it, you close the quotes and start a new line, again within quotes. Extended BASIC and some other higher-level languages permit you to edit and sort strings of text. Such functions are included in "word processing packages."

Referring back to the PRINT command, your computer is limited in what it can respond to without quotes. If you type

PRINT MY NAME IS JOHN HENRY

your computer will display

SYNTAX ERROR

or some other indication that you have asked for something that is outside the sequencing or other rules the machine must obey. BASIC has no connections that will permit it to PRINT unquoted text.

Mathematical problems are a different matter. Division, multiplication, addition, and subtraction fit right into a computer's hardware. The switches are designed to flip with relative ease for such problems. The answers will be displayed in familiar form. You probably are already familiar with three of the commands for these mathematical functions, + (plus), − (minus), and / (divided by). However, to avoid confusion with the letter *X*, BASIC uses an asterisk (*) to indicate multiplication. You have only one new symbol to learn and you can perform addition, subtraction, division, and multiplication on your computer.

The computer will also store parts of a problem until you need them. If you type

    A = 549
    B = 10

you can tell your computer to

    PRINT A*B

Since it has number equivalents of A and B stored in one of its handy switching systems, your computer (when you hit the RETURN key) will display

    5490

the multiplication of 10 times 549.

That's a handy thing when you're dealing with many numbers and many different operations on them. For you math buffs, BASIC in your computer also handles exponentials with ease. The symbol is an upward pointing arrow ↑ or ∧. Thus, 3 ↑ 5 is a short way of telling the machine to perform the following multiplication: 3*3*3*3*3 (3 multiplied by itself five times).

BASIC programs have rules (a syntax). When you want to type a complete program, you first type the command NEW and hit the RETURN key. This removes any other BASIC program already in internal storage. Now you can type the statements of your new program. The largest-numbered statements must be END on most machines.

You can also tell your computer to repeat an instruction by using the BASIC word GOTO. Thus, if you type

```
10 PRINT "HELLO"
20 GOTO 10
30 END
```

then command your short program to RUN, your screen will fill up with HELLOs. The 30 END instruction keeps your machine from flashing an ERROR signal. You can stop the repeated HELLOs by hitting the CTRL (control) key and the letter C simultaneously or by performing whatever appropriate BREAK command is outlined in your manufacturer's manual. It's very simple.

In this example, your computer is performing a controlled stutter. You have set up an endless loop. The machine, operating at its one-step-at-a-time limits, performs the instruction at line 10, then does what it's told to do at line 20, which tells it to repeat the instruction at line 10.

When we were telling you about the simpleton limits of computer logic, we pointed out that these machines are great at comparing. They can supply answers to questions about

less than $<$

greater than $>$

less than or equal to $<=$

greater than or equal to $>=$

not equal to $<>$

The BASIC symbols for these functions are shown at the right. These apply not only to numbers but to any other quantities you can feed into your computer. They can compare the lengths of textual strings and sort in many different ways for word editing. BASIC will also square numbers or round them off. It has another function that approximates randomness. You get this by typing RND (RANDOM). The machine plus program limits are the real limits to such random selection. Most good random programs will give you a statistically accurate randomness within usable limits. When you use the RND instruction, the machine displays a number chosen by its RANDOM program and within whatever limits you have set—a random number from 1 to 10, for example. With this program, it will flip an imaginary coin for you, indicating "heads" or "tails" ad infinitum. This function has been used in many computer games.

As you grow more skillful in writing programs, you will find that some simple programs can be used at many places in a longer program. To do this you save the simple program as a subroutine. Any time you want to reuse that short program without recopying it, you tell the computer to GOSUB and follow this with the proper statement number for the start of the subroutine loop.

The similarity between these BASIC words and their English language equivalents will not have escaped you. This makes them extremely easy to remember. You already have familiar hooks in your own memory upon which to hang these new words.

There are few delights to compare to having your instructions carried out precisely to the letter every time. Computers are famous for doing just that. It is up to you to make sure the instructions you give it reflect what you want it to do. That is the art of programming. The payoff is that once you have solved a particular problem with a program, the computer will faithfully solve that problem for you forevermore.

21

A BASIC Vocabulary

The vocabulary of the BASIC language consists of a list of *statements,* each of which has a definite function. Within many of the statements are modifiers that should be understood before you try to program.

A statement may be preceded by a statement number. This number identifies a particular statement and sets its fixed position in an orderly sequence of statements. A BASIC program starts at the statement with the smallest statement number and proceeds in sequence to the largest, unless the order is changed by one of the control statements. (See GOSUB and GOTO)

Some of the statements include *expressions.* This has become a catchall term. In different situations it may mean *integer, string, variable assignment,* or even *comparison.* Since all of these are quite different, we recommend that you use the specific term instead of *expression.*

Integer can be an actual integral number (in BASIC, integers range from −32K to +32K) or an *integer variable* (which see). It can also be the numerical result of an arithmetical operation on two or more other numbers, (say 5 + 7). When you tell your computer to PRINT 5 + 7, the 5 + 7 is itself a number (12). BASIC allows any operation that results in a number to be used wherever a number can be used.

A *string* is a group of characters. It has a beginning and an end. It may contain up to 255 characters in one continuous sequence on some computers. It can be referred to by a name that you give it, and it's called a *string variable.* This is a good example of obscurity in Computerese. We usually refer to the name of the string instead of to the string itself, and it might better have been called *string name.*

163

In integer BASIC variables come in two forms: string variables and integer variables. The contents of these variables can be changed at any time.

Following is a list of BASIC statements and what they do. The statements themselves are CAPITALIZED and the modifiers are in small letters.

CALL number

CALL transfers the program to a machine-language routine. On an Apple II computer, CALL −936 clears the screen. The integer(s) following CALL is the address for the start of the routine. Refer to your owner's manual for the different options.

DIM variable (number)

DIMension reserves space in internal storage for your variables. The number in parentheses gives the number of integer variables or characters in the string. String variable names must end with a dollar sign: $.

END

END is the final statement in a BASIC program. It must have the largest statement number in the program.

FOR variable-number TO number STEP number

FOR is the start of a FOR . . . NEXT loop. The variable is an integer variable and it starts with the value of the first number. The second number is the value that the variable will have when the last repetition of the loop is completed. The third number is the amount added to the variable at the end of each repetition. The third number and STEP may be omitted if you only add 1 each time.

GOSUB statement number

GOSUB transfers the program to a BASIC subroutine; The last statement of the subroutine is RETURN. This returns the program to the statement following the GOSUB.

GOTO statement number

GOTO transfers the program to the statement headed by the statement number. GOTO 10 transfers you to the statement numbered 10 in your program. The program then does what statement 10 tells it to do.

IF variable comparison THEN statement

IF . . . THEN first makes the variable comparison. If the comparison is accurate, the statement following the THEN is executed. If the comparison is not accurate, the statement after THEN is skipped. (For example, if the variable comparison says "A = 4" and the integer variable which you have named A does in fact equal 4, the statement is executed. If A does not equal 4, the statement is ignored.) You might pause and remember at this point that "A = 4" flips switches according to the rules which have been preset in your machine.

INPUT variable

The storage area assigned to the variable is there to receive your information. Whatever information you type on your keyboard is copied into the storage area. If it is an *integer variable,* a number between −32K and +32K must be typed. A *string variable* will accept any keyboard entry, just as long as the total number of characters is less than the total reserved with the DIMension statement. A carriage return ends the INPUT.

LET variable = number
LET string variable = string

LET copies a number to an integer variable or a string to a string variable.

NEXT integer variable

NEXT is the last statement of a FOR . . . NEXT loop. The integer variable is increased by the STEP value that is assigned in the FOR statement. If the result is less than the final value (also established in the FOR statement), the loop is repeated. Otherwise, the program continues with the statement following the NEXT.

POKE number, number

POKE stores the second number in the internal storage location (the address) that is equal to the first number. (It POKEs the number in there.)

PRINT variable
PRINT "THINGS IN QUOTES"

PRINT displays information on your screen or printer. Integer variables are displayed as numbers, string variables as strings, and anything enclosed by double quotes is printed just the way you typed it between those quotes.

REM anything

REMark lets you write reminders to yourself in the middle of your program. Anything after REM (which you can also think of as REMinder) is ignored by the computer up to the carriage return signal.

RETURN

RETURN transfers the program back to the statement after GOSUB. It is the last statement of a subroutine. (Not to be confused with directions referring to the RETURN key on your keyboard. The RETURN we refer to here is a word in BASIC that performs in the computer in a way similar to that key. With this word, you build the key's function into the program.)

TAB number

TAB moves the cursor to the horizontal position on the line equal to the number you assign. The number must be between 1 and 40 on most machines.

Now, let's have another look at this vocabulary. They are just words that have been assigned the job of flipping certain switches. The switches in their combinations, by performing certain actions, give *meaning* to the words.

In a real sense, CALL "calls up" a particular routine and performs whatever routine is designated by the number.

DIMension opens up a reserved space in the internal storage and holds that space for a particular use.

END is something like the period at the end of a sentence. It is the final stopping point in the program.

The FOR . . . NEXT loop is a bit more complicated, but an example should make it clear. Here's an example of a FOR statement:

```
10 FOR A = 1 TO 6
```

10 is the statement number.

This statement sets up a routine. It assigns the value 1 to the variable A. The number 6 is the high limit of A *and* the number of times the loop will be repeated.

The next statement in the routine could go this way:

20 PRINT "A ="; A

And after that:

30 NEXT A

The NEXT statement sets the end of the loop and increases the value of *A* by (*A* = *A* + 1). If *A* is still 6 or less, the program goes once more through the loop. When *A* exceeds 6 (the high limit that we have assigned to the variable named *A*), the program skips to the statement after the FOR . . . NEXT loop. Just remember that a FOR statement must always have a NEXT statement somewhere below it to tell where the loop ends *and* to send the program back to the FOR statement and another run through the loop.

FOR . . . NEXT is a method of constructing loops to perform tasks you want done. It has advantages. Such loops are easier to read in your program. You don't have to look all through the program to find out what the loop is doing. All you do is look for the NEXT that contains the same variable as the FOR.

GOSUB, GOTO, POKE, and PRINT all are sufficiently close in meaning to plain English equivalents that you should have no trouble remembering what they do.

IF . . . THEN makes a comparison. IF (something), THEN (do this other thing). IF (not something), THEN (go on about your business).

INPUT has become a part of the American vernacular. You're putting information into the machine.

To understand LET, remember that you are *writing* something after this word. What you write is copied by the machine because the switches that respond to LET have been arranged that way.

REMarks are just what they seem: REMinders that are supposed to elicit some response in your head, not in the computer.

If you can type on a typewriter, RETURN and TAB need no more explanation.

We think the few other words in this short vocabulary are self-explanatory. Try all of these words a few times on your own computer and the meanings will be fixed into your memory.

Now you can get into BASIC programming.

22

Getting Down to BASIC

There is a language associated with programming that is shared by most higher-level languages, including BASIC. As you now should recognize, an advantage of BASIC is that it introduces you to the vocabulary of this related language in a more pleasant and forgiving way than most of the more specialized higher-level languages. When you have mastered this related language with BASIC, much of what you have learned will carry over into almost any other language you may choose.

In this related language are such words as *instruction, statement, command, variable, constant, expression, string, number, source* and *object.* You may already understand every one of these words, but all of them are worth a review.

An *instruction* is information that, when coded and introduced as a related whole into your computer, causes that computer to perform its operations. It's easy to remember: An instruction is what tells the computer to work.

A *statement* is one line element of a program and is preceded by a statement number, which sets the sequence of when the statement will be used. Statements are put into operation sequentially from lower number to higher in Basic.

A *command* specifies the operation to be performed. Don't confuse a command with a statement. A command is smaller. It causes a pulse, a signal, or set of signals to start, stop, or continue some operation. Commands cause something to happen right away.

Variables and *constants* are equally easy to remember. Constants don't change, but variables might mean one thing one time and something else another time.

A *string* is a group of items that are set up in sequence according to some rule. Your computer will have a limit on the length of string it can accommodate.

A *number* is an expression of quantity: *how many*.

Numbers and strings come in both variable and constant form. A constant number appears in a BASIC program as itself. Just type it anywhere a number can be typed. It won't change unless you type another number in its place. In many systems, a variable number is represented by a letter. (Some systems allow more than one letter for a variable name.)

You've already seen examples of constant strings. Whenever you PRINT anything in quotes, the thing in quotes is a constant string. A variable string is represented by a letter followed by a dollar sign *($)*.

Variables change. The idea to remember is that you never know what the variable is, so you give it a name and always refer to it by its *name*, not its contents.

Constants work the other way around. You always know the contents of a constant, so there's no reason to give it a name. The only reason for quotes around a constant string is to separate it from the other symbols of the program. Anything in quotes is a constant string.

To understand *source*, think of it as the place from which things *flow*, and it can be the channel along which things flow. When applied to the coding of a program, the concept of a source code provides you with some flexibility. The thing you want to do does not have to be wired into the hardware logic. You can put together a *program* that lets you enter and modify the source code.

With a source you go to the elemental nature of your computer's operation. A *source program*, for example, is a program written in a language that is easy for you to use in expressing certain problems or procedures. It is also a program that can be *automatically* translated into machine language (where it becomes an object program).

The *object program* is the program you are aiming for. The source program is developed first. The object is the translation of the source into the machine program and it's made by the computer itself.

You will find source and object useful concepts in programming because they relate to how your machine uses what you tell it to do. They relate to how your program is translated into machine code. No matter the language in which you write your program, your aim is to have that program work at the machine code level where the computer flips its own switches.

The source code is what you write. The object code is what the computer does.

An *expression* is a group of program words and/or other symbols that are set out according to the rules—that is, in a required sequence and according to the syntax that is specific to the programming language you are using.

Now, to BASIC itself:

Earlier, we introduced you to PRINT and GOTO. On most machines these can be used as either commands or statements.

Recall our example of quoted text. When quotes are used in BASIC, the enclosed text never changes unless you change it by retyping the statement. It is a constant.

Constants are useful for displaying information that doesn't change. The prompt "TYPE NAME" will do nicely for any name. You cannot use a constant for the name to be typed, however. If you did, you would have to write a new program for each name you typed. That's where variables enter the picture.

String variables let you put new information into a program. If you set up this program sequence:

```
10 PRINT "TYPE NAME"
20 INPUT A$
30 END
```

this would prompt the person using the program to type a name and then wait for the name to be typed. It wouldn't make any difference which name was typed. In fact, it wouldn't make any difference what you typed just as long as the RETURN key was hit. Whatever you type in response to this program will be put into a variable string named *A$*.

String variable names end with *$* in BASIC. The name has to start with a letter, and some versions allow several internal variations.

The letter *A* might have different meanings in different contexts. By itself it names a variable number.

```
PRINT A
```

tells your computer to print the current value of the variable number named *A*.

PRINT "A"

would just print the letter *A*. Remember that it's a constant string when there are quotes around it.

PRINT A$

would print the current contents of the variable string named *A$*.

Now, recall that you can print the number equivalent to this expression:

PRINT 5*6

That prints the result of multiplying 5 times 6. The expression (in this case 5*6) is first broken down to its single-number answer and that answer is printed. Variable numbers or constant numbers may be used in such expressions.

You now have seen the four kinds of PRINT instructions possible in BASIC.

PRINTing constant strings is useful when you want to prompt the person using your program. If your program is at a point where it needs a particular piece of INPUT, you PRINT a few words in quotes, which tell that person what to do. This is common procedure even with quite complex and sophisticated programs.

If you are writing a program to save names, addresses, phone numbers, birth dates, and anniversaries, at some point you are going to have the names of people typed into a variable string. A reasonable sequence in such a program would be:

```
200 PRINT "TYPE NAME"
210 INPUT N$
```

The initial statement numbers would, of course, be determined by where you needed the name in the program. The END statement is assumed to be somewhat further along, with a higher number preceding it.

The INPUT instruction copies what is typed into a stored variable. It is in STORAGE and can be recalled when needed. This can be either a string variable or a number variable. If you are using a number variable and you type something other than a number, an ERROR message is displayed. *Any* symbols can be typed when you are using a string variable.

Statement numbers (those sequential numbers at the beginning of each line) usually go by tens. This leaves some openings between statements for adding things later. Don't put yourself into the position of having to retype a lot of statements that already work just because you decided to add another statement and there aren't any statement numbers left in the place where you want to make the insert.

Most versions of BASIC allow statement numbers as high as 32K. If you get into the habit of being liberal with your statement numbers, your programs will be easier to follow and to modify.

Programs usually have several major parts. If you start each of these parts on an even-thousand statement number, you have a visual reminder that a new thing is about to happen. This first statement of a new section should be a REMark to remind you what you're doing in the program segment.

The END statement has to be the highest-numbered statement in your program. If you make its statement number 32000, you can type it at the beginning and forget about it. The statement will always be there at the end of your program.

Remember that the GOTO statement lets you change the normal order of statements in your program. In the "HELLO forever" example it was used in a statement that created an endless loop. GOTO can also be used as a command. While you are writing statements (remember that you're in the command mode when you do this), you can GOTO any of the statement numbers of your program whenever you wish. This lets you test a small section of your program without having to wade through the whole thing every time.

GOTO is the "debugger's friend."

Where computers are concerned, some things are more equal than others. The equals symbol (=) can be used two ways. As the assignment operator, it copies things into variables where they are stored for later use. Just make sure the variable matches the thing being copied. If you're copying a number, you must use a number variable (no $), while strings must use string variables (letter $).

The equals sign can also be used to compare things. We now return to the conditional statement IF. This first compares a variable with a constant or with another variable. Equality is one of the conditions of comparison. Remember that we're flipping switches according to very elemental logic, it either is or it isn't. Your switches can go only one of two ways: on or off, yes or no.

Another way of assigning things to variables is with the LET instruction, but this really doesn't do anything except stick out in your program. When you see it, you know that whatever is on the right-hand side of the equals sign is being copied into the variable whose name is on the left.

Don't try to copy a number into a string or vice versa. Most computer systems will give you an ERROR if you do, but if your system lets you do this and you do it by mistake, the results are apt to be disastrous.

It may help to go a bit anthropomorphic and think of the IF statement as a demand that a decision be made. This is the statement that lets you write single programs that do one of two things. (Two-state switches; never forget it.) First, you set up a comparison between a variable and a constant or between a variable and another variable. The comparison can be set up any way you want, and we'll show you some examples later. When you RUN the program, the instruction at the end of the IF statement is run if the comparison is true. Otherwise, this instruction is skipped and your program goes to the next statement.

The syntax of the IF statement is as follows:

Statement number
IF
Comparison
THEN
Instruction

With some computer systems, the THEN is optional and serves merely to separate the comparison from the instruction.

You can use the IF statement to let the person using the program select one of several options. By making the instruction (see the foregoing) GOTO a statement number, the section of your program starting with that statement number will be used only when the input variable contains a preselected symbol. Here's what we mean:

```
1000 PRINT "TYPE FIRST LETTER OF SELECTION"
1010 PRINT "   ADD NEW RECORDS"
1020 PRINT "   LIST OLD RECORDS"
1030 PRINT "REPLY:"
1040 INPUT R$
1050 IF R$ = "A" THEN GOTO 2000
1060 IF R$ = "L" THEN GOTO 3000
1070 GOTO 1000
```

Statements 1000 to 1030 tell the person using this program what options are available by printing the constant strings. 1040 copies the user's selection into a variable string named *R$*. 1050 is a *conditional* GOTO. It goes to the first statement of the routine that adds a new record to a file. The only time it would GOTO 2000 is when the user types the letter *A*. If the variable string *R$* consists of the constant string "*A*", then the next statement number in the program is 2000. If not, the next statement is the next sequential number after 1050—in this case 1060.

1060 is the same as 1050 in its operation.

1070 returns to the 1000 statement when neither an *A* nor an *L* is typed.

If you commit to memory the definitions and the operations we have just explained, you will have a powerful tool in your possession for programming in BASIC. If you go no farther into programming, this will let you understand and modify many programs.

23

A Structure for People

There is a revolution going on in the computer industry called *structured languages*. Structured languages use a minimum of *types* of statements and emphasize the use of names that are developed by the programmer. They follow a certain format akin to grammatical structures. They are meant to include a visually obvious relationship between the various operations of a program.

We have developed another sort of structure that will work with any programming language. We call it *structured program development*.

First, the problem to be solved is stated in a verbal form. Just say what you want it to do. This can usually be done in a sentence or two.

Then make an outline of the steps that will be needed to do it. This will include such things as changing and displaying or printing recorded information, selections of different things to do, and establishing a general sequence for the final program. Some languages use statement numbers (BASIC included), and this stage will also assign numbers to the major parts of the program. If names are used instead of numbers to label things, the names will be assigned to the major pieces of your program.

The next stage is to make a map of the program. Using symbols that have been carefully designed to be universally understandable (such as international highway signs) and a structure that is easy to understand and visually informative, lay out the entire program step by step from beginning to end. If you're using statement numbers, include the major ones.

Finally, the program is written in the programming language. This is also done in stages. First, signposts are put up to help guide the way for the detailed work to follow. When this is complete, the program is "filled in" until it is finished. The program map is used as a tool in this stage.

Some of the stages will require two or more tries before you are satisfied that they are right. Don't be afraid to throw away the first attempt of any stage if you come up with a different and better way of doing it.

Each stage should be completed before the next is begun. Make sure it is right and that everything has been included; changes are always more difficult to effect when a later stage of greater detail has been reached. If you come up with a much better approach while writing the program, go back to the outline and change it to correspond to the new way. Then carry the change through the map (we call it the PROGRAMAP) and finally come back to the program with a good understanding of what must be done. Make the tools first.

Documentation (such as a flowchart) should be an integral part of the program's development. It should evolve with the stages, not come as an afterthought.

We make this point because many professional programmers, dismayed by the "standard" flowchart system, have stopped making them. Programmers find it too tedious to change the chart every time a minor modification is introduced into the program. The result: Charts often have been dropped altogether.

We addressed ourselves to changing the system because the present philosophy of flowcharting stinks. The truth is, most existing flowcharts were made after the programs were written. They provide the experienced programmer with a visual abstract of the program.

The *abstract* became the ideal: Pack as much information into as small a space as possible and make it tell you "at a glance" what is happening.

Some thirty abstract symbols were agreed upon to "represent" the different programming operations. Those symbols are so abstract that they sometimes confuse experienced programmers.

The idea behind the standard system is that you can write a great deal of information inside the symbols and pack the symbols side by side and above and below one another until you get the whole program abstracted down to a page or two.

This becomes part of the documentation package. Its sole purpose is to describe in as few words as possible what has already been done.

That, as one of our sainted ancestors once said, is "bassackwards." The visual representation of programs is a marvelous idea. But it should be a developmental tool, not an end product. The *program* is the end product. We object strongly to the way the industry uses flowcharts.

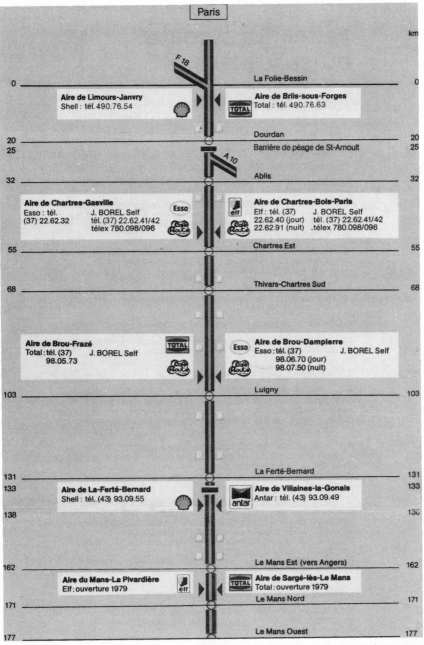

l'Océane A11. This graphic map of the French freeway from Paris south reveals features in common with computer flowcharts. It shows access points, start and end, special features along the way, and the distances between entry and exit points. No attempt has been made to show small geographic variations. Special signs (P), easily read, show rest stops *(aire de repos)*. Other features have their special symbols. What you *need* to know is right here.

Thus, the PROGRAMAP.

It should start at the beginning and flow step by step to the end of the program—just like the program itself.

It should bridge the gap between the verbal statement of the problem to be solved and the final program.

It should be easy to produce and easily understood.

It should have a structure, and its symbols should be as suggestive as possible of what they represent.

The examples we will provide you are typical of many things that come up in programming. We have chosen the BASIC language because of its ready availability and ease of understanding for the novice. Whatever your experience, neophyte or professional, we hope we have succeeded in showing you a straightforward way of program development that will make the task of programming easy and will thus open the door to your own creativity.

24

PROGRAMAP

The funny word we use as title for this chapter is the label for a new graphic way of laying out a computer program. We're talking about flowcharts. As we've indicated, most programmers get away from them because the symbols have been designed and arranged in a way difficult to use. Flowcharts became too much of a hassle. But the flowchart can be a superb tool. It can form an easily understood picture of what happens in your computer.

What do we do? Go along with the stiff and clumsy present system?

Our solution was to go back to the symbols and redesign the flowchart into a one-dimension diagram, taking the common, ordinary road map as our guide. We studied the symbols, comparing them with graphic forms that have come out of the International Convention on Graphic Symbols.

There's a general recognition all around the world that symbols transcend differences in languages, that they can be a marvelous instrument of quick and effective communication. This has given us easily understood highway signs, essentially the same in France, England, Germany, the United States, Canada—everywhere there is motor traffic.

Take a good look at the way those highway signs are designed. Particular shapes have been chosen to mean particular things. You don't have to see the word *stop* to know it's a stop sign. And they are positioned in a way that relates directly to what they tell you to do. Further, they contain easily recognized symbols; a hand, an arrow, an intersection T, a snake track for a winding road ahead. You see on the sign the *thing*

179

signified by that sign: a pedestrian, a leaping stag, a child, a symbolized steep hill with a car on it in outline, a gasoline pump, a wrench (for repair services), or a tent (indicating camp sites).

You see a recognizable thing.

This entire concept is adaptable to computer programming in a way that has never before been quite achieved. And it serves a multiple purpose here.

1. Carrying over the highway sign concept emphasizes the urgent need for a general understanding of computers. After all, understanding highway signs can be a life-and-death matter. We assure you that survival is involved in understanding computers.

2. No one imagines that highway signs are inherently intelligent. They are a tool of travel. And that's the way it is with computers: Such signs can be a reminder that we are using a tool and that we are engaged in movement.

3. The idea of "traffic flow" is extremely useful when using a computer. Keep in mind that you are routing electrical signals. The routing involves switch patterns that can be recognized and repeated. Traffic signs are adaptable to this in a natural way with which you are already familiar.

4. Because highway signs are designed for quick and urgent messages, they have been reduced to common ideas, often to things associated with mechanical or bodily movements. This is the principle of primitive sign languages and it makes such signs easy to learn and remember.

5. You probably already know many of the symbols we employ. Attaching them to your computer is simply a matter of using them yourself.

After coming to a decision on the symbols, we tackled the problem of how the chart flows. Conventional diagrams jump around a lot—up, down, sideways, over to that box, out of one symbol and branching into several others. They contain lots of little boxes filled with cryptic shorthand notes.

Very confusing the first time you try to use such a diagram. We have reduced all of that jagged movement to a straightforward, one-dimensional progression.

It may appear pretentious of us to address ourselves to such fundamental change. After all, the flowchart has been used for about a quarter of a century as a visual aid to the internal paths of computer programs. It has become standardized. Its symbols were adopted by the American

National Standards Institute in 1970 and were approved by the Federal Office of Management and Budget in 1973. Very heavy stuff. They are used everywhere.

But road maps have probably been evolving for at least ten thousand years. Sign languages have an even longer history. An illiterate person can understand such signs once the concept has been explained. They contain fundamental ideas, perhaps built into the way our thinking processes have evolved.

A computer program can be compared quite easily with a route across a section of terrain. Boundaries are defined and routes are visualized for getting from one place to another. A correct route can be found when you know the terrain. Our "road map" only needs some new symbols for *bridging* because a program can make extraordinary leaps from one place to another without touching any places between.

In a useful graphic system it's important that program statements appear step by step from beginning to end, that they be *structured*. We are convinced that the "structured languages" will soon dominate the more advanced uses of computers. A flowchart concept that follows the same idea will endure. Therefore, our PROGRAMAP follows a structured pattern starting at the top of the page and going down step by step toward the bottom. It does not split into separated multiple paths, as the standard diagrams often do.

Another important feature keeps track of what's happening outside your system—the inputs and outputs. They must be clear and unmistakable. They require a place of their own in the visual scheme.

Finally, there must be signposts—everyday words posted at important places along the way. These are commonly called comments or remarks. They should give a brief but clear description of what the program is doing. They should appear on both the flowchart and the program.

One of the things you'll notice right away about the written form of your program when you begin putting it on paper is that you can write notes to yourself all over the page and it's easy to distinguish such personal notes from the actual steps of the program. Writing such notes is an excellent habit to form. Remind yourself right on the flowchart and the program what it is you're doing. When it comes time to put the program into your computer, all you have to do is type three letters, REM, and put after it the same REMinder. The computer will treat the matter within the quote marks as text and will display that text for you in your program, an ongoing reference to the working steps shown right on your CRT.

All along, our goal has been an improved link between the verbal statement of the problem and the final program. In simplifying the procedure, we believe we have reached this stage:

If you can type a letter on a typewriter and tell a stranger how to get to your house, you can write your own programs. You know you don't have to be a math whiz to do those things.

You begin the PROGRAMAP by carefully defining what you want to do. You need a general statement of the problem—some such thing as "I want to keep track of my auto servicing records and have a reminder about maintenance." Give the program a title, perhaps "Car MAINTE-NANCE."

(We have supplied a complete sample program on car maintenance in Appendixes F and G. You may want to refer to it as you read this chapter.)

The next step involves an outline. Outlines are important because of a fundamental difficulty that has been recognized in programming. People rarely if ever think in the required tightly logical steps. You have to get organized before you can put yourself in a computer frame of mind. Part of your organization must include an overall strategy. There can be no foggy areas. You must understand what is taking place in the machine at all times.

That's why we start you with an objective. You want a reminder program for car maintenance? Why? You know your car will last longer if you follow a good maintenance policy. And in fuel-crunch times you know you'll get better mileage that way.

Our preliminary sketch can be based on the owner's manual:

1. Change oil and lube every three months or 3,000 miles.
2. Change oil filter every second oil change.
3. Rotate tires and check brakes every 6,000 miles.
4. Change radiator coolant every fall.
5. Repack wheel bearings and change transmission fluid every 24,000 miles.

This list provides the rules from which the maintenance times and/or mileage can be figured. The program will use records of when service was last performed and these rules will be used to calculate when the next service must be done.

Both the objective and the outline must be verbal. We are not yet into the PROGRAMAP proper. The outline will go on to break the objective into manageable pieces that will contain every switching operation. We will give each piece a name and carry that name through to the final program. We will give statement numbers to each step, starting at 1000 and counting by thousands for major steps and giving the intervening smaller numbers to the smaller steps.

We will include notes about what will be displayed. We will show the *what* and the *where* of each input. We will indicate what is to be saved and what calculations and rearrangements will be made.

We are setting out to establish the order (sequence) in which things will happen. There is usually a good reason for one particular order. Think it through before making arbitrary decisions, but don't expect to hit it perfectly on the first try every time. Just keep in mind that your computer has been designed to follow a coldly logical order and that you will regret illogical choices.

You are required to describe the steps in their proper sequence, a sequence that leads directly to the desired result. The computer must deal with yes or no answers and no middle ground.

When you're doing it right, you are conforming perfectly to the popular myth about Germans, the idea expressed by Vicki Baum when she said she looked out the window of her Berlin hotel and saw the German robins piling the leaves according to size.

(Math aficionados among you know such particular problem-solving procedures by the buzzword *algorithm*. But just like the Baum robins, you can follow such a procedure without knowing either the word or its meaning.)

Two functions will be needed for our program to work across a period of time. There must be a way to revise when a particular maintenance has been completed, and the new schedule must be figured from the rules and displayed.

Since the revision depends on information gathered when you figure the new schedule and display it, you might want to put the second routine in the first position.

It really makes no difference.

However, it's wise to get into the habit of simply making a choice whenever there is more than one way of doing something, *even if your choice is purely emotional.* If you want to change things later, you will remember those emotional decisions and they will help you find your way through the program. And with two distinct functions you must make a choice right at the beginning.

You now have enough of an idea about what's to be done that you can follow the preliminary verbal outline. This will serve as a guide in our flowchart.

1. Display title and provide a choice between two functions.
2. Complete maintenance function:
   A. Select which maintenance was completed.
   B. Revise "maintenance last done" record.
   C. Figure new "next maintenance" mileage and/or date.
3. Display "next maintenance" schedule.

You should note that this outline points up the difference between the way people think "in the round" and how computers are forced to operate—limited to handling one thing at a time. In the completed program a choice must be made between five different maintenance operations. You could do it easily, but your computer must go through five separate selection and rejection steps in turn. While the outline makes sense to us in spite of its five-way choice problem, programming it requires us to break down the list into a series of "yes-no" questions.

Here's where a flowchart comes into its own. It shows you visually how your program will be written. It breaks the problem into graphic individual steps and shows you the sequence of steps.

It's time for you to meet the PROGRAMAP.

We separate our PROGRAMAP symbols into four columns. The first column is reserved for accessories. Each device is designated by a graphic symbol in a square. Whenever you see a square, you know you're dealing with an accessory. The symbol in the square will picture the device—phone, tape deck, TV screen, and so on.

The second column is reserved for things done by the central processing unit (CPU), our old familiar SWITCHING. All symbols in this column contain some curved element. Whenever you see these curved lines, you know you're in the CPU.

To the right of CPU is a column we call REROUTE. Here's where we get into the bridging leaps your program can make. Every symbol in this column is triangular. When you see a triangle on the flowchart, you know your program is being rerouted.

To the right of REROUTE we reserve a wide column for statement numbers and verbal descriptions. Here's where you write notes to yourself. Here are the brief and clear descriptions of what the program is doing and the names of the things being done. After you have gained some skill with these descriptions, they will often contain some of the exact wording for your program. The statement numbers in this column are all enclosed in ovals to set them off.

Here's how the symbols look:

PERIPHERAL   CPU   REROUTE   DESCRIPTION

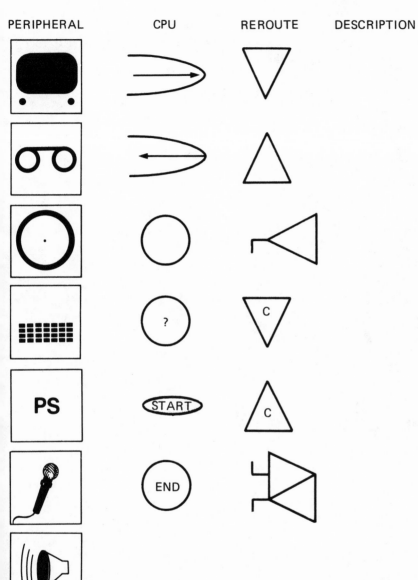

We have chopped a number of symbols off the standard system. Thus, the visual basis of the PROGRAMAP not only is easier to recognize, but you have fewer things to learn.

This is what the symbols mean:

SCREEN (CRT)

TAPE

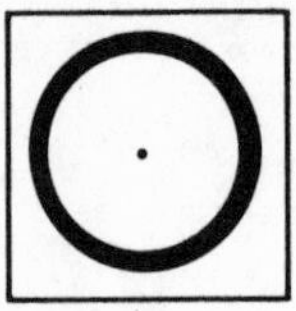

DISK

KEYBOARD

PS PRINTER

MICROPHONE

SPEAKER

TELEPHONE

(We decided to put *PS* in the "printer" square because of the number
f languages that begin their word for printing with either a *p* or an *s*.
nglish has both *print* and *stamp*.) And *PS* in English stands for a verbal
ddition to a letter. It's an easy thing to remember.)

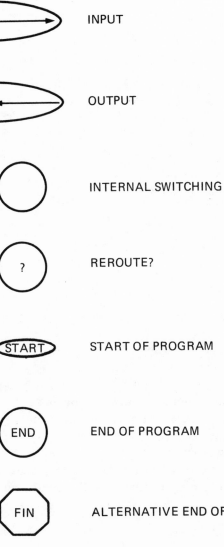

INPUT

OUTPUT

INTERNAL SWITCHING

REROUTE?

START OF PROGRAM

END OF PROGRAM

ALTERNATIVE END OF PROGRAM

Down—to a higher statement
number in the program.

 Up—to a lower statement
number in the program.

 Entry point

 Reroute to a higher number when
a condition (C) is met.

Reroute to a lower number when
a condition (C) is met.

 Subroutine detour

In the fourth (right-hand) column, reserved for statement numbe
and verbal descriptions of the program, these are the rules:

When you are prompting the program user to do something, you p
that something in plain English and bracket it with quotation marks. Whe
it comes time to translate from flowchart to program, you merely ty
PRINT and put the prompt (quotes and all) in the program.

All reminders to yourself start with REM.

All entry points for the program get statement numbers on th
flowchart. Major sections of your program count by thousands, min
entry points count by round hundreds.

All dimension statements go at the beginning. (In BASIC these are called DIM statements. They assign the maximum number of characters that can be contained in a SET series, which means a series of symbols to be placed in storage.)

With variables, you use the actual name. (We will go into this in more detail presently.)

All REROUTEs are labeled with the statement number of the destination—where the program will GOTO.

A line connects each sequential step in the chart. Put an arrow on the line to show the direction of traffic flow. Think of that line as a street sign on one-way streets.

When you REROUTE, you move to the appropriate column and indicate direction of flow by where the triangle points.

Use of the REROUTE column and symbols will probably take you the most time to master if you're a rank beginner. For that reason, we'll go into it in a bit more detail.

REROUTE is where you symbolize many of the IF statements (if this, then that . . .). These all involve decisions to be made—yes or no, true or false. They direct your program to another place *if a condition has been met.*

In conventional flowcharts, this operation has been indicated by a *Y* (for yes) or *N* (for no) contained in a box of some sort. We find that confusing and unnecessarily complex. When you get to such a point in a program, you actually have only one question to answer: Is the condition met or isn't it? The letter *C* seems appropriate to stand for a condition. If there's a *C* in our triangle, that tells you there's a condition to be met. The description column *describes* that condition. If there's no *C* in the triangle, that triangle stands for anything else your program is about to do in its REROUTing.

You proceed from there.

Now, go back to the illustrations of the symbols and note the question mark in the switching circle. That's what signals a shift into the REROUTE column. You have a question to answer, a condition to be met.

REROUTE has many functions. It lets one program do several things, depending on a decision *you* make at that point. You have a routing choice. (Our section on conditional statements, pages 172-74, explains this more fully.)

REROUTE also lets you create subroutines that save a lot of time and space. We apply another label to these subroutines. We call them

DETOURs. The process of switching to a subroutine and coming back to the mainstream is akin to making a detour around a roadblock. The next statement after the GOSUB is eventually reached in a roundabout way with the RETURN statement at the end of the subroutine DETOUR.

REROUTE lets you jump around quite remarkably in your program, touching down only where you want, searching out and presenting things the way you require.

For example, the IF statement allows you to find the smallest of a group of variables. (Don't be confused by the word *variable*. It is simply a symbol standing for an entity that can assume a number of different values. It can *vary* depending on how it's used.)

Here's how you find the smallest:

Enter the first variable on your list into a special variable. This special variable is compared in turn with each of the other variables on your list. If the special variable is larger than the one being tested in its turn, the smaller one gets copied into the special variable. It *then* becomes the standard for the next comparison. You come out the other end with the smallest on your list, and you can start with that one when you stack according to size. (We're only joking.)

The actual program statement to find the smallest could go this way:

```
1100 IF S  > A(I) THEN S = A(I)
```

In this example, S is the special (smaller) variable and $A(I)$ is the one being tested for comparative size. 1100 is the statement number.

While this example uses number variables, the same statement with the string variables $S\$$ and $A\$(I)$ would copy the first (alphabetically) string into $S\$$.

That is a very valuable tool for finding things lost in a jumble of other things. Knowing how to use REROUTE with the other programmable features of your computer lets you sort and rearrange all kinds of variables.

REROUTE, with its ability to set up conditional questions in ways they can be answered, uses the statements IF and FOR. Those two statements in the BASIC language allow you to make programming decisions.

Remember that the FOR statement creates a loop.

In more precise programming terms, FOR is the initializing statement of the FOR . . . NEXT loop. NEXT is the *last* statement of a FOR . . . NEXT loop. You can put any number of statements between the FOR and the NEXT, limited only by the storage capacity of your system.

That buzzword *initializing* is essentially simple. It stands for the preliminary steps used in arranging instructions and information in storage when those things are not going to be repeated. You want those things in storage to be used over and over—a loop.

FOR is actually a shortened form of a sequence of statements used so often that a shorthand abbreviated term is desirable. You've already met the sequence in the chapters on BASIC, (Chapters 21 and 22) where we explored counting and the counting variable.

When you use FOR, the counting variable is initialized. It is arranged in storage in such a way that you can use it without having to repeat it. You do this to limit the number of times your loop will play. You don't want the loop repeating endlessly the way we did with the "HELLO forever" example.

If we call this variable L (for loop), all we have to do is set it equal to some number at the beginning. That's the lower limit of the variable.

Unless there's good reason to start your loop at something other than the number 1, that's a desirable lower limit and it makes the loop easier to write. Later on, we'll show you how a loop looks on a flowchart. Right now, this is how the start of a loop appears in a program statement:

```
1000 L = 1
```

An alternative would be

```
1000 LET L = 1
```

You then pick up the next statement number:

```
1010
```

which is the first statement of your loop.

After you have composed all of the things that are supposed to happen in your loop, you need two more statements to tie it off:

```
1100 L = L + 1
1110 IF L < = N GOTO 1010
```

N indicates a variable limit to your loop. N could be a constant, provided you know in advance the number of times your loop will have to play.

The same thing happens with two statements when you use the FOR
. . . NEXT loop:

```
1000 FOR L = 1 TO N
1010
   •
   •
   •
1100 NEXT L
```

NEXT L adds 1 to L loop and returns the program to 1010 (the
first statement after FOR) unless L is then larger than N.

Note that the FOR statement starts the loop at 1 and establishes the
final value of L as the value of N. These examples presume that you gave
a value to N somewhere else in the program. By changing the value of N,
you can change the number of times your loop will play. This makes the
loop a flexible tool that can be used and reused as you require.

Now, here's how the IF appears in a flowchart:

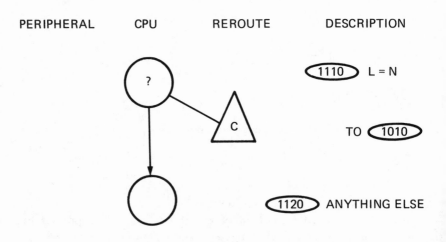

Note that the triangle containing the conditional *C* points upward toward a
smaller statement number. Loops always start at a smaller number (a
previous statement). All IF statements take this form in the chart.

Here's how you could chart the loop itself:

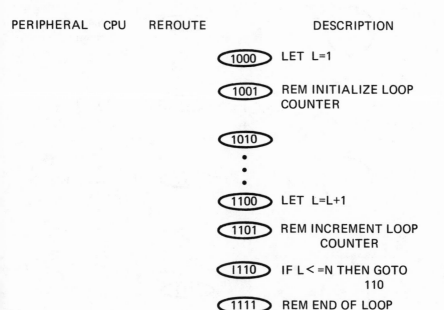

PERIPHERAL   CPU   REROUTE   DESCRIPTION

1000   LET L=1

1001   REM INITIALIZE LOOP
        COUNTER

1010
    •
    •
    •

1100   LET L=L+1

1101   REM INCREMENT LOOP
              COUNTER

1110   IF L< =N THEN GOTO
              110

1111   REM END OF LOOP

Instead of calling the left-hand column PERIPHERAL, you could get closer to computer function with a shorter label by calling it I/O for INPUT/OUTPUT. The symbols in the column would not change.

Here's how you chart your loop in more detail with PROGRAMAP symbols:

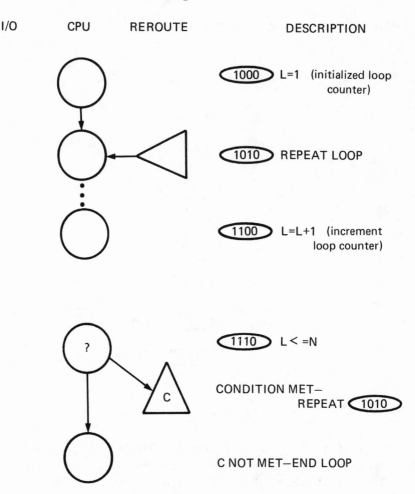

I/O	CPU	REROUTE	DESCRIPTION

1000 L=1 (initialized loop counter)

1010 REPEAT LOOP

1100 L=L+1 (increment loop counter)

1110 L< =N

CONDITION MET—
REPEAT 1010

C NOT MET—END LOOP

Note that if you fail to make a perfectly vertical column and CPU wanders off into I/O or into REROUTE, the shape of the symbol prevents any confusion. That's why we standardize shapes of highway signs, too.

When you've completed your first program chart and outline, compare them with your objective. Did anything change? Do you see a better way to do the outline or the chart? If you see a better way, try it. Then compare. Did you do a messy job with either one? Recopy until you can read your work easily. While recopying, you will come to think about previous programs you have written. Does something remind you of a clearer way to do this?

Don't hesitate to change either outline or chart. Play with the verbal versions of your program before trying to translate into a computer language. There are often better ways of doing these things, and programmers have been known just to stumble on those better ways while playing with a program in verbal form.

There comes a point of diminishing returns in such play, however, and you will have to determine that point. Just remember that the best time to make changes is while you're working on your outline. And changes at the chart level are easier than changes in a programming language.

Don't start the chart until you're sure the outline leads you to your chosen objective. Don't start the program until you're sure the chart answers the same demand.

As you draw the picture of your program, put switching operations in the same order as they appear in the outline. Include statement numbers and names of the major divisions in your program. Describe each step.

When the picture is complete, compare it with your outline. Make sure you haven't left anything out.

NOW—go back and look at all of your REROUTEs.

Is there a good reason for each one?

A program can often be simplified by eliminating unnecessary REROUTEs. Sometimes you can do this by changing the sequence in your program. If you change the sequence in the chart, be sure to make the same change in your outline. Outline and chart form a handy cross-check system, and they should be dealing with the same things in the same order.

Sometimes you will want to convert a section of your program into a subroutine. If a procedure happens several times in your program, a subroutine can be a real saver of time and space. Sometimes you can scan back toward the start of a program and find a place before a branching where a procedure can be written once and performed in several different branches after the split.

Just remember that subroutines add REROUTEs, and these make your chart harder to follow. Use subroutines sparingly.

You have just completed one of the hardest chapters in this book, and *we did not flag it to keep you from reading it.* No, we are not cheating. Even if you avoid all aspects of personal programming, there are things in this chapter that will help you all through your association with computers. If you do no more than learn how things flow, you will have accomplished something very valuable. But if you learn to understand and use these PROGRAMAP symbols, if you master the steps from outline to flowchart to program, you will be the unquestioned master of your computer. We recommend that you review this chapter, studying the illustrations and the examples. You will find a PROGRAMAP dictionary in Appendix C. It takes you through the meanings of the individual symbols and the various combinations in greater detail.

25

Writing Up a Storm

All through the writing of this book we have been designing and assembling the pieces for a computer to be used by authors. In doing this, we know we are going to arouse controversy. There will be protests even from some authors and a lot of the usual garbage based on the belief that computers can "think."

Wags will say: "Ohhhh, so you're going to let a computer write your books!"

This tiresome stupidity is a mental trap we hope you can avoid. A computer does nothing more than process what you give it. If you give it garbage, it returns garbage that has been processed by a computer.

Garbage stays garbage no matter how you process it. Always remember GIGO.

Our approach to the new computer has been rooted in the driving concept of this book: The machine must be fitted to you, not the other way around.

Think about what's happening here.

We are writing.

We are writing about computers.

One of this team is a successful author and amateur electronics-computer buff; the other member is an acknowledged expert in both computer engineering and programming with some fifteen years of experience in the field.

That's a powerful combination for this designing job. We are engaged in doing many of the things we would turn over to the computer—tedious,

197

routine tasks that should be done at higher speed. And we believe that the best way to learn is to *do*.

Computers can be made to direct the performance of any machine—a typewriter, for instance. Computers work very fast. With computer control, a fast printer can type a long novel in a couple of hours. That can take two or more weeks with a conventional typewriter and human typist.

The possibilities in having an extremely sophisticated and very fast typewriter that is also a highly responsive filing system for notes *and* a rapid source for reference material make the computer extremely attractive to an author.

Here are some of the problems you face in writing a book:

1. The creative process often demands that you work at breakneck speed, a speed that makes every petty interruption a bitterly resented nuisance.

2. Complex developments in a book often demand that you use many notes and references—your original notes on the characters, a dictionary, encyclopedias, specialized reference works relating to geography, physics, psychology, medicine, astronomy . . . It's an open-ended list.

3. As you write, you often want to make extensive changes in earlier portions of your work—eliminate a character, add a character, combine characters into one person, change dialog, introduce new dialog, and other business.

Since you can program your computer to whip through the storage systems where information is kept, and since you can do this in almost limitless ways, the possibilities for editing and word management are awesome.

Writing employs both intuition and logic in a highly individualized balancing act. A writer tends to develop a style that can be recognized. If you can use a computer for an ongoing check on your logic and as a storage system for all the other essentials (including the manuscript itself), you have a marvelous tool that will not slow you down or otherwise cramp your style.

The manuscript for an entire novel can be automatically scrolled upward or downward on your screen. You can scroll rapidly or slowly.

You can jump into the manuscript anywhere you choose. With clever editing cues you can dart to any part of your work that you want to see, and you can do this in seconds. No fumbling around with papers; you just push a few keys. The computer does your bidding automatically.

Once you have located a place where you want to work on the manuscript, you can open a space to insert new material, you can rewrite the portions around the new insertion, and then you can rapidly scroll forward to make the new material appropriate at every other necessary place.

Finding those necessary places is a task you turn over to your computer and your editing program. It is accomplished with dazzling speed. A new character can be integrated into your work in a quarter of an hour.

You want a change?

You can make that change (even a highly involved one) at such speed that you do not lose the flow of your own creation.

Now, let's say that you get near the end of the book and you suddenly realize that you have characters with quite similar names—Tim and Jim. Believe us, it can happen. One very popular American author admitted to us in confidence that he was into the last chapter of a book before he realized that he had a Sam and a Ham in his work. It was an easy mistake to make, he said. When they came onstage, the characters were Samuel and Hamilton. But familiarity bred confusion because the other characters were always referring to them as Sam and Ham.

With the old manuscript method you laboriously search through the lines of typescript and change one of the names. There is a strong possibility that you will miss one of the changes. The author referred to above did just that, and none of the copy editors or proofreaders caught it.

Ahhhhh, but with a computer, you can direct the machine to do this *automatically*. No mistakes. It won't miss a one. The entire job will require only a few minutes at most while you go on to something else.

The machine is an editor and proofreader that responds to your every need.

It is also a very fast secretary.

Notes and other reference materials can be called up onto the screen as you need them. You hit a few keys and the needed material is there in front of you, separated from the manuscript by a horizontal line on the screen.

Because writing is rooted strongly in an *oral* tradition—you talk to the ears through the eyes—many authors tend to make homonymic errors in spelling: *their* for *there* and the like. Other spelling idiosyncrasies can crop up from time to time for any number of reasons. When these mistakes produce *real words,* they can be missed quite easily. Copy editors and proofreaders will spot a *teh* without much trouble and change it to *the.* But what if you intended to write *they* and dropped the *y?*

Rest easy.

You can incorporate an entire dictionary into your computer and program a system cued to your particular problems. If the context of what you're writing makes the meaning of a word clear, the computer will automatically correct what you type. If there's a doubt about the word, your computer will flag that word in such a way that you can come back to every decision point at the end of the day and make your own corrections.

What you store in your computer is there in a fixed form and can be recalled at your demand.

Rafael Sabatini, the Italian-born master of English prose, could never remember whether he had already killed off a particular character in his work. He is noted for handling a large number of characters in intricate relationships. To keep himself from inadvertently bringing a dead character back to life in a later chapter, Sabatini kept a row of dolls on his desk. Each doll was labeled with the name of a character. When Sabatini killed off a character, he searched out the appropriate doll and pushed it over. Keeping an eye on the dolls that were still standing told him which ones were still "alive" in his book.

A computer can store your "dolls" for you. If you try to reintroduce the deceased without first arranging a "second coming," the computer will stop you with ringing bells and flashing ERROR messages.

Any logical business of your work can be assigned easily to the computer's programs and storage system, leaving you free to get on with the business of drama.

For a science fiction writer, the computer is a "dream machine." That becomes clear if you follow what we are doing with this new computer and what has been done with other computers to augment the dramatic effect.

First, we are building the large storage capacity for sophisticated computer graphics into our new machine.

Computer graphics—the production of computer-managed images on the CRT—offers an open-sesame to the simulation of imaginary settings. This already forms a mainstay of Hollywood's attempts to translate science fiction into movies. Some of the things Hollywood calls science fiction are really comic books for the screen, akin to some early pulp stories in their primitive assumptions and laughable mistakes in science. But it's obvious that these crude attempts to translate imaginative images into film are still in their infancy. The written form of science fiction has left the pulp training ground and errors far behind. Films will do the same.

But we have seen the "image writing" on the screen.

Our "author's computer" has a system to simulate visually some of science fiction's requirements—the display of exotic solar systems, for example.

With a computer you can create a multibody solar system—let us say, two suns, eight planets, many minor satellites—and you can choose among these places for the settings of your drama. You can build into one of these planets a number of exotic conditions—variable gravity, dramatic differences in atmospheric thickness, strange seasonal progressions . . .

You then let your computer roll this system through its orbits, displaying your chosen settings on the screen at every stage of the yearly passages. You will *know* when it's spring on Planet X or when the tides rise four hundred feet on Planet Y.

The same facility that lets you do this with an imagined solar system lets you create exotic spaceships and turn those ships to any desired angle of view on your screen. You can examine the outside skin of your ship or look into its rooms and corridors. You can move that spaceship from one planet to another. Your computer will supply the *logical* elapsed time according to the program(s) you have supplied. No more laborious figuring of such flight times.

As a time-saving boon to the science fiction author, this facility alone is worth the price of admission into the computer age.

The writing of *Dune,* for instance, required years of research, mountains of notes, tedious hours of careful computations, and a number of educated guesses. A computer would not have eliminated the research, but it would have condensed and organized the notes for quick recall, and it would have helped enormously with the guesses. The computations could have been done in minutes.

Here, then, are the things we are building into our new computer:

A reliable keyboard with some extra keys that allow quick access to support facilities: notes, graphics, dictionary, and the like.

The CRT is on a vertical format.

A page of manuscript is on a vertical format, why not the screen?

The CRT will display both capital and lower-case letters on a large matrix—seven by eleven dots. A separating line can be introduced onto the screen to set off a place for notes. Without notes, the screen will carry type for about three normal typewriter pages at one time.

Any place in a long manuscript can be brought onto the screen while you go on with other work. The search will not take more than a minute and often only a few seconds, depending on the complexity of your demand.

The printer is a spinwriter. It will produce a completed manuscript on bond paper in familiar typed appearance. An editor, seeing nothing but the manuscript, would not know it had been typed by a computer—except that there might be some comment about the neatness and clarity of the typing.

This printer will type a completed novel in about two hours. By changing the type ball, it offers a wide selection of different type faces: italic, roman, plain, or fancy.

The computer is actually several computers tied into a single system. One chip can be managing notes while another goes on with other work.

To keep all of this running smoothly, we set a lower limit of twenty-one million bytes for external storage on disks. Internal storage will also be relatively large. At this writing, we have not yet fixed an upper limit for it.

What about loss of work through a machine malfunction or other problem?

Writers are notoriously paranoid about the loss of completed work. There have been some horror stories to reinforce this paranoia. Work has been lost in fires—all of Jack London's manuscripts were destroyed by an arson blaze. Wine has been spilled on the paper, reducing it to pulp—this happened to Truman Capote. Manuscripts have been lost in the mails or even stolen. One was held for ransom. They have even been scattered out a window by a sudden wind storm.

As a protection against loss of work through any such breakdown, including electrical failure or other mechanical malfunction, our system is backed up by cassette tape. The tape makes a record of everything that's done—every word typed, every command to the computer(s), all of a day's labor. In the event of a breakdown, the tape will restore that work in just a few minutes. You can carry an entire novel on a couple of tapes and lock them in a fireproof vault every night if that's your wish.

What has even more interesting potential is the fact that a publisher can use our completed disks to set the actual type for a book. The editor would need only a disk driver, a computer of sufficient capacity for a simple editing program, a good keyboard, and a CRT.

Although this new computer is built on an eight-bit format, it can simulate sixteen bits and thus can "talk" to larger machines, providing access to necessary programs and information through the long-distance telephone lines. (Yes, a disk on the West Coast of the United States could transfer its information to a disk in New York City in a few minutes.)

As a bonus, the keyboard of our machine is silent. There's no rattle of a typewriter to distract you while you compose your deathless prose. This is important to some writers. For instance, Robert Heinlein writes on a silenced typewriter, the kind built for use in mortuaries. Some authors feel so strongly about this that they write only with a pen.

We don't feel that silence is absolutely necessary, but it's a pleasant feature.

There are some other bonuses.

With twenty-one million bytes we can have a second terminal and a time-sharing system on which to do all of the household bookkeeping.

The system also gives access to a large personal library in four ways: by author, by publisher, by title, and by a précis of subject matter. With special reference works it provides a cross-index to page numbers.

All of these books are filed in computer storage by Library of Congress numbers—a program commercially available and widely used—and this actually provides a fifth means for calling up the stored books.

We have taken the time to acquaint you with this machine for several reasons. Since there was no computer on the market tailored to quite these demands, we have alerted you to the fact that you can have a machine designed precisely to your needs. The cost need not be prohibitive, especially for tax-deductible business equipment. We hesitate to put an actual price on it now because mass production methods and refinements are sure to reduce that price.

It was also our desire to show you the design process in action— fitting the computer to personal needs. It would be difficult to overemphasize how strongly we feel about this approach.

MAKE THE MACHINE FIT YOU!

Accept nothing less. If you get a salesman or "computer expert" who balks at this, go somewhere else. The computer industry needs *you;* you don't need any particular one of them.

Lastly, make it fun. Being the first kid on your block with a time cruncher should at least provide you with considerable enjoyment, not to mention time saved for other pleasurable activities.

Go and compute.

26

PS

Did we write this book on a computer?

No.

This book was partly a test project to set the design requirements for a writer's computer. This required that we use conventional methods while comparing those methods to available computer methods.

Have we been redundant in our presentation of what you need to know before you can run your own computer?

Yes, of course.

We conformed to a well-tested educational technique usually expressed as:

"Tell them what you are going to tell them."

"Tell them."

"Tell them what you told them."

"Reinforce this with repetitious examples."

We don't want to conceal any of this process from you because we really don't think of you as "them." You are somebody who could profit from the use of a personal computer. Our basic motive has been to help you do just that.

If you take us up on our challenge in sufficient numbers, we expect a "Tansley effect" to result. This is named for an Englishman who noted about a hundred years ago that when many amateurs get together with common interests and avocations, their combined individual insights result in a vastly increased understanding of a particular field. It's synergistic, a benefit both individual and collective.

The information age is upon us.

With more and more people becoming interested in home computers, more organized information will come into the hands of an increasing number of people. With books such as this one and in many other ways, people are sharing what they have learned. The Tansley effect will certainly come into full force. Computers are playing an increasingly important role in amateur societies by distilling large masses of individual insights into useful packages.

Quality is sure to dominate such a trial-and-error process.

Our hope is that you get your own computer and join the information age as soon as possible.

Note that we have attached supportive appendixes to our book. Although they are more complex than the necessary essentials already detailed, we urge you at least to dip into them. You might keep the glossary (Appendix J) handy while you make your first attempts at operating your new machine.

Appendix A
The Biomachine

Someday we will attach a computer directly to the human nervous system. Computer storage will flow directly into your thoughts—in graphic symbols, in words written or oral, in pictures projected onto your "inner eye," and in sounds uttered for "your ears alone." High-speed computer sorting will respond to your unspoken mental demand.

On that day your personal computer will probably be a pea-size device implanted in your flesh. Mass storage and the data banks will be someplace outside your body, linked to you by something like microwave.

That is a clear direction of research and development. The major barrier to this prediction is not the hardware, but the software—the programs.

Before that day comes we will have to match our high-data-rate and multichannel system to the computer's one-step-at-a-time but high-speed system. We will have to mesh extremely different ways of coding information. That is a problem in translation, and *that* is primarily a software concern.

It is a monumental interface task, especially in view of the fact that we do not know our own mental coding system. The speed/exchange problem is daunting. Your nervous system is composed of biological elements having a reaction-response-relaxation time of some two hundred milliseconds, about six orders of magnitude slower than most present computers. Despite this relatively slow use-and-recovery rate, you can achieve a very high effective speed while maintaining a large data rate.

You can handle a lot of information very fast. The smoothly expanding continuum is available to you, not to the computer.

There is no doubt that this linkage between flesh and machine will occur—a kind of ultimate prosthesis. Several current developments make this apparent.

An electroencephalograph (EEG for short), an instrument for detecting your brain's electrical activity, can distinguish between your decision-making and your action signals. This has been recognized for some time.

This predicts that an EEG linked directly to a computer can produce information out of which the computer can determine whether you have spare mental capacity available from moment to moment. The implications in biofeedback training are awesome. This says that you can be trained to use your mental capacity to its limits.

Since computers can also be set up to detect nonverbal signals—those commonly associated with stress analyzers and autonomic responses—it is likely that a computer can be programmed to assess your decision-making and associated responses. In plain English, your computer will read you and produce information out of which you can judge the effectiveness of your decision making.

The possibilities of such developments are legion, especially in education.

This says the biomachine will come, a mixture of you and computer in an extremely tight relationship. Trying to stop this evolution is like trying to play King Canute. As the good king demonstrated to his sycophantic courtiers, when the tide's rising, words won't stop it.

None of this says computers will give you an instant education in a foreign language or any other skill. It will give you instantaneous access to a dictionary, but you will still have to learn how to convert what the dictionary provides into the spoken and written words.

Don't imagine that this evolution can be outlawed. The first brain surgeon able to engage a tight instantaneous link with his medical library and other surgeons *while he is operating* will lead the way for all other surgeons to follow. When that surgeon demonstrates a computer-assisted ability to operate at a microscopic level, perhaps even at a cellular level, there will be a stampede of surgeons to join him.

Countless lives have already been saved through the computer's ability to sort great masses of medical data, but that is only a crude beginning.

What about our lawmakers? Can they be induced to try blocking this computer evolution? The first attorney able to do an instantaneous sorting through his entire law library while he stands in the courtroom will make it certain that his fellows acquire the same ability.

Present concepts of "intelligence" and "brain" do not apply to what we are describing. What we have with computers is an interactive evolutionary process. It applies equally to us and to computers. It is deeply involved with our desires, some of which are instinctual and unconscious. Because of this, a tight symbiotic relationship between human and computer can be predicted with certainty. We will become increasingly dependent upon computers and they upon us.

The mutual adaptation between humankind and computers will be far-reaching. There appear to be few arenas of our activity where computers cannot improve the sorting-comparison-reaction rate.

Much of the information management in this evolutionary development is being turned over to computers—rapidly growing mountains of information plus faster and faster sorting and comparison. This means that the speed of development is following an exponential growth curve. The first group to make the adaptation may never be caught by its competitors. Whoever moves first will be out in front and gaining speed faster than anyone coming up from behind.

Does that mean we have a tiger by the tail?

Perhaps. But the fur is already between our fingers.

There will be conflict over this evolution. A great many careers are tied to "things as they are." Jobs, rank and prestige, profits and power, are involved. And computers in the hands of people who wish to use them as weapons are, indeed, dangerous instruments. We don't doubt for a minute that the organized management of great masses of information has destructive potential.

To what uses will this tool be put?

Will a pharmacist and biotechnician in some small, emerging nation use this new ability to produce a world-threatening plague? Will a displaced dictator use it to develop a way to cause great seismic sea waves? Will a "military genius" think he has the key to world conquest?

In an age of weapons that can destroy the entire planet, submitting to "military instinct" is obviously suicidal and not very intelligent. There will be no real estate left where a *victor* can stand and beat his chest.

Of course it's possible that a nut with a computer will do something monumentally insane. And if one person can use a computer for violence, others can retaliate. There we go back into the adolescent murk of our bloody past.

We say that this is already the insane course upon which our world is embarked, and we are holding out for the individual and for intelligence. We define intelligence as the ability to adapt to change. Computers are great for managing the conditions of change. In the sense that they provide quick access to massive amounts of information, they can amplify this kind of intelligence. They can be instruments of survival.

There appears little doubt, though, that the age of the biomachine will be ushered in by severe times.

We assume that intelligence is really a survival characteristic, but this turns upon itself. Those who adapt survive. Survivors are the ones who write the rules and write even the descriptions of intelligence. Our argument turns on the observation that some kind of information processing appears to be at work in our adaptability, at work on both a conscious and unconscious level. We see a severe screening process imposed on the ability to sift through information for the survival knowledge (again, our definition of intelligence). Even if you assume that good instincts may be quite as workable for survival as good intelligence, you are still operating on a base of information.

The implication here is that the computer/biomachine is a consciousness machine. If you identify instinct as an awesome deposit of information gathered from evolutionary experience, then the computer offers you the opportunity to manage that amount of information *consciously*. It can provide the ultimate marriage between conscious and unconscious.

This brings us back to square one and our definition of intelligence, back to our argument for the widely disseminated use of computers. We say that the uninhibited broadcast spread of computers to everyone in our worldwide society offers a way out for a civilization that suffers from the false idea that we live in a universe where absolute rules can be determined.

Admittedly, this is an open-ended argument and fraught with peril. But we live in a world where our differences are precious for the survival of the species. Anything that strengthens our individualism becomes precious for us all, and computers are certainly a powerful instrument for the individual.

Visibly, the computer is already here and appears to be unstoppable. The biomachine is coming. We are entering the age of the Chinese curse:
"May you live in interesting times."

Appendix B
Computers Are Not
People

There exists a real question whether the fundamental processes in your brain are even remotely comparable to the mechanical and electronic switching of computer circuits.

Calculating and memory are only a small part of what we must use to feel human. The way we view our universe is surrounded by grand assumptions and screened by vaguely glimpsed inferences that emotion-in-the-guise-of-logic frequently denies, and we often deal in ideas that Authority mistakenly punishes. Today, few would question Galileo if he called the Church Fathers of his day "power-hungry monsters suppressing ideas for personal gain."

The best medical specialists in today's world still don't know how your brain works. They may never know. The subjective complexity of that unique anatomical creation—YOU—is like an ever-unfolding mystery, without beginning, without end. The more we discover, the more we find there is to discover.

It has been suggested that we are "colloidal computers" using an electrochemical system. According to this theory, we mediate the transfer of ions through a chemical medium to produce our data bits. Any first-year chemistry student knows this would have to be a very slow process when compared with purely electronic data juggling. Computers are already into the trillionths-of-a-second range and may go faster.

Colloidal systems are confined to the millisecond range (*milli* = thousandth).

Yet it's obvious that we can operate in some respects at an effective speed much faster than computers—perhaps by bridging much larger pans of "unknowns." If the computer comparison is to hold, we would have to make up for our shortcoming in speed by being multichannel, multidimensional, or by some means yet to be discovered.

At an operational level we know that your brain uses chemical as well as electrical processes. You may even have capacities similar to those demonstrated in holograms. For those of you who have never before met this term, *hologram* labels a three-dimensional photographic process involving lasers. When you break the "negative" of a hologram, each shattered part contains the three-dimensional image of the whole original, although sometimes in less detail.

There is even a new suggestion arising out of research in particle physics that your brain shares in a "cosmic data bank" that is linked to the universe by tachyon phenomena.

Tachyon refers to a concept proposed on the basis of an implication in Einstein's special theory. The suggestion is partly responsive to observations of a rare particle behavior in cloud chambers. These observations can be explained if you assume that some particles travel backward in time. The suggestion is that if signals or information can travel backward in time, that would be equivalent to particles going faster than light. If the suggestion is verified, it makes precognition possible—not *certain* but possible.

There are indications that various types of memory are localized in specific areas of our brains, but the current theoretical model of our brains is approximately equivalent to the flat-earth theory, which began going out of vogue about the time of Columbus. We don't even know what form the actual signals take within the brain. The decoding process remains a mystery.

Whichever way we turn, we are forced to ask even more difficult questions about the brain-computer comparison.

Compared with your brain, a computer is a simple, one-dimensional thing restricted to linear pathways and movement one step at a time. Even the dullest human does not suffer such restrictions.

Primarily because of its speed and storage capacity, your computer has an edge on you in the exhaustive analysis of the possibilities that you have laid out for it in some fashion. It will not, however, examine *every* possibility because we don't know how to program for every possibility and, by extension, will never know how to do this. This is an elemental fact about infinity that we can face but a computer cannot.

But given any system with known limits or known to have limits, your computer can exhaust the possibilities within those limits. That's a computer's strength. You can program it to do such things. The machine flips switches. It simulates. It obeys your commands and can even contr other machines within these limits.

Computers break down when confronted with such problems as th construction of workable plans. Logical systems can deal only wit limited word definitions, and they can do that just so long as there are n evolutionary changes in grammar or definitions. Much to the dismay o absolutists in Linguistics and the French Academy, all words and lan guages are in a process of evolutionary change, sometimes slow, some times rapid. Computers keep getting left behind. They are outpaced by th human plan.

Furthermore, our languages do not always stick to their theoretica descriptions or to "known rules." Languages are notorious for perform ing outside their theoretical descriptions. This is much more than problem of discovering rules. Every reader of this book should be able t produce examples of where the rules of grammar have been broken, ofte dramatically, without the least influence on understanding.

Your computer is based squarely on a logical system, confined t those logical rules. Logical systems are in serious difficulty when you ca break their rules without seriously affecting understanding. And those rules are in even greater trouble when breaking the rules improve understanding. This is especially true in poetry (try e.e. cummings) and ir urgent survival commands.

"Watch out!"

"Keep clear!"

Yes, we talk to each other and have been doing this since we were quite young. Now, you can even *talk* to a computer. However, there is a telling observation that must be made about our use of language.

We practice a form of communication that requires agreements about shared experiences. Anyone who has tried to translate from one of our languages into another knows the severe limits placed on quite useful languages by this shared-experience agreement.

There is an amusing story told about the project to design a computer system that would translate Russian into English and vice versa. To test the system, the designers fed the translations back into the computer, setting the machine to restore the translations to the originals.

In one case, they went from English to computer Russian, then from computer Russian back into computer English. The computer produced a new word: *watergoat*. The designers knew they had nothing like that in the English original. They went back to that original and found the offending words: *hydraulic ram*.

They started with a term for a mechanical pump and ended by inventing a new animal form.

When you assume that a translation can form a perfect two-way bridge between you and a machine, you are confronting this agreement on shared experiences. You also are assuming there will be no changes in definitions or grammar and that computer evolution can follow precisely in the tracks of animal evolution.

Your brain juggles a vastly more subtle and highly differentiated mass of information than computers can handle. Look at it briefly.

Through light rays, your eyes screen for countless variable rhythms in your surroundings: colors, written words, pictures, animate and inanimate objects (the difference is often a key to survival), and much more.

Through sound waves your skin and ears juggle another spectrum of variables: spoken words, deep reverberations, the meanings hidden in subtle tones, the magic of music, the calls of animals and birds, the signals of horns and bells.

Your nose is just as wide a window on your world, sensing those external hormones called pheromones, sensing the gross insults of ozone and smog, responding to the fine distinctions in floral perfumes.

Not only does your skin sense sounds, but it responds to temperature, touch, and other fine gradations of pressure changes, and it may even be able to detect light. There are some interesting experiments suggesting this.

These are just a few of the conscious parts of the human system. There remains that vast reservoir of unconscious cataloguing that accompanies your consciousness, which monitors and influences your behavior—that great inheritance which we sometimes pass off with the inadequate label of "instinct." This, in turn, is rooted in a bioevolutionary history that has modified us throughout our racial development.

How do we compare all of that with computers?

It is easy to see, though, how the comparison attempts developed, how the false image of computers was built up in our minds. Like you, a computer receives information from the universe around it. The computer is programmed to classify that information, store it, and then act (in a programmed way) to influence the outside world. It became easy to call the storage process "memory," even though human memory is a far more complex affair. Programming is easily likened to conditioning. The behavioral psychologists have had a field day with that comparison. And it's quite attractive to call *data input* "reading" or "listening."

Out of this came the concept of artificial intelligence and the other anthropomorphic forms now commonly used to describe computer performance.

We suggest that you must impose clearly unrealistic limits on your own abilities before you can make such comparisons. The machine does not *understand*. It cannot *know* or *plan*. It has no *judgment* that you can trust to look out for your best interests. The machine has no such *interests*.

This is a problem in semantics carried to a dangerous extreme. Computer simulation (essentially a complex of labels) will never be the *thing* at which it points in our flesh-and-blood universe. No complex of computer circuits nor of our brain cells can ever be that thing which the symbols try to describe.

Guide your reactions by this fact and you will always be at least one jump ahead of your computer.

Despite the elementary and obvious nature of this observation, the computer industry and many computer experts appear united in an effort to deny it. It's as though they were trying to break down some final semantic barrier, trying to create a symbol which is in fact what the symbol describes.

To the extent that this is an attempt to make symbols predict events in our universe, it is praiseworthy. To the extent that it confuses computer performance with what people do, even going a step beyond into an emotional belief in the reality of the symbols, this is a sad commentary on wishful thinking.

Whether this illusion game turns out to be destructive depends in large part on the beliefs we invest in the computer's symbols before we test what those symbols create.

If computers ever acquire something we could understand as intelligence, it will be profoundly different from our mental activity, and issuing from something distinctly not a brain. The mechanical roots are too different from the animal roots; the experience framework will be too divergent.

Whatever it is your brain does, you experience *life*, you embody this. We suggest, though, that you do not know life. This is something you can share with your computer. There is a Zen axiom that you can embody truth but you cannot express it. This conforms to Heisenberg's theory that at some point our own observations distort what we are observing. That places real limits on what we can express, limits we should always test and attempt to expand, but *what you cannot express you cannot convert into a program.*

Appendix C
PROGRAMAP
Dictionary

PROGRAMAP DICTIONARY

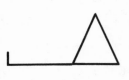

GOTO (larger statement number)

GOTO (smaller statement number)

IF (condition) GOTO larger
statement number

IF (condition) GOTO smaller
statement number

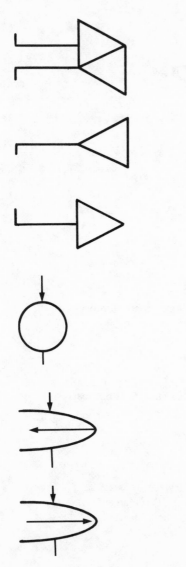

GOSUB (statement number)

ENTRY POINT

RETURN FROM SUBROUTINE
to main program

INTERNAL SWITCHING

OUTPUT

INPUT

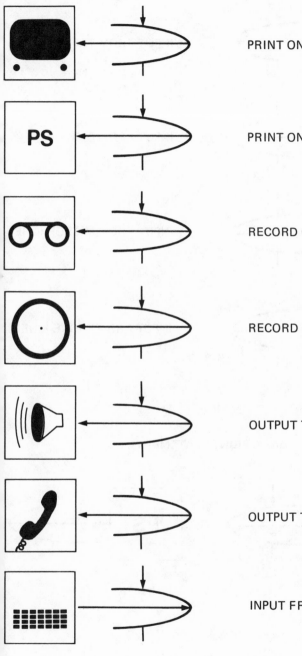

PRINT ON SCREEN

PRINT ON PRINTER

RECORD ON TAPE

RECORD ON DISK

OUTPUT TO SPEAKER

OUTPUT TO PHONE LINE

INPUT FROM KEYBOARD

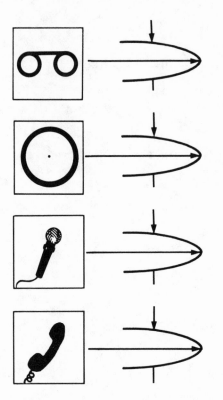

INPUT FROM TAPE

INPUT FROM DISK

INPUT FROM MICROPHONE

INPUT FROM PHONE LINE

BASIC PRINT STATEMENT

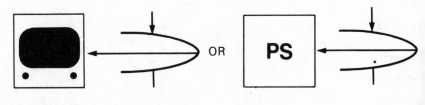

OR

PS

CRT SCREEN

PRINTER

BASIC GOTO STATEMENT

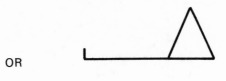

OR

smaller number

bigger number

BASIC GOSUB STATEMENT

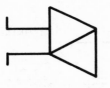

BASIC RETURN STATEMENT

BASIC IF STATEMENT

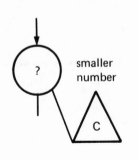

smaller
number

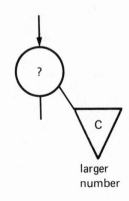

larger
number

BASIC FOR . . . . . . NEXT STATEMENT

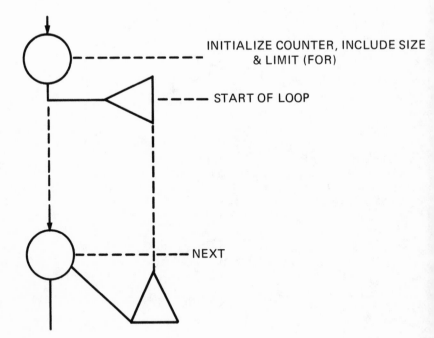

INITIALIZE COUNTER, INCLUDE SIZE
& LIMIT (FOR)

START OF LOOP

NEXT

BASIC <u>END</u> STATEMENT
(alternatives)

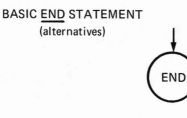

ALL OTHER BASIC STATEMENTS

Appendix D
Computer Magazines

Note: Names and addresses are based on latest information available at pre time. Due to delays for production there may be inaccuracies.

BYTE
Byte Publications, Inc.
70 Main Street
Peterborough, NH 03458

Calculators / Computers
DYMAX
PO Box 310
Menlo Park, CA 94025

Computer Music Journal
Peoples Computer Co.
PO Box E
Menlo Park, CA 94025

Computer Notes
MITS Inc.
2450 Alamo S.E.
Albuquerque, NM 87106

Creative Computing
Creative Computing
PO Box 789-M
Morristown, NJ 07662

Digital Design
Benwill Publishing Corp.
167 Corey Road
Brookline, MA 02146

Dr. Dobbs Journal
Peoples Computer Co.
PO Box E
Menlo Park, CA 94025

EDN
Chaners Publishing
270 St. Paul Street
Denver, CO 80206

Elementary Electronics
Davis Publications, Inc.
PO Box 2630
Greenwich, CT 06830

Electronic Design
Hayden Publishing Co.
50 Essex Street
Rochelle Park, NJ 07662

Electronics
  McGraw-Hill Inc.
  1221 Avenue of the Americas
  New York, NY 10020

Ham Radio
  Communications Technology
  Greenville, NH 03048

IEEE Computer
  IEEE
  345 E. 47th Street
  New York, NY 10017

Interface Age
  McPheters, Wolfe & Jones
  16704 Marquardt Avenue
  Cerritos, CA 90701

Kilobaud
  Kilobaud Inc.
  Peterborough, NH 03458

Mini-Micro Systems
  5 Kane Industrial Drive
  Hudson, MA 01749

Peoples Computer (PCC)
  Peoples Computer Co.
  PO Box E
  Menlo Park, CA 94025

Personal Computing
  Benwill Publishing
  167 Corey Road
  Brookline, MA 02146

Popular Computing
  PO Box 272
  Calabasas, CA 91302

Popular Electronics
  One Park Avenue
  New York, NY 10003

Radio Electronics
  Gernsback Publications
  200 Park Avenue S.
  New York, NY 10003

ROM
  ROM Publications Inc.
  Route 97
  Hampton, CT 06247

SCCS Interface
  Southern California Computer
    Society
  1415 Second Street
  Santa Monica, CA 90401

73 Amateur Radio
  73, Inc.
  Peterborough, NH 03458

Appendix E
Microcomputer
Accessories and
Manufacturers

Note: Names and addresses are based on latest information available at press time. Due to delays for production there may be inaccuracies.

Apple Computer Company
770 Welch Road
Palo Alto, CA 94304

Applied Microtechnology
100 N. Winchester Boulevard
Suite 260
Santa Clara, CA 95050

Bitech, Inc.
1440 State College Boulevard
Bldg. 6
Anaheim, CA 92806

Byte, Inc.
1261 Birchwood Drive
Sunnyvale, CA 94086

CGRS Microtech
PO Box 368
Southampton, PA 18966

Commodore
901 California Avenue
Palo Alto, CA 94304

Compucolor Corp.
Subsidiary of Intelligent Systems
   Corp.
5965 Peachtree Corners E.
Norcross, GA 30071

Computer Data Systems
c/o Robert Boyer
English Village Apts.
Atram Hall #3
Newark, DE 19711

Computer Power and Light
12321 Ventura Boulevard
Studio City, CA 91604

Control Logic, Inc.
9 Tech Circle
Natick, MA 01760

Cramer Electronics
85 Wells Avenue
Newton, MA 02159

Cromenco
One First Street
Los Altos, CA 94022

Cybersystem, Inc.
4306 Governors Drive
Huntsville, AL 35805

Data General Corp.
Southboro, MA 01772

Digital Electronics Corp.
2126 Sixth Street
Berkeley, CA 94710

Digital Equipment Corp.
146 Main Street
Maynard, MA 01754

The Digital Group
PO Box 6528
Denver, CO 80206

E&L Instruments
61 First Street
Derby, CT 06418

EBKA Industries, Inc.
6920 Melrose Lane
Oklahoma City, OK 73127

EBNEK, Inc.
254 N. Washington Street
Wichita, KS 67202

ECD Corp.
196 Broadway
Cambridge, MA 02139

Electronic Control Technology
PO Box 6
Union, NJ 07083

Electronic Memories & Magnetics
Corp.
12621 Chadron Avenue
Hawthorne, CA 90250

Electronic Products Associates, Inc.
1157 Vega Street
San Diego, CA 92110

Electronic Tool Co.
4736 W. El Segundo Boulevard
PO Box 1315
Hawthorne, CA 90250

Fabri-Tek, Inc.
5901 S. County Road 18
Minneapolis, MN 55436

Fairchild Microsystems Division
1725 Techology Drive
San Jose, CA 95110

Futurdata Computer Corp.
11205 La Cienaga Boulevard
Los Angeles, CA 90045

Hal Communications Corp.
Box 365
807 E. Green Street
Urbana, IL 61801

Heath Company
Benton Harbor, MI 49022

Heurikon Corp.
700 W. Badger Road
Madison, WI 53713

Hewlett-Packard Corp.
1501 Page Mill Road
Palo Alto, CA 94304

Hughes Aircraft Co.
Aerospace Group
Culver City, CA 90230

IMS Associates, Inc.
1922 Republic Avenue
San Leandro, CA 94577

IMSAI Manufacturing Corp.
14800 Wicks Boulevard
San Leandro, CA 94577

Infinite, Inc.
1924 Waverly Place
Melborne, FL 32901

Intel Corp.
3065 Bowers Avenue
Santa Clara, CA 95051

Intelligent Systems Corp.
5965 Peachtree Corners E.
Norcross, GA 30071

International Data Systems, Inc.
400 N. Washington Street
Suite 200
Falls Church, VA 22046

International Microsystems, Inc.
122 Hutton Street
Gaithersburg, MD 20760

Intersil, Inc.
10900 N. Tantau Avenue
Cupertino, CA 95014

M&R Enterprises
PO Box 61011
Sunnyvale, CA 94088

Martin Research
336 Commercial Avenue
Northbrook, IL 60062

Microcomputer Associates Inc.
2859 Scott Boulevard
Santa Clara, CA 95050

Microdata Systems
2 Mack Road, #101
Woburn, MA 01801

Microkit Inc.
2180 Colorado Avenue
Santa Monica, CA 90490

Midwest Scientific Instruments
220 W. Cedar
Olathe, KS 66061

MITS, Inc.
2450 Alamo S.E.
Albuquerque, NM 87106

Monolithic Systems Corp.
14 Inverness Drive E.
Englewood, CO 80110

MOS Technology Inc.
950 Rittenhouse Road
Norristown, PA 19401

MOSTEK Corp.
1215 W. Crosby Road
Carrolton, TX 75006

Motorola Inc. Microsystems
2200 W. Broadway
Mesa, AZ 85202

Multisonics, Inc.
6444 Sierra Court
PO Box 2295
Dublin, CA 94566

National Semiconductor Corp.
2900 Semiconductor Drive
Santa Clara, CA 95015

Noval Inc.
8401 Aero Drive
San Diego, CA 92123

Ohio Scientific Instruments
11679 Hayden Street
Hiram, OH 44234

Pacific Cyber/Metrix, Inc.
180 Thorup Lane
San Ramon, CA 94583

Pertec Computer Corp.
12910 Culver Boulevard
PO Box 92300
Los Angeles, CA 90066

Polymorphic Systems
737 Kellogg
Goleta, CA 93017

Process Computer Systems (PCS)
750 N. Maple Road
Saline, MI 48176

Processor Technology
6200-T Hollis Street
Emeryville, CA 94608

Pro-Log Corporation
2411 Garden Road
Monterey, CA 93940

Quay Corporation
PO Box 386
Freehold, NJ 07728

Radio Shack
2617 West Seventh Street
Fort Worth, TX 76107

Realistic Controls Corp.
3530 Warrensville Center Road
Cleveland, OH 44122

Rockwell International
 Microelectronic Devices
PO Box 3669
Anaheim, CA 92803

Signetics Corp.
811 E. Arques Avenue
Sunnyvale, CA 94086

Southwest Technical Products
 Corp.
219 W. Rhapsody
San Antonio, TX 78216

Sphere Group
791 S. 500 W.
Bountiful, UT 84010

STS Systems
Mount Vernon, NH 13057

System Integration Associates
Little Conestoga Road and
   Adams Drive
Glenmore, PA 19343

Systems Research Inc.
1010 Westwood Boulevard
Los Angeles, CA 90024

Technical Design Labs
Research Park Bldg. H
1101 State Road
Princeton, NJ 08540

Terak Corp.
PO Box 3078
Scottsdale, AZ 85257

Texas Instruments Inc.
8600 Commerce Park Drive
Houston, TX 77036

TLF
PO Box 2298
Littleton, CO 80161

Tranti Systems, Inc.
1 Chelmsford Road
North Billerica, MA 01862

Vector Graphic, Inc.
717 Lakefield Road
Suite F
Westlake, CA 91361

Veras Systems
PO Box 74
Somerville, MA 02143

Warner & Swasey Co.
30300 Solon Industrial Parkway
Solon, OH 44139

Wave Mate
1015 W. 190th Street
Gardena, CA 90248

Western Data Systems
3650 Charles Street, #2
Santa Clara, CA 95050

Wyle Computer Products
3200 Macgruder Boulevard
Hampton, VA 23666

Appendix F
Car Maintenance
PROGRAMAP

In the next appendix we will get into an actual program you can run on your machine. But first we want you to go through the PROGRAMAP for that program. Remember that the symbols in a flowchart provide an overview. They show the "whole picture" and must be set out in a clear and uncluttered way. If the flowchart is cluttered, your picture of the program will be blurred.

Specific descriptions accompany the flowchart. Without translating the program language you can read these descriptions to tell what's happening. The descriptions will also appear in the program as comments or remarks. They provide a cross-reference. Always go through these detailed steps. Six months later, when you decide you want to make your program do something more complex, the time saved with a matching flowchart and program remarks will more than compensate for the original effort. The flowchart also saves time in the actual program writing.

We strongly recommend that you try our symbol system rather than the industry standards. The reasoning behind our system is known as *top-down*. In it, you solve the problem first, then write the program that does the problem solving automatically.

Here's how it goes:

The first thing on the outline (page 184) is "Display title." The program's beginning is indicated on the chart by an oval box containing the word START. Since BASIC programs always start with the smallest-numbered statement and proceed sequentially to the largest, we start with that smallest number in this way:

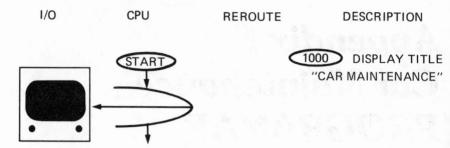

I/O   CPU   REROUTE   DESCRIPTION

START

1000 DISPLAY TITLE
"CAR MAINTENANCE"

The object of the PROGRAMAP is to provide a smooth transition from outline to program. The description column is vital for this transition. Overall program strategy is contained in the outline. The PROGRAMAP follows that same strategy and elaborates on details needed in the program. In the description column such things as main statement numbers, variable names, REROUTEs, and SWITCHING operations are identified. The resulting map will translate easily into BASIC or other programming language.

Note that information is first given to the program user via the screen, just one step with the PROGRAMAP. Other details include the START symbol and beginning statement number, which is circled. When output is to the screen or printer, remember that the things you put in quotes constitute a *constant string,* always displayed or written verbatim.

We now let the program user choose between two things: (1) recording completed service, *or* (2) displaying the upcoming maintenance. We also must copy existing maintenance records from cassette tape storage. You need two tapes: one for the program and one for the maintenance records.

The program tape will be copied using the BASIC "LOAD" statement. The record tape will be controlled by the program. (Note that the first time you use this program you will have to provide appropriate information on the record tape for the program to RUN.)

Since both functions use the information stored on the record tape, it's best to copy the records at this stage. That way the copying operations have to be in the program only once. The program tells the user to put the cassette into the recorder and rewind the tape. We must also stop the program while this is done and provide a way to restart it from the keyboard when the cassette is ready. Look at the description column. The INPUT symbol for this step is accompanied by a descriptive WAIT FOR RETURN.

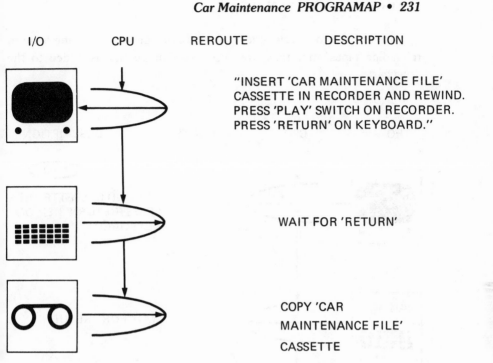

I/O	CPU	REROUTE	DESCRIPTION
			"INSERT 'CAR MAINTENANCE FILE' CASSETTE IN RECORDER AND REWIND. PRESS 'PLAY' SWITCH ON RECORDER. PRESS 'RETURN' ON KEYBOARD."
			WAIT FOR 'RETURN'
			COPY 'CAR MAINTENANCE FILE' CASSETTE

Let's say you accidentially insert the wrong tape. Here's the program solution to that problem:

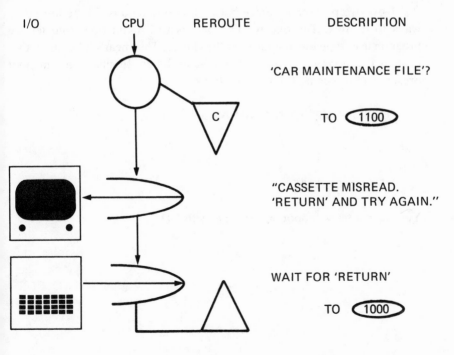

I/O	CPU	REROUTE	DESCRIPTION
			'CAR MAINTENANCE FILE'?
	C		TO 1100
			"CASSETTE MISREAD. 'RETURN' AND TRY AGAIN."
			WAIT FOR 'RETURN'
			TO 1000

Tapes have to be rewound. It's good practice to get into the habit of rewinding tapes after they are used. This instruction is added to the flowchart:

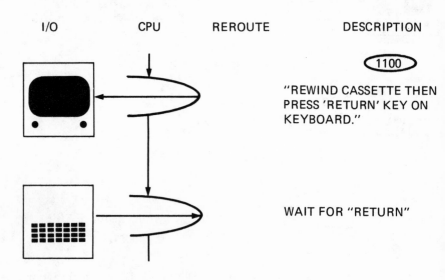

I/O	CPU	REROUTE	DESCRIPTION

1100

"REWIND CASSETTE THEN
PRESS 'RETURN' KEY ON
KEYBOARD."

WAIT FOR "RETURN"

Now, we provide a choice between two functions. There are many ways to do this. The one we like best is to list functions and let the program user type the first letter of the choice. This means, of course, that no two functions can start with the same letter. In this program, that presents no problem. The two functions are:

RECORD COMPLETED MAINTENANCE

and

DISPLAY SCHEDULE

Your computer will not confuse an *R* with a *D*.

I/O	CPU	REROUTE	DESCRIPTION

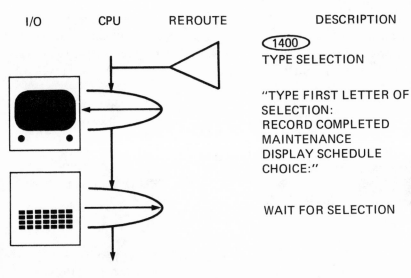

1400
TYPE SELECTION

"TYPE FIRST LETTER OF
SELECTION:
RECORD COMPLETED
MAINTENANCE
DISPLAY SCHEDULE
CHOICE:"

WAIT FOR SELECTION

Part 1 of the outline now contains only the one item: We must check the selection and reroute the program to the correct routine. If you have not typed one of the two required letters, the program should return to the point where a selection is made. We will reroute twice:

I/O	CPU	REROUTE	DESCRIPTION

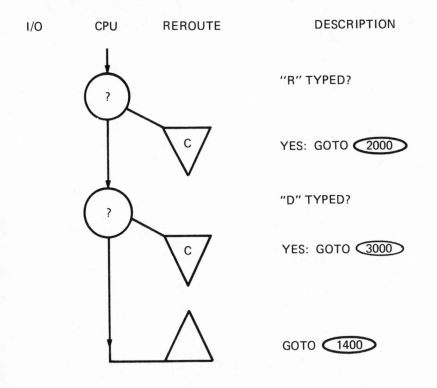

"R" TYPED?

YES: GOTO **2000**

"D" TYPED?

YES: GOTO **3000**

GOTO **1400**

We now go on to part 2 of the outline, which is more complex. It must provide access to each maintenance record individually and compute the next maintenance. It should start with a title (good practice for every routine) and the list of maintenance functions from which you can choose.

I/O   CPU   REROUTE   DESCRIPTION

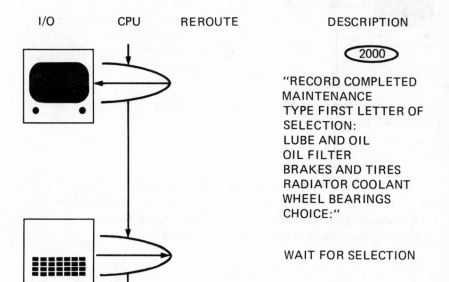

2000

"RECORD COMPLETED
MAINTENANCE
TYPE FIRST LETTER OF
SELECTION:
LUBE AND OIL
OIL FILTER
BRAKES AND TIRES
RADIATOR COOLANT
WHEEL BEARINGS
CHOICE:"

WAIT FOR SELECTION

The five selections need five "REROUTE?" symbols in the flow-chart, ending again with return for typing mistakes:

I/O	CPU	REROUTE	DESCRIPTION

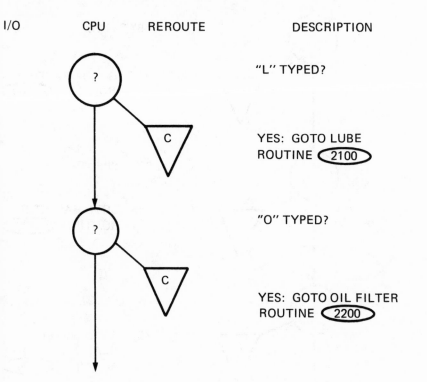

"L" TYPED?

YES: GOTO LUBE
ROUTINE ⟨2100⟩

"O" TYPED?

YES: GOTO OIL FILTER
ROUTINE ⟨2200⟩

I/O   CPU   REROUTE   DESCRIPTION

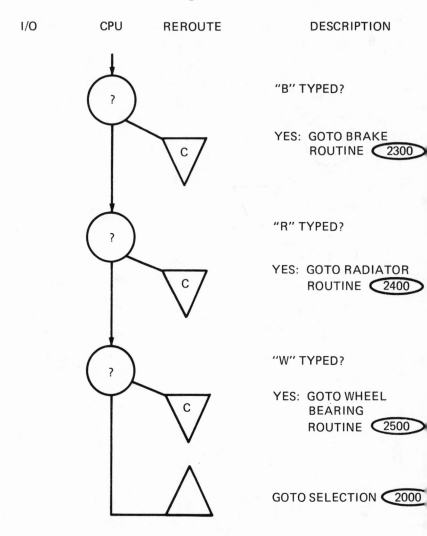

"B" TYPED?

YES: GOTO BRAKE
ROUTINE 2300

"R" TYPED?

YES: GOTO RADIATOR
ROUTINE 2400

"W" TYPED?

YES: GOTO WHEEL
BEARING
ROUTINE 2500

GOTO SELECTION 2000

Maintenance routines work with information pertaining to each routine. The information is organized in groups corresponding to each maintenance function. Each group is known as a *record*. The complete collection of records is called a *file*. We have five maintenance records in the maintenance file.

The rest of the routines use the various maintenance records. Part 2 of the outline changes the information in the records to reflect completed servicing. Part 3 displays the record information on the screen.

Routines in part 2 request the necessary information from the program user. This information on services performed together with the rules from the owner's manual on the car establish the next date and/or mileage for a servicing. This information is stored in the relevant record, an updated record file on a CAR MAINTENANCE FILE cassette.

The first routine is LUBE AND OIL CHANGE. This must be done (in our example) every three thousand miles or three months, whichever comes first. It must request date and mileage from the program user. It will then calculate the date and mileage for the next such servicing *and* automatically put these into the LUBE AND OIL record.

I/O	CPU	REROUTE	DESCRIPTION

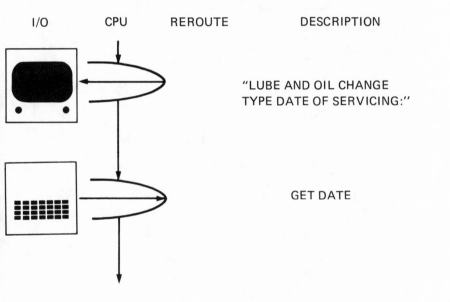

"LUBE AND OIL CHANGE
TYPE DATE OF SERVICING:"

GET DATE

I/O	CPU	REROUTE	DESCRIPTION

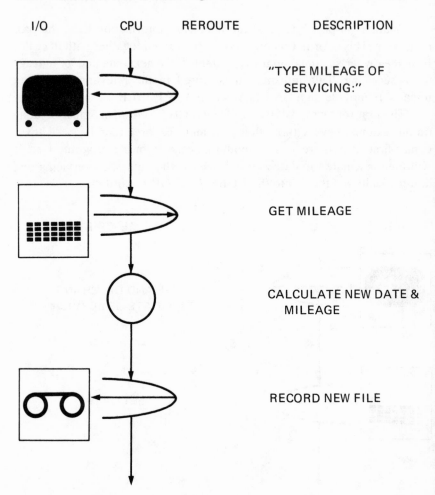

"TYPE MILEAGE OF
SERVICING:"

GET MILEAGE

CALCULATE NEW DATE &
MILEAGE

RECORD NEW FILE

Finished with the LUBE AND OIL CHANGE function, the program can either END or go back to part 1 of the outline, where you choose between the two functions. We must not forget to rewind the cassette tape if we go back to the choice point. Going back to the start also makes it possible to run this or another part of the program without restarting. Since the information tape must be read again if the program is restarted from the beginning, the program is easier to use if it is returned to the function choice, thereby eliminating unnecessary operations.

I/O   CPU   REROUTE   DESCRIPTION

GOTO 1100

The OIL FILTER routine might best be included in the LUBE AND OIL CHANGE routine, but for now we will make it separate just to outline the operations. Make a note that this sort of thing happens routinely in the writing of programs. Changes and condensations can come later.

For this step we again need date and mileage:

I/O   CPU   REROUTE   DESCRIPTION

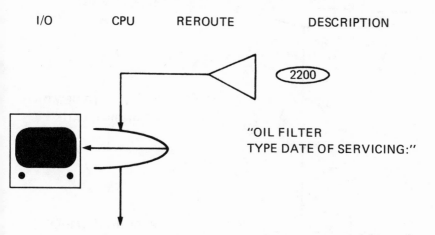

2200

"OIL FILTER
TYPE DATE OF SERVICING:"

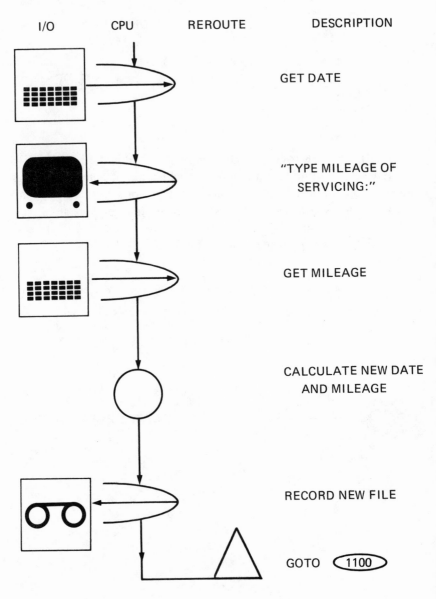

TIRE ROTATION AND BRAKE INSPECTION uses mileage only:

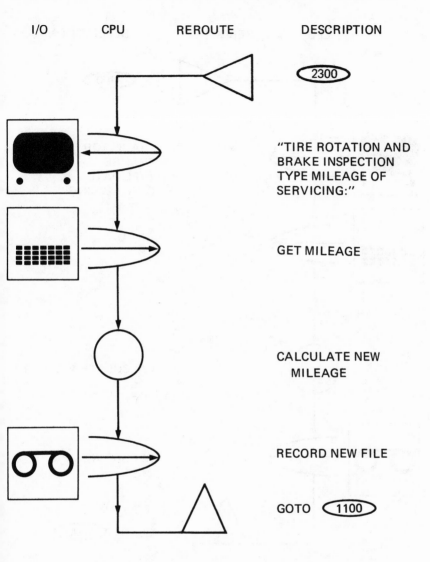

I/O	CPU	REROUTE	DESCRIPTION

2300

"TIRE ROTATION AND
BRAKE INSPECTION
TYPE MILEAGE OF
SERVICING:"

GET MILEAGE

CALCULATE NEW
MILEAGE

RECORD NEW FILE

GOTO 1100

The RADIATOR COOLANT routine needs only the date:

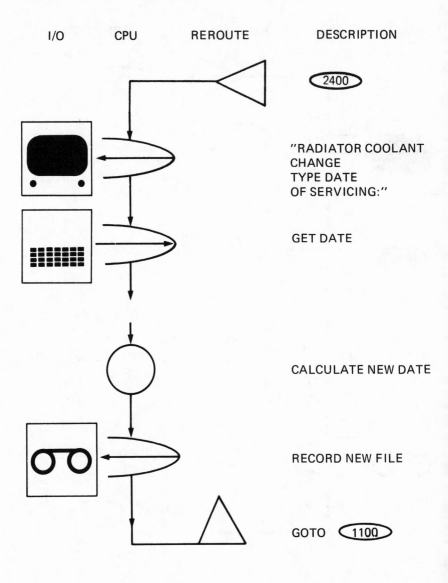

I/O	CPU	REROUTE	DESCRIPTION
			2400
			"RADIATOR COOLANT CHANGE TYPE DATE OF SERVICING:"
			GET DATE
			CALCULATE NEW DATE
			RECORD NEW FILE
			GOTO 1100

The WHEEL BEARING REPACKING routine uses mileage only:

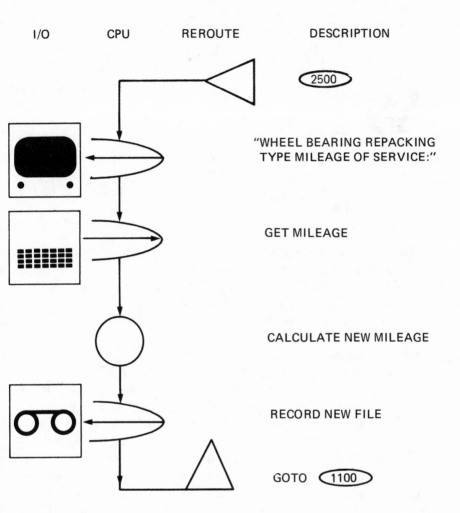

I/O	CPU	REROUTE	DESCRIPTION

2500

"WHEEL BEARING REPACKING
TYPE MILEAGE OF SERVICE:"

GET MILEAGE

CALCULATE NEW MILEAGE

RECORD NEW FILE

GOTO 1100

Part 3 of the outline, the final part of the program, requires display of NEXT MAINTENANCE schedule. This uses information from each maintenance record and displays it on the screen, then returns to the function selection. There is no cassette tape rewind at this point.

I/O   CPU   REROUTE   DESCRIPTION

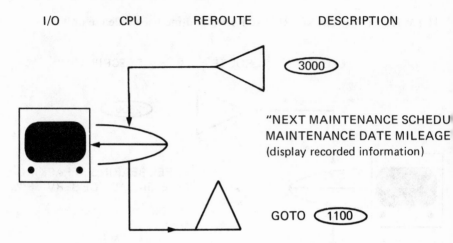

"NEXT MAINTENANCE SCHEDU
MAINTENANCE DATE MILEAGE
(display recorded information)

GOTO ⬭1100⬭

We have now completed a flowchart.

This is the point for removing redundant steps.

As it stands, the flowchart goes from one end of the program to the other in a continuous way. This is known as *straight-line programming.* When you are starting to write your first programs, this is the recommended way to do it. But now that the flowchart is complete, you can see if there are any sections that are repeated.

We mentioned earlier that it might be good to put LUBE AND OIL CHANGE and OIL FILTER routines together. Except for title, the flowchart shows that they are identical. This doesn't mean the programs would also be identical, since the rules for the calculations differ. If we set up the LUBE AND OIL CHANGE routine to ask: "OIL FILTER CHANGED? (Y OR N):," then we can address the problem another way. Since the filter is changed only at alternate oil changes, if the filter was changed this time, it doesn't have to be changed next time. The conditions can be written into the program using the answer to the FILTER CHANGED? question. Verbal information in the record must be made to conform. We do this by using the words "LUBE, OIL CHANGE, AND FILTER" when it's time to replace the filter, and just "LUBE AND OIL CHANGE" when the filter is not to be changed.

Since we have combined FILTER with LUBE AND OIL, the control routine now contains one less reroute. This saves programming space and time. The first two routines now look like this in the PROGRAMAP:

I/O	CPU	REROUTE	DESCRIPTION

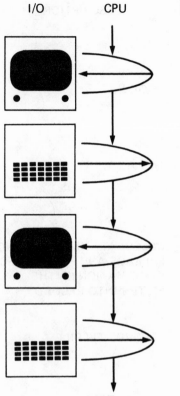

"LUBE, OIL CHANGE AND FILTER, TYPE DATE OF SERVICING:"

GET DATE

"TYPE MILEAGE OF SERVICING:"

GET MILEAGE

I/O	CPU	REROUTE	DESCRIPTION

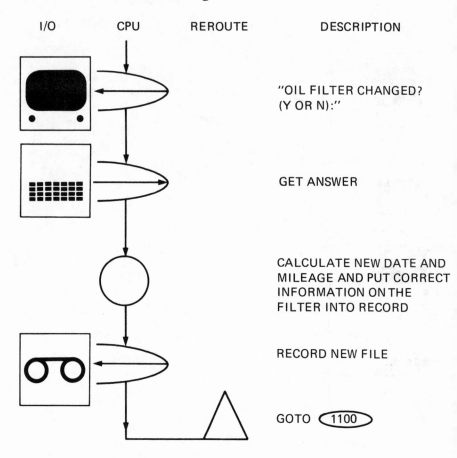

"OIL FILTER CHANGED? (Y OR N):"

GET ANSWER

CALCULATE NEW DATE AND MILEAGE AND PUT CORRECT INFORMATION ON THE FILTER INTO RECORD

RECORD NEW FILE

GOTO 1100

Our program still contains repetitions. The combinations "TYPE DATE OF SERVICING:"–GET DATE and "TYPE MILEAGE OF SERVICING:"–GET MILEAGE are each used several times. They could be done more easily with subroutines.

We have already seen examples of a program going to another place and then returning to the main selection. Subroutines also do this, but in a slightly different way.

If we call part 1 of the outline the *control routine* (this is where it's determined which function will be performed), then each routine in parts 2 and 3 is reached from the control routine and returns to it. It's as if the routines that perform the functions were right there in the control routine. They could have been put there in the preliminary PROGRAMAP. We didn't do it that way because we're too lazy to try and keep track of the whole thing all at once. It's easier to break programs into smaller groups, each performing a specific function.

The control routine embodies the whole program. It is the main part of the structured concept. The rest of the routines merely "detail" the functions that can be selected from the control routine.

Detail routines "know not from whence they come." This is what separates them from subroutines. A subroutine contains detailed operations that are encountered many times in a program. A subroutine is set up in a way that lets you reach it from any place in the program. You return to that same place whenever you need the automatic performance stored there.

Our flowchart representation of a subroutine excursion consists of two REROUTE symbols, the first going to the subroutine and the second returning from it. The comment specifies which subroutine:

I/O	CPU	REROUTE	DESCRIPTION

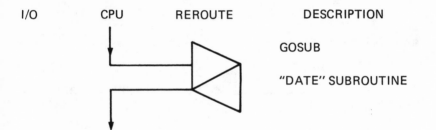

GOSUB

"DATE" SUBROUTINE

The subroutine contains the detailed operations and REROUTE symbols from and to the program:

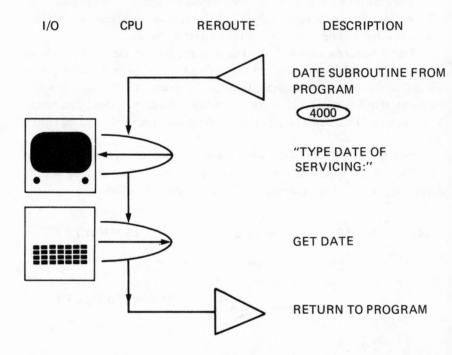

The mileage subroutine is the same, but with MILEAGE replacing DATE where appropriate and, of course, with a different series of statement numbers.

A final redundancy involves recording the new file on cassette tape. This is done at the end of each RECORD MAINTENANCE routine. We could handle this by a subroutine, the same way as the date and mileage. That would involve a GOSUB to the recording steps, a return to the maintenance routine, and then the final GOTO the control routine.

Since the next step after recording is always a return to the control routine, we could simply make this part of the program another detail routine, with the last step a GOTO returning the program to the control routine. We have chosen to put the GOSUB at the return point in the control routine. It will go in at the start of the control routine right before the "REWIND CASSETTE" message.

The control routine PROGRAMAP now begins with:

I/O	CPU	REROUTE	DESCRIPTION

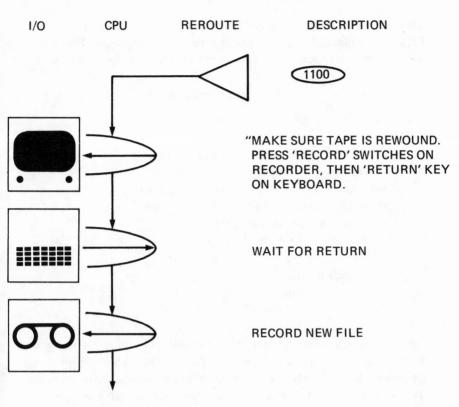

"MAKE SURE TAPE IS REWOUND.
PRESS 'RECORD' SWITCHES ON
RECORDER, THEN 'RETURN' KEY
ON KEYBOARD.

WAIT FOR RETURN

RECORD NEW FILE

We then go to the "REWIND CASSETTE" message and the rest of the control routine as before.

Each of these modifications has improved the program. We didn't require them to make the program work, but without redundant steps the program will be much easier to write. However, before we start to write the program, we should make a new outline and PROGRAMAP to reflect the improvements. This method of starting over with the outline when the final shape of the program has been decided is what is meant by the top-down concept.

This new outline will be more detailed than the original. The steps have been rearranged and renumbered, and the new operations added. PROGRAMAP and final program will follow the same sequence. Numbers on this outline will be the statement numbers of the final PROGRAMAP and program.

Initialization is the first step. It starts with statement number 1000.

There are often more statements in initializations because of DIMensions, REMarks, reading files, and establishing string constants. Therefore, we will skip 200 statement numbers (an extra 100) to the first entry point.

CAR MAINTENANCE OUTLINE

1000 Control routine—initialization
1200 Control routine reentry—record file
1300 Control routine reentry—rewind cassette tape
1400 Control routine reentry—mode selection
2000 Recording routine—maintenance selection
3000 Lube, oil change, and filter maintenance
4000 Brake and tire maintenance
5000 Radiator coolant maintenance
6000 Wheel bearing maintenance
7000 Display schedule
8000 Date subroutine
9000 Mileage subroutine

Other entry points appear in the program, but these are in the detail routines and we don't need them in the outline. When the program is typed into the computer, statement numbers on the outline should contain REMs with brief descriptions of the new outline. This outline is less verbally descriptive than the original, but its main purpose is to provide signposts for the steps you will follow.

The PROGRAMAP, too, must be made to conform. Here's the reworked flowchart:

I/O	CPU	REROUTE	DESCRIPTION

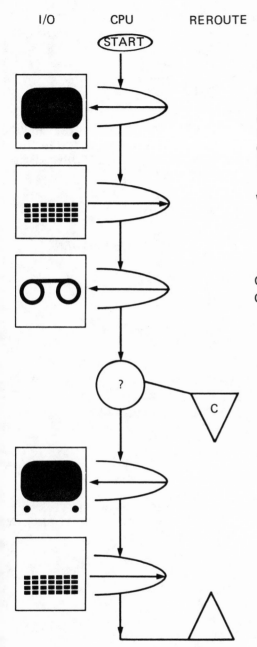

START

1000

INITIALIZATION

"CAR MAINTENANCE
INSERT 'CAR MAINTENANCE FILE'
CASSETTE INTO RECORDER AND
REWIND. PRESS 'PLAY' SWITCH
ON RECORDER. PRESS 'RETURN'
KEY ON KEYBOARD."

WAIT FOR RETURN

COPY 'CAR MAINTENANCE FILE'
CASSETTE

CASSETTE TITLE =
'CAR MAINTENANCE FILE'

C

YES:
TO 1300

"CASSETTE MISREAD.
'RETURN' AND TRY AGAIN."

WAIT FOR RETURN

TO 1000

I/O	CPU	REROUTE	DESCRIPTION

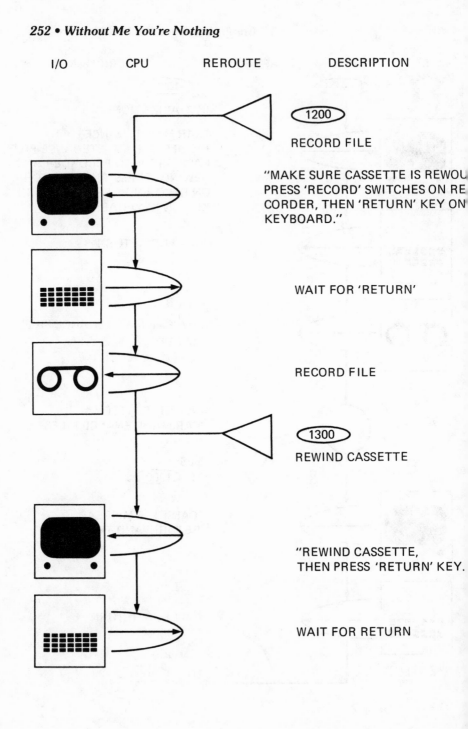

1200
RECORD FILE

"MAKE SURE CASSETTE IS REWOU
PRESS 'RECORD' SWITCHES ON RE
CORDER, THEN 'RETURN' KEY ON
KEYBOARD."

WAIT FOR 'RETURN'

RECORD FILE

1300
REWIND CASSETTE

"REWIND CASSETTE,
THEN PRESS 'RETURN' KEY.

WAIT FOR RETURN

I/O   CPU   REROUTE   DESCRIPTION

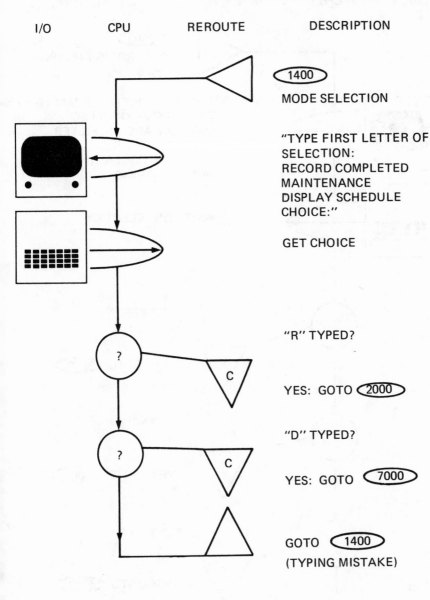

1400

MODE SELECTION

"TYPE FIRST LETTER OF
SELECTION:
RECORD COMPLETED
MAINTENANCE
DISPLAY SCHEDULE
CHOICE:"

GET CHOICE

"R" TYPED?

YES: GOTO 2000

"D" TYPED?

YES: GOTO 7000

GOTO 1400
(TYPING MISTAKE)

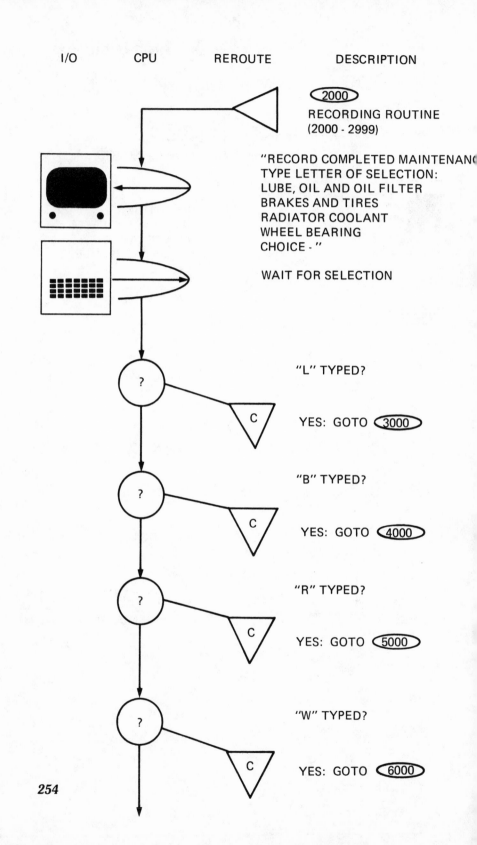

I/O	CPU	REROUTE	DESCRIPTION

2000
RECORDING ROUTINE
(2000 - 2999)

"RECORD COMPLETED MAINTENANC
TYPE LETTER OF SELECTION:
LUBE, OIL AND OIL FILTER
BRAKES AND TIRES
RADIATOR COOLANT
WHEEL BEARING
CHOICE - "

WAIT FOR SELECTION

"L" TYPED?

YES: GOTO 3000

"B" TYPED?

YES: GOTO 4000

"R" TYPED?

YES: GOTO 5000

"W" TYPED?

YES: GOTO 6000

254

| I/O | CPU | REROUTE | DESCRIPTION |

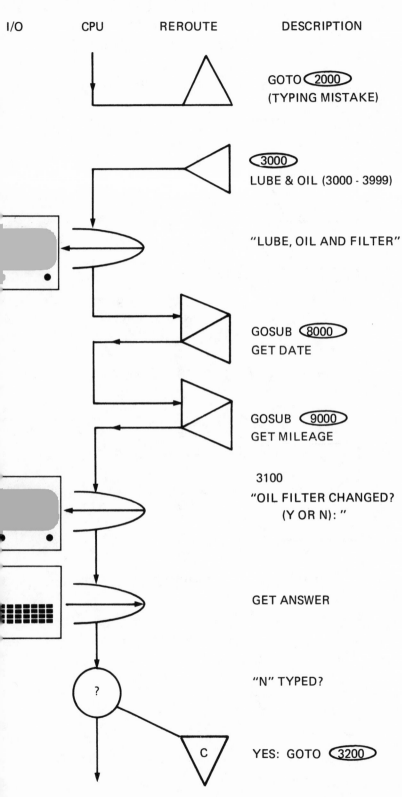

GOTO ⟨2000⟩
(TYPING MISTAKE)

⟨3000⟩
LUBE & OIL (3000 - 3999)

"LUBE, OIL AND FILTER"

GOSUB ⟨8000⟩
GET DATE

GOSUB ⟨9000⟩
GET MILEAGE

3100
"OIL FILTER CHANGED?
   (Y OR N): "

GET ANSWER

"N" TYPED?

YES: GOTO ⟨3200⟩

I/O	CPU	REROUTE	DESCRIPTION

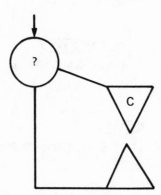

"Y" TYPED?

YES: GOTO 3300

GOTO 3100

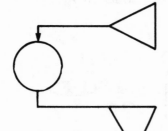

3200

REM COPY "LUBE, OIL & FILTER" INTO RECORD

GOTO 3400

3300

REM COPY "LUBE & OIL"

COPY "LUBE & OIL CHANGE" INTO RECORD

3400

COPY AND CALCULATE NEW DATE

MONTH < = 12?

GOTO 3500

MONTH = MONTH − 12
YEAR = YEAR +1

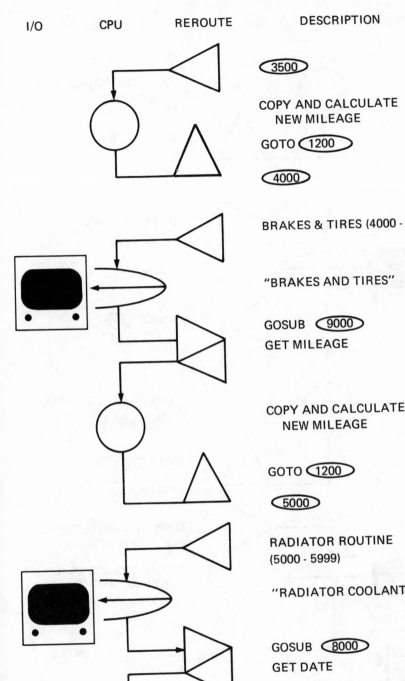

I/O	CPU	REROUTE	DESCRIPTION

3500

COPY AND CALCULATE
NEW MILEAGE

GOTO 1200

4000

BRAKES & TIRES (4000 - 4999)

"BRAKES AND TIRES"

GOSUB 9000
GET MILEAGE

COPY AND CALCULATE
NEW MILEAGE

GOTO 1200

5000

RADIATOR ROUTINE
(5000 - 5999)

"RADIATOR COOLANT"

GOSUB 8000
GET DATE

257

I/O	CPU	REROUTE	DESCRIPTION

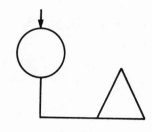

COPY AND CALCULATE
NEW DATE

GOTO ⟨1200⟩

⟨6000⟩

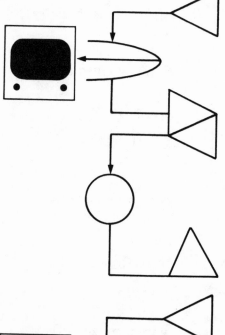

WHEEL BEARINGS
(6000 - 6999)

"PACK WHEEL BEARINGS"

GOSUB ⟨9000⟩
GET MILEAGE

COPY AND CALCULATE
NEW MILEAGE

GOTO ⟨1200⟩

⟨7000⟩

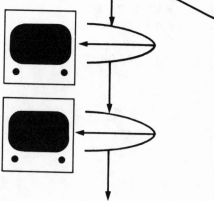

DISPLAY MAINTENANCE
SCHEDULE (7000 - 7999)

"MAINTENANCE SCHEDULE"
"NEXT MAINTENANCE
MILEAGE DATE"

DISPLAY MAINTENANCE
SCHEDULE

I/O	CPU	REROUTE	DESCRIPTION

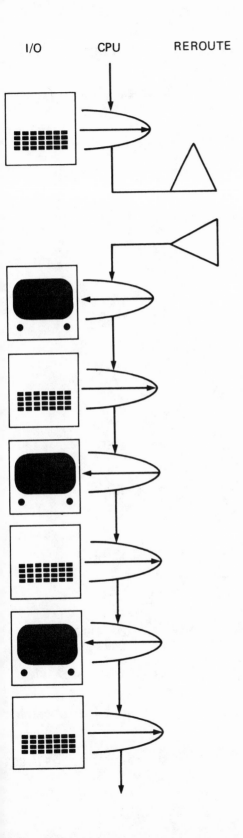

WAIT FOR RETURN

GOTO  1400

8000

DATE SUBROUTINE
(8000 - 8999)

"MONTH NUMBER?"

GET MONTH NUMBER

"DAY OF MONTH?"

GET DAY OF MONTH

"YEAR?"

GET YEAR

259

| I/O | CPU | REROUTE | DESCRIPTION |

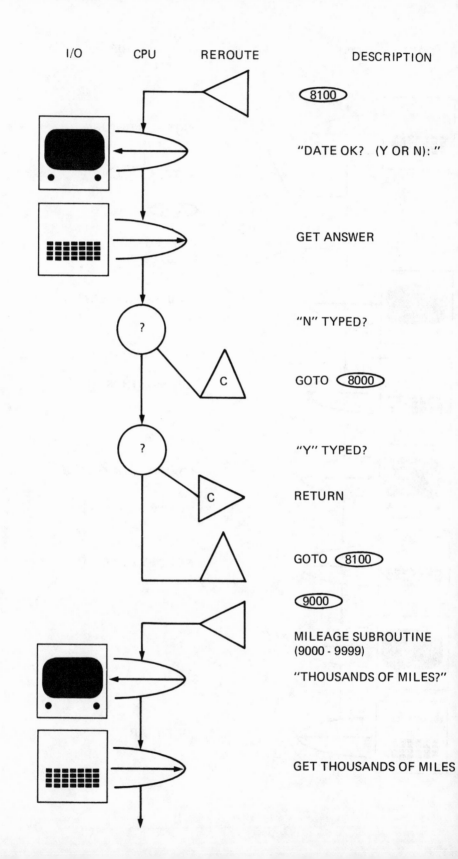

8100

"DATE OK? (Y OR N): "

GET ANSWER

"N" TYPED?

GOTO 8000

"Y" TYPED?

RETURN

GOTO 8100

9000

MILEAGE SUBROUTINE
(9000 - 9999)

"THOUSANDS OF MILES?"

GET THOUSANDS OF MILES

| I/O | CPU | REROUTE | DESCRIPTION |

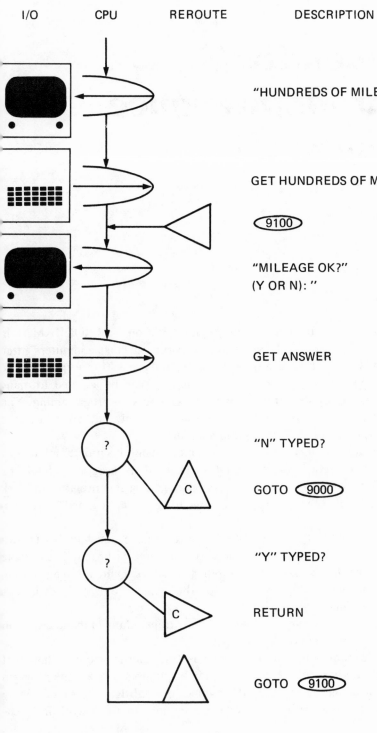

"HUNDREDS OF MILES?"

GET HUNDREDS OF MILES

9100

"MILEAGE OK?"
(Y OR N): "

GET ANSWER

"N" TYPED?

GOTO 9000

"Y" TYPED?

RETURN

GOTO 9100

Appendix G
Car Maintenance
Program

Now, we can get into the actual program built on the PROGRAMAP in the preceding section. This program will run on most computers fitted with BASIC. Just type it into the computer and use it. Our purpose was to supply you with an example. The techniques can be adapted to many other uses. Study this program with the chapters on programming. You will not only see how software appears in print, but you'll get the essentials of an important programming format.

You don't really need to know any more about this program than how to type it into your computer and RUN it. Many programs should be available to you in that form. But practice getting this program to work will teach you other things than how to make a "canned" program operate.

This is a good place to advise you that once you have your own computer, you should not be afraid to try out some of the readily available software that has been written for other machines. Quite often a program written for one machine will work on the competition's product just as long as the same language is used.

There are, however, occasional booby traps. Many of those traps can be disarmed with minor adjustments.

For example, if your machine has less internal storage than that required by a particular program, it may be possible to adapt the program to your machine by reducing the number of records to be saved, or by splitting the program into two or more sections that can work independently.

Don't expect your machine to grow a printer for your bare-bones system just because you give it a program that requires a printer. Equally, don't be surprised if the output intended for a printer can be put onto a screen with only two or three small changes.

This CAR MAINTENANCE PROGRAM was written for an Apple II computer with 48K RAM with Integer BASIC. If you have trouble putting it into your machine, reread these paragraphs and act accordingly.

Before we get into the program, we want to take you through the essentials about PRINT control. This is good practice and will pay off every time you use a computer.

You already have seen the four types of PRINT statements:

1. You can print a constant string (anything in quotes).

2. You can print the numerical answer to an algebraic expression (a number constant).

3. You can print the contents of a variable string.

4. You can print numerical variables.

Each time a PRINT statement is executed, it starts printing one place and finishes printing somewhere else. PRINT control symbols allow you to establish where things will be printed.

Most machines use two special symbols: commas and semicolons. These are typed immediately after the thing you are printing. A comma causes the cursor to move to the right for the next column. A semicolon leaves the cursor in the position immediately to the right of the final character printed. If neither symbol is used, the cursor moves to the left end of the next line down on the screen ending the line it started on.

You also have special statements that control the position of the cursor before the PRINT statement is executed. The TAB statement moves the cursor to any position on the line and the VTAB moves it to the beginning (left side) of any line on the screen.

With that information in mind, here's how the program goes:

If you make the first statement of a BASIC program a DIMension statement, the variable names that have been reserved are easily found. You just look at the beginning of the program.

To begin, statement number 1000 is the DIMension statement. We will come back to it from time to time and add the variable names as they are needed.

```
1000 DIM
```

Referring to the PROGRAMAP, you will see that the first thing the program does is display the title and instructions on how to get the file into storage. Your computer will have a special statement that clears the screen of all previous material. This clear-screen statement varies from machine to machine. It is a "machine-dependent" instruction, and we will merely bracket the required function in parentheses, leaving it to you to find the particular instruction for your machine. It will be in your programming manual.

    1010 (clear screen)

Most machines leave the cursor at the upper left corner of the screen after this instruction. To make the display pleasing, the title should be centered. Since our title, CAR MAINTENANCE, has fifteen letters and there most often are forty character positions across a screen, the first letter of the title should start in the thirteenth position. The cursor can be moved to that position with the TAB instruction:

    1020 TAB 13

Now, we display the title with a PRINT instruction:

    1030 PRINT "CAR MAINTENANCE"

When the print statement ends without a comma or semicolon, the cursor returns automatically to the left end of the next lower line on the screen. However, we want some space below the title. To get that, we use the VTAB (vertical TAB) instruction. VTAB 4 gives us a gap of two lines between the title and the next instruction. If your computer does not incorporate the VTAB instruction, two PRINT " " statements do the same thing.

    1040 VTAB 4
    1050 PRINT "INSERT 'CAR MAINTENANCE FILE' CASSETTE"

Double quotation marks cannot be printed on most systems; the apostrophe is a substitute.

At this point you don't have a 'CAR MAINTENANCE FILE' cassette. We'll show you how to make one presently.

    1060 PRINT " INTO RECORDER AND REWIND."

If you want to start a line a little to the right, it is often easier and more readable to put a few spaces inside the quotation marks instead of using TAB. TABs should be reserved for wide gaps.

Next, we display new information. This requires another vertical gap, just one line this time. Either PRINT " " or VTAB 7 will work. However, PRINT " " has the advantage of being independent of things happening around it. You don't have to count back the number of lines already used and supply an appropriate number. When PRINT " " is used, there will always be one blank line between the line you have just completed and the next one, even if a line is later added or removed.

```
1070 PRINT " "
1080 PRINT "PRESS 'PLAY' SWITCH ON RECORDER."
1090 PRINT " "
1100 PRINT "PRESS 'RETURN' KEY ON KEYBOARD."
```

When the program is RUN, by the time it reaches this point, all the instructions necessary to copy the CAR MAINTENANCE FILE into internal storage will be on the screen. An INPUT statement will stop the program until the person using it is finished with the instructions. When the RETURN key on the keyboard is pressed, the program continues:

```
1120 INPUT Z$
```

The variable name *Z$* has not been used before in this program. You now can go back to the DIMension statement at the beginning and enter it. Remember that when you retype that original statement number 1000, this wipes out whatever was already there. Statement 1000 now looks like this:

```
1000 DIM Z$ (1)
```

Z$ will provide for single-letter inputs wherever they come up in the program.

Now, since most program "bugs" result from typing errors rather than mistakes in logic, it's a good idea to try your program at various stages. If you do too much program without testing it, the mistakes tend to stack up. Correcting them can be tedious. But before testing you need an END statement:

32000 END

You can type RUN at this point and see how the program is coming. Your screen should show:

CAR MAINTENANCE

INSERT 'CAR MAINTENANCE FILE' CASSETTE
INTO RECORDER AND REWIND.

PRESS 'PLAY' SWITCH ON RECORDER.

PRESS 'RETURN' KEY ON KEYBOARD.

If you now press the RETURN key, the BASIC prompt should come back because the END statement has been reached.

A look at the display on the screen tells us what to do next. The file must be copied from the cassette into internal storage, another machine-dependent operation. Your manufacturer's manual should tell you how to do this.

The same variables with space reserved by the DIMension statement will be contained in the CAR MAINTENANCE FILE cassette. Since we still don't know all of those variables, a label will do for now to keep the statement number reserved:

1130 (copy car maintenance file)

We can come back to this after we know what has to be kept in the file.

Some identification should be written on the outside of all cassettes and stored on the tape itself. Program cassettes generally play the title at the start. Data cassettes can also be identified with a title. Since we are already calling this one CAR MAINTENANCE FILE, we can put this on the tape.

Now the program can check the variable that contains this identification, making sure we have the correct tape. Here's how the detection routine works:

Something is checked to see if its value is the same as a constant that is known to be correct. If the values match, everything's OK. If they're different, something is displayed that roughly corresponds to a descripion of your problem. Everything is brought to a screeching halt until the problem is corrected.

On most large computer installations, such problems usually crop up around four A.M. Generally, the system programmer is rousted from the ck by a phone call. A frantic voice comes on the line, often smack in the middle of a sentence: ". . . and that's all I did, but maybe I shouldn't ave hit the RETURN, but it happened about an hour ago, and I've tried everything because I didn't want to wake you again, and . . . you there?"

The system programmer usually goes down to the computer installation and spends the next few days trying (often in vain) to figure out what appened. Of course, the main reason he became system programmer was because he knew where to hide the working, *bugless* version of the operating system—a place where nobody else could find it and destroy it n the middle of a panic.

Tape verification is straightforward.

The variable name to hold cassette identification can be *I$*. Add it at he DIMension list, which now becomes:

```
1000 DIM 1$(20), Z$(1)
```

The 20 after *I$* reserves space for twenty letter inputs at this variable. To make the comparison, you need an IF statement:

```
1140 IF I$ = "CAR MAINTENANCE FILE" THEN GOTO 1300
```

This continues your program at the point where the REWIND CASSETTE message is displayed when the correct information is on the tape. If the wrong tape has been copied, chances are good that the program would not have made it this far because the operating system would have discovered the mistake in the number of bytes on the tape. It would then have displayed a somewhat cryptic message, sending you to your manual to find out what went wrong.

In case your system has no such error-catching features, you can provide your own message:

```
1150 PRINT "CASSETTE MISREAD."
1160 PRINT " 'RETURN' " AND TRY AGAIN.";
1170 INPUT Z$
1180 GOTO 1010
```

This will return you to the original display, giving you another chance
to get the right cassette.

On the PROGRAMAP, the next operation is to record the file on the
cassette. As with copying, the recording routine varies with the machine.

```
1200 (clear screen)
1210 VTAB 4
1220 PRINT "MAKE SURE CASSETTE IS REWOUND."
```

The sequence of clearing screen and positioning the cursor before
displaying a new instruction is quite common. It's much like erasing the
blackboard between the history and arithmetic lessons.

```
1230 PRINT "    "
1240 PRINT "PRESS 'RECORD' SWITCHES ON RECORDER,"
1250 PRINT "    THEN 'RETURN' KEY ON KEYBOARD."
1260 INPUT Z$
1270 (record car maintenance file)
```

The routine from 1200 through 1270 records the new version of the
file after a servicing has been recorded. This same routine can be used
later to create the CAR MAINTENANCE FILE cassette.

The 1300s just display the REWIND CASSETTE message. This is
needed when the file tape is read (when the program is first run) and after
recording.

```
1300 (clear screen)
1310 VTAB 4
1320 PRINT "REWIND CASSETTE, THEN PRESS 'RETURN' KEY."
1330 INPUT Z$
```

The rest of the routine lets you select which program function to use.
The two options are (1) recording a completed new maintenance; or (2)
displaying the schedule for the next servicing.

```
1400 (clear screen)
1410 VTAB 4
1420 PRINT "TYPE FIRST LETTER OF SELECTION:"
1430 PRINT "    "
1440 PRINT "    RECORD COMPLETED MAINTENANCE"
```

```
1450 PRINT "    DISPLAY SCHEDULE"
1460 PRINT "    "
1470 PRINT "CHOICE:    ";
```

On most systems, the semicolon stops the cursor after the last letter ıs printed. Using it at the end of statement 1470 makes your reply appear ɔn the line with CHOICE:.

This time, the reply will be compared with the constant strings *R* and ꓘ in order to determine the next step. If something else is typed by mistake, the last statement loops the program back to the start of the display. You get another chance to type either an *R* or a *D*.

```
1480 INPUT Z$
1490 IF Z$ = "R" THEN GOTO 2000
1500 IF Z$ = "D" THEN GOTO 7000
1510 GOTO 1400
```

The control section is now complete.

The next part of the program (numbers in the 2000s) provides another selection. Its structure is similar to that of the previous section, although ɪonger because there are more options:

```
2000 REM RECORD SELECTION (2000-2999)
2010 (clear screen)
2020 PRINT "RECORD COMPLETED MAINTENANCE."
2030 VTAB 4
2040 PRINT "TYPE FIRST LETTER OF SELECTION:"
2050 PRINT "    "
2060 PRINT "    LUBE, OIL AND FILTER"
2070 PRINT "    BRAKES AND TIRES"
2080 PRINT "    RADIATOR COOLANT"
2090 PRINT "    WHEEL BEARING REPACKING"
2100 PRINT"    "
2110 PRINT "CHOICE:    ";
2120 INPUT Z$
2130 IF Z$ = "L" THEN GOTO 3000
2140 IF Z$ = "B" THEN GOTO 4000
2150 IF Z$ = "R" THEN GOTO 5000
2160 IF Z$ = "W" THEN GOTO 6000
2170 GOTO 2000
```

Again, the last statement loops us back through the display if something other than *L, B, R,* or *W* is typed.

Numbers in the 3000s are reserved for recording lube-and-oil servicing.

```
3000 REM LUBE & OIL (3000–3999)
3010 (clear screen)
3020 PRINT "LUBE, OIL CHANGE, AND FILTER"
3030 VTAB 4
```

After displaying the title, the program detours to the date and mileage subroutines. Each will return with the numbers typed into the integer variables named *Z(1)* through *Z(5)*.

```
3040 GOSUB 8000
3050 PRINT "   "
3060 GOSUB 9000
3070 PRINT "   "
3100 PRINT "OIL FILTER CHANGED? (Y OR N):   ";
3110 INPUT Z$
```

This time, *Z$* should contain a *Y* or an *N*. You can do this in a way you've already used:

```
3120 IF Z$ = "N" THEN GOTO 3200
3130 IF Z$ = "Y" THEN GOTO 3300
3140 GOTO 3100
```

Following is a different type of comparison with one less REROUT-ing. After *Y* is compared, the input variable is checked to see if it's different from *N*. If it's different, neither *Y* nor *N* were typed, and it loops back to the question. When *N* is typed, instead of looping back, it continues with the next statement:

```
3120 IF Z$ = "Y" THEN GOTO 3300
3130 IF Z$ < > "N" THEN GOTO 3100
```

If the first method makes more sense to you, use it. The extra statement makes no difference unless you run out of storage room when you've reached the end of the program. In that case, the shorter version lets you eliminate some steps and fit the program to your machine.

Statement 3200 puts "LUBE, OIL FILTER" into a string named *A$*. If the answer to the "OIL FILTER CHANGED?" question is *N*, the program goes here. If you did not change the filter this time, that should be done at the next lube-and-oil maintenance. With 3210 the program then skips ahead to 3400 so that "LUBE AND OIL CHANGE" do not get put into *A$*.

```
3200 A$ = "LUBE, OIL & FILTER"
3210 GOTO 3400
```

If the OIL FILTER CHANGED? answer is *Y*, the filter does not have to be changed at the next servicing, and the words "LUBE AND OIL" are put into *A$*.

```
3300 A$ = "LUBE AND OIL"
```

The rest of the lube-and-oil section copies the date and mileage from *Z(1)–Z(5)* into *A(1)–A(5)*. The date is copied first with the number 3 added to the month number:

```
3400 A(1) = Z(1)+3
3410 A(2) = Z(2)
3420 A(3) = Z(3)
```

If the number of the resulting month is larger than 12, then 12 must be subtracted from the month and the number 1 added to the year. If the month is still less than or equal to 12, this part is skipped in statement 3430 and the mileage is copied:

```
3430 IF A(1) <= 12 THEN GOTO 3500
3440 A(1) = A(1)-12
3450 A(3) = A(3)+1
```

While the mileage is copied, 3 is added to the thousands:

```
3500 A(4) = Z(4)+3
3510 A(5) = Z(5)
3520 GOTO 1200
```

Statement 3520 returns us to the file-recording part of the control routine, ending the lube-and-oil section.

The 4000s record the brake-and-tire maintenance. We have set this up every six thousand miles using the mileage subroutine. There is no date.

```
4000 REM BRAKES AND TIRES (4000–4999)
4010 (clear screen)
4020 B$ = "BRAKES AND TIRES"
4030 PRINT B$
4040 VTAB 4
4050 GOSUB 9000
4060 B(4) = Z(4) + 6
4070 B(5) = Z(5)
4080 GOTO 1200
```

The new things are the addition of a 6 instead of a 3 to the thousands integer of mileage, and Bs are used for the variable names.

Radiator coolant servicing comes up once a year. You need only the date subroutine:

```
5000 REM RADIATOR (5000–5999)
5010 (clear screen)
5020 C$ = "RADIATOR COOLANT"
5030 PRINT C$
5040 VTAB 4
5050 GOSUB 8000
5060 C(1) = Z(1)
5070 C(2) = Z(2)
5080 C(3) = Z(3) + 1
5090 GOTO 1200
```

The wheel bearing routine is almost identical to the brake-and-tire routine. You add 24 to the mileage thousands instead of 6.

```
6000 REM WHEEL BEARINGS (6000–6999)
6010 (clear screen)
6020 D$ = "PACK WHEEL BEARINGS"
6030 PRINT D$
6040 VTAB 4
6050 GOSUB 9000
6060 D(4) = Z(4) + 24
6070 D(5) = Z(5)
6080 GOTO 1200
```

The display routine consists mainly of PRINT statements. You display the contents of the records, using their respective variable names. First, you display the column headings:

```
7000 REM DISPLAY MAINTENANCE SCHEDULE (7000–7999)
7010 (clear screen)
7020 PRINT "MAINTENANCE SCHEDULE DATE   MILEAGE"
```

The information in the records is then displayed line by line:

```
7030 VTAB 4
7040 PRINT A$, A(1);"/";A(2);"/";A(3),A(4);",";A(5)
```

The commas between *A$* and *A(1)* and between *A(3)* and *A(4)* cause the information to be displayed in columns by tabbing the function. Semicolons keep the cursor from moving after the last character of the preceding data has been printed. Check your manufacturer's manual to see if your machine uses other print-control characters.

The first variable, *A$*, contains the words "LUBE AND OIL" or "LUBE, OIL & FILTER". This describes the servicing to be done by the date and mileage shown on the rest of the line.

A(1) contains the month number. The comma before it moves the cursor to the beginning of the next column and the semicolon after it prints the next part of the display immediately after the number. The "/" is a constant string. This causes a slant bar (/) to be printed after the month number. The semicolon keeps the cursor from moving, and the *A(2)* prints the day number immediately after the slant bar. Another / is printed after the day, and the *A(3)* prints the year after the day. The comma moves the cursor to the next tabulation, and *A(4)* prints the number of thousands of miles. A semicolon insures that the comma will be printed immediately after the thousands. Finally, a semicolon puts the hundreds digit immediately after the comma. The absence of any print-control character at the end causes the cursor to move to the beginning of the next line on your screen.

The rest of the records are printed in much the same way:

```
7050 PRINT "   "
7060 PRINT B$, B(4);",";B(5)
7070 PRINT "   "
7080 PRINT C$, C(1);"/";C(2);"/";C(3)
7090 PRINT "   "
```

```
7100 PRINT D$, D(4);",";D(5)
7110 VTAB 14
7120 PRINT "PRESS 'RETURN' TO CONTINUE."
7130 INPUT Z$
7140 GOTO 1400
```

Statement 7130 stops the program until the RETURN key is hit. This keeps the display on your screen until you finish looking at it. When the RETURN key is hit, the program goes back to the function-selection part of the control routine (which clears the screen). Without the INPUT statement, the display would flash by so quickly you would not be able to read the schedule.

This completes the schedule display section.

The two subroutines are all that remains. First, the date subroutine:

```
8000 REM DATE SUBROUTINE (8000-8999)
8010 PRINT "MONTH NUMBER?";
8020 INPUT Z(1)
8030 PRINT "DAY OF MONTH?";
8040 INPUT Z(2)
8050 PRINT "YEAR?";
8060 INPUT Z(3)
8100 PRINT "DATE OK? (Y OR N):";
8110 INPUT Z$
8120 IF Z$ = "N" THEN GOTO 8000
8130 IF Z$ = "Y" THEN RETURN
8140 GOTO 8100
```

The date is now stored in variables $Z(1)$ through $Z(3)$. When Y is typed in response to the "DATE OK?" question, the first statement after the GOSUB 8000 becomes the next step on the program. The Zs must then be copied to the appropriate integer variables.

The mileage subroutine is similar:

```
9000 REM MILEAGE SUBROUTINE (9000-9999)
9010 PRINT "THOUSANDS OF MILES?";
9020 INPUT Z(4)
9030 PRINT "HUNDREDS OF MILES?";
9040 INPUT Z(5)
9100 PRINT "MILEAGE OK? (Y OR N):";
```

```
9110 INPUT Z$
9120 IF Z$ = "N" THEN GOTO 9000
9130 IF Z$ = "Y" THEN RETURN
9140 GOTO 9100
32000 END
```

There's your completed program. Once it's in your computer, it will keep track of the servicing and the general maintenance on your car. You can get at the information rapidly, change it easily, and/or adapt it to another vehicle.

What is more important, this shows you how a general information storage/reminder program is written. There are many uses for such programs—for example, work scheduling, inventory control, maintenance and repair of buildings—and no doubt you can come up with adaptations of your own.

With slight alterations, such a program could keep you posted on what it's costing to operate your chariot. It also could monitor fuel costs for your home.

We did not forget to complete the DIMension statement. We have put it on the next page. Don't look at it just now. First, see if you can go back through this program and supply the missing DIMensions.

Complete DIMension statement for CAR MAINTENANCE program:

```
1000 DIM 1$(20),A$(30),A(5),B$(29),B(5),C$(23),C(5),D$(21),D(5),Z$(1),
Z(5)
```

If you happen to have an Apple II computer, the following statements will put this program into your machine. You could just type them in series now (after typing in the earlier parts of the program). Your computer will insert them in their proper order automatically.

Statements 1130 and 1270 each have five instructions. They read and write the information on the CAR MAINTENANCE FILE cassette. Colons are used to separate the instructions.

```
1010 CALL − 936
1130 POKE 60,0: POKE 61,8: POKE 62,200: POKE 63,8: CALL − 259
1200 CALL − 936
1270 POKE 60,0: POKE 61,8: POKE 62,200: POKE 63,8: CALL − 307
1300 CALL − 936
1400 CALL − 936
2010 CALL − 936
3010 CALL − 936
4010 CALL − 936
5010 CALL − 936
6010 CALL − 936
7010 CALL − 936
```

POKE and CALL are explained in the computer's programming manual. Equivalent functions are handled differently in different machines. For an Apple II computer, these statements copy the file and clear the screen. CALL −936 just happens to be the "clear screen" method on this machine. POKE "pokes" the required information into storage.

Before the program will work, a CAR MAINTENANCE FILE cassette must be made. We have allowed two hundred bytes of information for this file. Now that the recording routine is completed, we can use it to make the file cassette. This will take two extra statements at the beginning of the program.

First, we need the DIM statement (number 1000) to establish the variable sequence. Then the title must be supplied as a constant string copied into the tape identification variable, which is named *I$*. This can be done with:

1001 LET I$ = "CAR MAINTENANCE FILE"

Now, if we REROUTE to 1200 and put a new tape in the recorder, the recording routine will make a tape with two hundred bytes of information on it. The first twenty bytes will contain the identification CAR MAINTENANCE FILE. The statement for the REROUTE is:

1002 GOTO 1200

Now, just run the program and follow the instructions on the screen to make the file. When you are done, remove the statements 1001 and 1002 and the program can be used as it was intended.

Appendix H
Mortgage Hill

In our community there is a district named Morgan Hill, which is better known throughout the area as Mortgage Hill because of all the bank loans on the property there. This is just another sign that mortgages are a fact of life in our world. That's one of the reasons we decided to include a mortgage-calculating program in our book. You'll learn something about such programs while you study this appendix and, when you get through, you'll have an actual program that will tell you everything you need to know about a mortgage except how to pay it.

We will take it from the beginning in our top-down system—first the outline, then the PROGRAMAP, and finally the actual program.

The Outline

Our objective is to keep track of the interest paid on a mortgage. The program should calculate the payment if that's unknown. It must make a table of interest amount, the date, and the amount of the new balance. It must show totals of interest and of principal payments.

The program will, of course, use calculations typical of the accounting world. These calculations must have ten digits of accuracy in order to insure that the cents will come out right for dollar amounts up to a million dollars. (Who knows? There may be some high flyers among you. And there *is* inflation.) Our program will work on a floating point system with ten digits of accuracy.

Rules

1. If number of payments is known, calculate amount of monthly payment with

$$PMT = \frac{\text{Principal} \times i}{1-(1+i)^{-N}}$$

where i = monthly interest,
PMT = monthly payment,
N = total number of payments,
Principal = starting balance.

2. If amount of monthly payment is known, calculate number of payments with program loop as follows:

xxxx B = B*(1 + i) − PMT
      N = N + 1
      If B > 0 THEN GOTO xxxx

(xxxx represents an appropriate statement number in your program)

For this calculation, B = balance,
i = monthly interest,
PMT = monthly payment,
N = total number of payments.

When the loop is finished (that is, when $B <= 0$), the variable N will accurately reflect the number of payments.

3. Each line (monthly):

Interest payment = (prev. bal.) × (monthly int.)
Payment = (PMT) − (interest payment)
Balance = (prev. bal.) − (principal payment)

4. End-of-year totals:

Yearly interest paid = sum of monthly interest payments.
Yearly principal paid = sum of monthly principal payments.

5. End-of-contract totals:

   Total interest = sum of yearly interest.
   Total principal = sum of yearly principal.

Working Outline

1. Get starting balance of yearly interest.
2. If monthly payment known, get it. Otherwise get number of payments and calculate payment.
3. Get starting month and year.
4. Calculate and display date, interest payments, and new balance. Sum interest and principal for year totals and final total.
5. Stop when end of year. Allow keyboard input to start new year.
6. Display overall totals after last payment.

The PROGRAMAP

I/O	CPU	REROUTE	DESCRIPTION

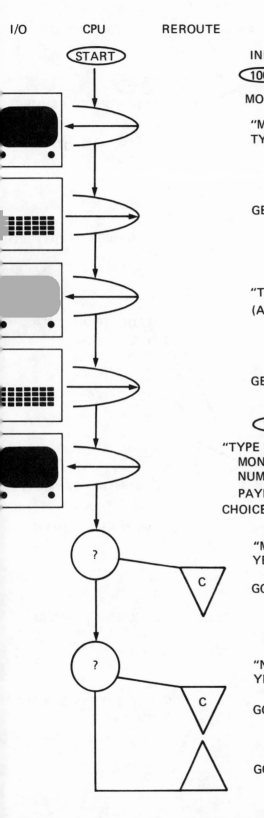

INITIALIZATION ROUTINE:

1000

MORTGAGE INFORMATION (1000 - 499

"MORTGAGE PAYMENT
TYPE PRINCIPAL"

GET PRINCIPAL"

"TYPE INTEREST
(ANNUAL %)"

GET ANNUAL INTEREST

1200

"TYPE FIRST LETTER OF CHOICE:
MONTHLY PAYMENT AMOUNT
NUMBER OF MONTHLY
PAYMENTS
CHOICE: "

"M" TYPED?
YES:

GOTO 3000

"N" TYPED?
YES

GOTO 2000

GOTO 1200

281

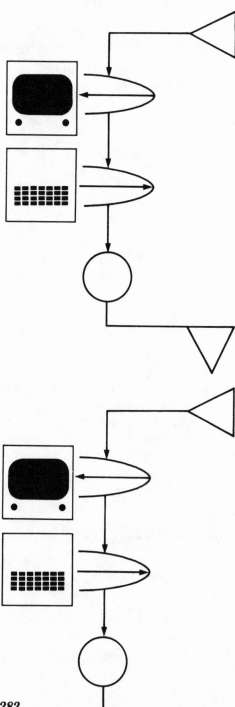

2000
GET NUMBER OF PAYMENTS

"TYPE NUMBER OF
PAYMENTS:"

GET NUMBER OF PAYMENTS

CALCULATE MONTHLY
PAYMENT

GOTO 4000

3000
GET MONTHLY PAYMENT

"TYPE MONTHLY PAYMENT:

GET MONTHLY PAYMENT

CALCULATE NUMBER OF
PAYMENTS

I/O	CPU	REROUTE	DESCRIPTION

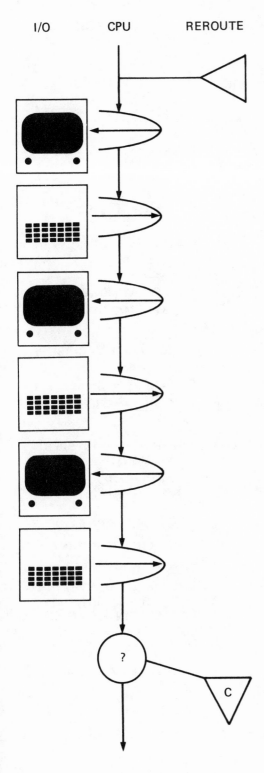

4000

GET STARTING DATE

"TYPE STARTING MONTH
NUMBER (1-12):"

GET MONTH

"TYPE STARTING YEAR
(TWO DIGITS):"

GET YEAR

"INFORMATION CORRECT?
(Y OR N): "

GET ANSWER

"Y" TYPED?
YES:

GOTO 5000

I/O	CPU	REROUTE	DESCRIPTION

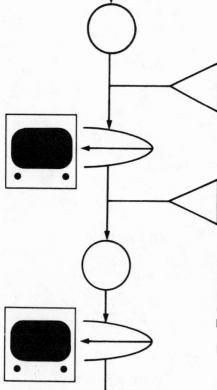

"N" TYPED?
YES:

GOTO ⟨1000⟩

GOTO ⟨4100⟩

⟨5000⟩
DISPLAY MORTGAGE
INFORMATION

INITIALIZE VARIABLES

⟨5100⟩   START YEAR

"PRINC=$ INTEREST= %
NO. MONTHS=   PMT=$

DATE   INT   BALANCE
            AMOUNT"

⟨5200⟩   PRINT LINE

CALCULATE INT AMOUNT
& BALANCE

(INT AMT)=BAL* (MONTHLY INT RATE
(YR INT)=(YR INT)+(INT AMT)
(PRINC AMT)=(MNTH PMT)−(INT AMT)
(YR PRINC)=(YR PRINC)+(PRINC AMT)
BAL=BAL−(PRINC AMT)

PRINT DATE, INT AMT, BALANCE

I/O	CPU	REROUTE	DESCRIPTION

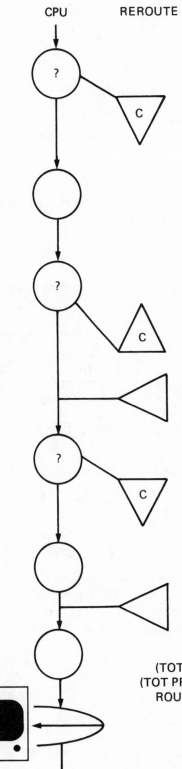

BALANCE < = 0?
YES:

GOTO 6000

MONTH=MONTH+1

MONTH < =12?
YES:

GOTO 5200

6000
IF B < =0
CALCULATE LAST PMT

B > 0?
YES:

GOTO 6100

CALCULATE LAST PMT &
ROUND OFF

6100 YEAR SUMS

CALCULATE TOTALS:

(TOT INT)=(TOT INT)+(YR INT SUM)
(TOT PRINC)=(TOT PRINC)+(YR PRINC SUM)
ROUND OFF YEARLY SUMS

"YEAR: INT= $
PRINC= $"

285

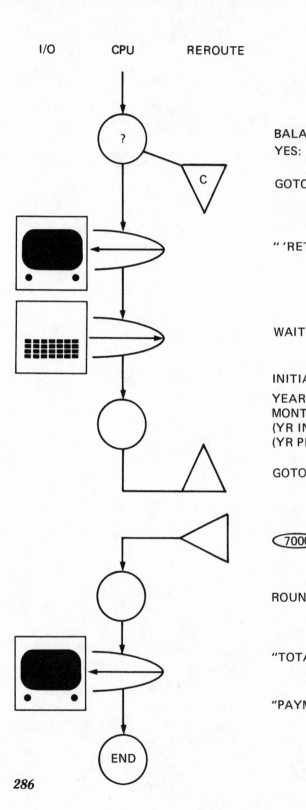

I/O   CPU   REROUTE   DESCRIPTION

?

C

BALANCE < =0?
YES:

GOTO 7000

" 'RETURN' FOR NEXT YEAR."

WAIT FOR RETURN

INITIALIZE YEAR VARIABLES:
YEAR = YEAR +1
MONTH = 1
(YR INT SUM) = 0
(YR PRINC SUM) = 0

GOTO 5100

7000 GRAND TOTALS

ROUND OFF TOTALS

"TOTAL: INT= $
              PRINC= $ "

"PAYMENT: LAST= $
              TOTAL= $"

END

Appendix I
Mortgage Payment
Program

You could just type this program into your machine and RUN it. Since machines of different manufacture have slight variations in their function requirements, we have enclosed "machine-dependent" functions in parentheses in small letters. See statement 1010 below for an example. Check your owner's manual before trying to put this program into your machine.

```
1000 REM MORTGAGE PAYMENT PROGRAM
1010 (clear screen)
1020 HTAB 12
1030 PRINT "MORTGAGE PAYMENT"
1040 PRINT "   "
1050 PRINT "TYPE PRINCIPAL:   ",
1060 INPUT P
1070 PRINT "   "
1080 PRINT "TYPE INTEREST (ANNUAL %):   ",
1090 INPUT I
1100 J = I / 1200
1110 PRINT "   "
1120 PRINT "TYPE FIRST LETTER OF SELECTION:"
1130 PRINT "   MONTHLY PAYMENT AMOUNT"
1140 PRINT "   NUMBER OF MONTHLY PAYMENTS"
1200 PRINT "CHOICE:   ";
1210 INPUT C$
1220 IF C$ = "M" THEN GOTO 3000
1230 IF C$ = "N" THEN GOTO 2000
```

```
1240 GOTO 1200
2000 REM GET NUMBER OF PAYMENTS
2010 PRINT "   "
2020 PRINT "TYPE NUMBER OF PAYMENTS:   ";
2030 INPUT N
2040 PRINT "   "
2050 REM CALCULATE MONTHLY PAYMENT
2060 M = (J*P)/(1 − (1 + J)↑(− N))
2070 GOTO 4000
3000 REM GET MONTHLY PAYMENT
3010 PRINT "   "
3020 PRINT "TYPE MONTHLY PAYMENT:   ";
3030 INPUT M
3040 REM CALCULATE NUMBER OF PAYMENTS
3050 N = 0
3060 B = P
3070 B = B*(1 + J) − M
3080 N = N + 1
3090 IF B > 0 THEN GOTO 3070
4000 REM GET STARTING DATE
4010 PRINT "   "
4020 PRINT "TYPE STARTING MONTH NUMBER (1–12):   ";
4030 INPUT D
4040 PRINT "   "
4050 PRINT "TYPE STARTING YEAR (TWO DIGITS):   ";
4060 INPUT Y
4070 PRINT "   "
4100 PRINT "INFORMATION CORRECT?(Y OR N):   ";
4110 INPUT C$
4120 IF C$ = "Y" THEN 5000
4130 IF C$ = "N" THEN 1000
4140 GOTO 4100
5000 REM DISPLAY MORTGAGE INFORMATION
5010 B = P
5020 DIM A(2),C(2),S(2),T(2)
5030 DIM M$(12)
5040 M$(1) = "JAN": M$(2) = "FEB": M$(3) = "MAR": M$(4) = "APR":
   M$(5) = "MAY": M$(6) = "JUN": M$(7) = "JUL": M$(8) = "AUG":
   M$(9) = "SEP": M$(10) = "OCT": M$(11) = "NOV": M$(12) = "DEC"
5100 REM START YEAR
```

```
5110 (clear screen)
5120 PRINT "PRINC = $";P, "INTEREST = "; I; "%"
5130 M = INT (M*100 + .5)/100
5140 PRINT "NO. MONTHS =   ";N," PMT = $";M
5150 PRINT "   "
5160 PRINT "DATE", "INT", "BALANCE"
5170 PRINT "   ", "AMOUNT"
5180 PRINT "   "
5200 REM PRINT LINE
5210 A(1) = B*J
5220 A(2) = M − A(1)
5230 S(1) = S(1) + A(1)
5240 S(2) = S(2) + A(2)
5250 B = B − A(2)
5260 C(1) = INT (A(1)*100 + .5)/100
5270 C(2) = INT(B*100 + .5)/100
5280 IF C(2) < 0 THEN C(2) = 0
5290 PRINT M$(D); "   ";Y,C(1),C(2)
5300 IF B <= .005 THEN GOTO 6000
5310 D = D + 1
5320 IF D <= 12 THEN GOTO 5200
6000 REM IF B<= 0 CALCULATE LAST PAYMENT
6010 IF B > 0 THEN GOTO 6100
6020 S(2) = S(2) + B
6030 M = INT((M + B)*100 + .5)/100
6100 REM YEAR SUBTOTALS
6110 T(1) = T(1) + S(1)
6120 T(2) = T(2) + S(2)
6130 S(1) = INT(S(1)*100 + .5)/100
6140 S(2) = INT(S(2)*100 + .5)/100
6150 PRINT "   "
6160 PRINT "YEAR:   INT = $";S(1);
6170 PRINT " PRINC =   $";S(2)
6180 IF B<= .005 THEN GOTO 7000
6190 PRINT "   "
6200 PRINT " 'RETURN' FOR NEXT YEAR";
6210 INPUT C$
6220 REM INITIALIZE NEXT YEAR
6230 Y = Y + 1
6240 D = 1
```

```
6250 S(1) = 0
6260 S(2) = 0
6270 GOTO 5100
7000 REM GRAND TOTALS
7010 T(1) = INT(T(1)*100 + .5)/100
7020 T(2) = INT(T(2)*100 + .5)/100
7030 PRINT "TOTAL: INT = $;T(1);
7040 PRINT " PRINC = $";T(2)
7050 PRINT "PAYMENT: LAST = $";M;
7060 PRINT "  TOTAL = $";T(1) + T(2)
32000 END
```

Appendix J
Glossary

A

accessory—any piece of equipment that is attached to a computer. Sometimes called *peripheral equipment,* or merely *peripheral.*

accumulator—special group of switches used for arithmetic and logical manipulations of information.

action—switching operation resulting from a command or instruction.

adder—circuit that performs the operations necessary to add two (usually binary) numbers together.

address—switch pattern identifying the location of a particular piece of information or program step.

address bus—group of wires with a voltage level corresponding to an address *(see).*

ALGOL—higher level programming language that uses instructions especially adapted to "number crunching."

alphanumeric—symbol group consisting of letters, numbers, and punctuation marks.

ALU—arithmetic logic unit: consists of adder, accumulator, and control and logic circuitry used in mathematical switching operations.

analog—continuous signal with a voltage corresponding to a measurement of something observed or monitored. *Also,* a device which, by its performance, can represent the performance of some other device. A model airplane can be the analog of its full-size counterpart.

analog computer—computer designed to operate directly on a continuous voltage. Analog computers represent numbers by continuous quantities, by mechanical quantities, or by models.

ANSI—American National Standards Institute: a corporation that compiles guidelines for the computer industry and other fields.

APL—a structured higher-level programming language.

applications program—program written to accomplish a specific task (usually in a higher-level language).

arithmetic logic unit—*see* ALU.

ASCII—American Standard Code for Information Interchange: a list of switch positions corresponding to each standard symbol.

assembler—machine-language program that converts mnemonics (abbreviated descriptions) to corresponding machine-language switch patterns.

assembly language—list of mnemonics (abbreviated descriptions) corresponding to the machine-language instructions.

assignment, variable—the copying of information into switches reserved for variables.

assignment operator—the *equals* symbol: causes the information on the right side to be copied into the switches reserved for the variable named on the left side.

asynchronous—exchanging information piece by piece instead of in long trains.

B

BASIC—Beginner's All-purpose Symbolic Instruction Code: an easily learned higher-level language designed to be used in "number crunching" and business-oriented problems.

BASIC, Extended—an enhanced version of BASIC that provides for accessories and floating-point numbers *(see)*.

BCD—binary-coded decimal: list of switch positions corresponding to the ten decimal digits.

binary—number system in which all digits are either 1s or 0s.

binary-coded decimal—*see* BCD.

binary digit—*see* bit.

bistable—electronic device having two different stable voltage outputs.

bit—*bi*nary *d*igit: single element of a binary number with a value of either 1 or 0.

branch—synonym for REROUTE operation.

branching—makes as much sense as GOTOing.

BREAK (BRK)—special symbol sent from a terminal to the computer indicating that the person using the terminal is finished.

buffer—special group of switches used to keep information until it can be used.

bug—program error.

bus—conductive pathway that distributes information to several different devices.

bus, address—*see* address bus.

bus, control—*see* control bus.

bus, data—*see* data bus.

byte—group of (usually) eight bits that, when taken together, represent a piece of information (ASCII character or binary or BCD number) or a machine-language program step (or part of one).

C

C—a structured higher-level programming language corresponding closely to machine language.

calculator—numeric computational device.

CALL—synonym for detour.

card—paper rectangles with information permanently fixed to them in the form of holes, a system rapidly being phased out.

card reader—machine that copies information from a card by sensing the positions of the holes.

case, lower—small letters; dates from the days of hand-set type, when the small letters were kept in a case that was racked at a lower position than the case holding the capital letters.

case, upper—capital letters (*see* case, lower).

central processing unit—*see* CPU.

character—a single symbol.

chip—electronic circuit enclosed by a ceramic or plastic package.

circuit—electronic device performing a predetermined function.

CLK—clock: electronic device that emits electrical pulses at a specific rate.

clock—*see* CLK.

COBOL—common business oriented language: a higher-level programming language especially suited to information processing instead of to number crunching.

code—symbolic representation.

command—instruction to the monitor that causes something to happen immediately.

comparator—*see* relationship symbols.

comparison—determination of the relationship between two pieces of information.

compiler—program that converts source-language statements (statements that can be read by people) into machine-language instructions.

complement—a number the same size as but the opposite sign of another number.

computer—machine that automatically processes information in a programmable way.

CONTROL (CTRL)—special key on keyboard; it alters the normal switch patterns of other keys so that they can be used as signals to the computer.

control bus—group of conductors that transmit control signals to the various parts of the computer.

control diagram—chart used by computer technicians; it gives correct signals for troubleshooting the hardware.

controller—program that checks the output of a machine outside the computer and keeps it within specified limits by changing the power supplied to that machine.

control section—part of a program that establishes access to detail routines.

counter—group of switches in a circuit that accumulates electrical pulses.

counter, program—*see* program counter.

CPU—central processing unit: main switching circuitry; it includes the ALU, instruction decoder, program counter, clock, and other elements.

CRT—cathode ray tube: a glass screen upon which output information is displayed.

cursor—special symbol displayed on screen indicating the position where the next character will be displayed.

cycle—the smallest complete element of a repeating electrical signal.

D

data—input information; often refers to numeric input.

data bus—conductive pathway for information.

debugging—process of finding and correcting program errors.

decimal—pertaining to the base-10 numbering system.

decision—programmed selection of one of two alternatives according to the positional content of a switch or switches.

decoder—circuit that converts coded information into a form that can be read by humans.

decoder, instruction—*see* instruction decoder.

decrement—the reduction of a numeric value in a set of switches by a fixed amount.

demultiplexer—circuit that switches information to one of several devices.

dendrite—branching protoplasm of the nerve cell.

description—verbal plain-language explanation of a program step.

detour—the process of going to a subroutine and returning from it.

device management—software procedure for scheduling and using particular accessories for different programs as these are needed.

diagram, control—*see* control diagram.

digit—single element of a number.

digital—relating to the separate and discrete "counting" numbers instead of continuously variable numbers.

digital computer—machine that automatically processes discrete information in a programmable way. A digital computer follows a definite numbering system built into the hardware. It employs discrete symbols.

DIM (DIMension)—higher-level language statement that sets aside specific storage space for named variables.

discrete—numbering system in which different numbers must differ by at least a certain definite amount.

disk—external storage accessory for a computer.

disk driver—machine that stores information on disks.

documentation—verbal and pictorial information describing how a program works and what the program does.

E

editor—program that modifies textual material according to commands.

encoder—circuit that converts input information into switch patterns that can be processed by a computer.

encoder chip—chip containing the encoder.

END—statement defining the last place in a higher-level language program.

ENTER—the process of transferring information into a computer.

erase—removing information from a computer.

ERR, MEM FULL—program mistake; attempting to put more information into internal storage than can be accommodated by the storage system.

ERR, RANGE—mistake resulting from trying to enter a larger or smaller number than allowed.

ERR, STR OVFL—(string overflow error); mistake resulting from trying to put more information into a string than it can hold.

ERROR—mistake in a program statement or the format of information input.

ESCAPE (ESC)—key on the keyboard often used with other keys for special functions.

execute—the process of running a program or part of a program.

expression—algebraic formulation that results in a number.

Extended BASIC—an enhanced version of BASIC that permits more high-level functions or accessories.

F

field—part of a record containing a specific type of information.

file—collection of similar records on external storage device.

firmware—machine-language program stored on ROMs.

first generation—term referring to earliest computers, which used vacuum tubes.

flip-flop—simple storage switch.

floppy disk—small external mass-storage medium.

flowchart—pictorial representation of a program.

font—in printing, a complete assortment of type in one style and size.

FOR . . . NEXT—first and last statements of a program loop.

FOR–TO–STEP—first statement of a program loop in a higher-level language.

FORTRAN—Formula translator: higher-level language designed to crunch numbers easily; primarily used to express computer programs in arithmetic formulas.

G

gate—circuit performing a logical function with two or more input and one output.
GIGO—Garbage in—garbage out: Input errors produce false answers.
glitch—a hardware error.
GOSUB—higher-level language statement that causes a detour.
GOTO—higher-level language statement that causes a reroute.

H

handler—program that makes an accessory work.
hard copy—output on paper.
hardware—physical piece of equipment.
hexadecimal—pertaining to a numbering system that uses sixteen digits instead of ten.
higher-level language—programming language that uses standard written statements that are translated by a compiler or interpreter into the machine's language.
holograph—three-dimensional image produced by a laser photographic process.
housekeeping—pertaining to the "bookeeping" aspects of programming.

I

IC—integrated circuit; synonym for chip.
IF . . . THEN—higher-level language statement that permits the programmed selection of one of two alternatives according to the contents of a variable.
illegal operation—synonym for error.
increment—increase of a numeric value in a set of switches by a fixed amount.
information—that which is processed by a computer.
initialize—to start the processor in a known way that does not have to be repeated.
input—information put into a program.
instruction—single element of a language: a command or the operational part of a statement.

instruction decoder—program that translates an instruction into the corresponding machine operation.

instruction set—a complete language.

integer—whole number without any fractional part.

integrated circuit—*see* chip.

interface—that which connects one thing to another thing.

interpreter—program that translates higher-level language statements one by one into machine language. It causes each statement to be executed before the next statement is translated.

interpretive language—higher-level programming language that is translated and executed one statement at a time.

interrupt—a signal from an accessory that stops the execution of a program temporarily, permitting the program to transmit or receive information from the computer.

I/O port—input/output port; connector for an accessory.

J

joystick—input accessory that transmits to the computer the information on how the stick has been moved.

K

K—kilo (1,024)

keyboard—the typewriterlike keys used to put information into a computer.

keyboard interpreter loader—circuit that translates signals from the keyboard into standard switch patterns and puts those patterns into internal storage.

L

language—complete set of instructions describing standard machine operations.

LET—higher-level language instruction that copies information into a variable.

light pen—an input accessory used with a screen; it transmits information relative to its position on the screen.

light pencil—another name for light pen.

light wand—another name for light pen.

line printer—high-speed output accessory that prints information on paper.

loader—program that copies other programs from an external device to internal storage.

logic—mathematical rules governing circuit functions and program operations.

logical state—the on or off condition of a switch.

logic circuit—circuit designed to perform a specific mathematically defined function.

lower case—*see* case.

loop—section of a program that can be repeated as needed; it reroutes to an earlier step in the program.

M

machine language—complete set of instructions that the machine can execute directly.

magnetic core—type of internal storage using small donut-shaped rings that can be magnetized.

magnetic disk storage—synonym for disk.

magnetic tape storage—external storage system on magnetic tape. An ordinary cassette recorder can work as this kind of storage system.

mass storage—external storage accessory such as disk or magnetic tape systems.

master control program—program that controls the entire system including accessories.

matrix—general term for coding circuits or arrays.

MEM FULL ERR—programming mistake. *See* ERR, MEM FULL.

memory—synonym for internal storage.

menu—table of contents listing a program or parts of a program.

microcomputer—small- to medium-capacity computer with its major circuitry on chips.

microcomputer chip—small-capacity computer with complete circuitry on a single chip.

microprocessor—the central processing unit (SWITCHING) of a microcomputer.

microprocessor chip—a microcomputer central processing unit on a single chip.

mnemonic—abbreviated description of a machine-language step used in an assembly language.

monitor—There are two different kinds: One is a piece of hardware, the other is a type of program. The hardware monitor is the display screen. The software monitor is a nickname for "system monitor" *(see)*.

monitor program—another term for "system monitor."

MPU—microprocessor unit: *see* microprocessor chip.

multiplexer—circuit that takes information from any of several places and puts it onto a single bus.

MUMPS—Multi-user multi-processor system: an operating system that integrates several computer systems in a way that lets them share information efficiently.

N

NEW—command in a higher-level programming language. NEW removes previous applications programs from internal storage; allowing you to put a new program into that storage.

NEXT—higher-level language statement used at the end of a FOR . . . NEXT loop to return to the start of the loop.

nibble—between a *bit* and a *byte:* a piece of information that is four bits long.

NO END ERR—error message indicating that a higher-level language has no END statement where the syntax of the language requires such a statement.

number—a mathematical entity that may indicate quantity, value, or amount of units.

O

object program—machine-language translation of a source program *(see)*.

operating system—group of (usually machine-language) programs that perform housekeeping functions: run accessories, translate or interpret higher-level language programs, and perform commands.

operator—person using a computer.

optical scanner—input accessory that uses light to convert printed information into switch patterns that can be processed by a computer.

OUTPUT—information transferred out of a computer to an accessory for storage, display, or printing.

OUTPUT section—that part of a program which transfers information from internal storage to an output accessory.

P

panel—section of a screen reserved for specific displays.

paper tape—long thin strip of paper with information permanently stored on it in the form of punched holes.

paper tape reader—input accessory that copies information stored on paper tape.

parallel processing—two or more programs running at the same time on a computer that has two or more central processors.

parity bit—an extra bit in a byte of information; it is used for verification of the coded message in the byte.

PASCAL—a structured higher-level programming language.

peripheral—synonym for accessory.

prompt—instruction or special symbol printed by the program to inform the operator what is needed.

pulse—electrical signal used to transmit a bit of information.

R

RAM—random-access memory: internal storage device with switches that can be changed.

random—a group of things each element of which can be selected as easily as any other element; a random number is one of a sequence believed to be free from conditions that might bias the selection of that number.

random-access memory—*see* RAM. (This is actually a synonym for direct-access memory, or direct-access storage.)

RANGE ERR—*see* ERR, RANGE.

read—the process of copying information from a storage or input device.

read-only memory—*see* ROM.

read-write memory—synonym for RAM.

record—collection of information about one element in a file.

register—set of switches reserved for a special purpose.

relationship symbols—less than <
> greater than >
> less than or equal to < =
> greater than or equal to > =
> not equal to < >

REM—REMinder; REMark; a higher-level language statement used for a description of a program operation. REMs are displayed, not otherwise acted upon.

REROUTE—a PROGRAMAP column depicting changes in the normal sequence of a program.

RETURN—higher-level language statement used at the end of a subroutine; it ends the detour by rerouting to the statement following the GOSUB. The RETURN key on a computer keyboard tells the computer that the operator has completed a particular operation.

ROM—read-only memory: internal storage device with stuck switches.

rotate—a machine-level instruction that shifts a group of switch patterns a specified number of places to the left or right.

RUN—higher-level language command used to start a program in internal storage.

S

SAVE—higher-level language command that transmits a program from internal storage to an external storage device.

scanner, optical—*see* optical scanner.

second generation—computers that used transistors rather than vacuum tubes.

sequential logic—train of circuits in which the output of each circuit is determined by an immediately preceding input; held to consecutive operations.

serial processing—the manipulation of information one piece at a time.

software—programs that are used in read-write storage and that can be modified.

solid state—semiconductor circuitry consisting of transistors, diodes, chips, and the like.

sorting—programming process used to organize information in a way determined by the operator.

source program—untranslated version of a higher-level language program. Source programs are written in a language the operator can read.

statement—single instruction of a higher-level language program.

storage—that part of the computer hardware where information is kept.

storage device—any of the internal or external pieces of hardware in which information is kept.

string—specific chunk of information.

string variable—chunk of information that can be referred to by name and changed by the program.

STR OVFL ERR—*see* ERR, STR OVFL.

structured language—a higher-level language that uses a multilevel syntactical structure.

subroutine—part of a program that is used in several different places of the program; it is separated from the main part of the program in order to make it available for use at any point.

switch, two-state—simple switch with two positions called "on" (represented by a binary 1) and "off" (represented by a binary 0).

switching—information manipulation by switch patterns.

synchronous—several switching operations that happen regularly (at a constant time interval) or predictably with respect to one another.

syntax—required structure of a command, instruction, or program.

system monitor—program that controls the switching of information between accessories and internal storage.

system software—software version of operating system *(see)*.

T

TAB—higher-level language instruction that controls the horizontal position where the next symbol will be printed on a screen or a printer.

teletypewriter—input and output printing terminal often used for transmitting information over long-distance cables.

terminal—input and output device with keyboard and printer or screen.

third generation—type of computer that uses integrated circuits for most of its circuitry.

transistor—semiconductor device used for switching in a digital computer.

two-state switch—*see* switch, two-state.

U

UNIX—multiuser operating system developed at Bell Laboratories and based on the structured language C.
upper case—capital letters; *see* case.

V

variable, string—*see* string variable.
variable assignment—the process of copying information into a specified variable.

W

word—basic unit of information handled by a computer; it contains the same number of bits as there are lines on the data bus.
write—process of copying information into RAM internal storage or of sending information to an output accessory.

FRANK HERBERT lives in Washington, the state of his birth. He is probably most famous for his series of novels dealing with the desert world Arrakis: *Dune, Dune Messiah* and *Children of Dune*. These books have sold in the millions of copies. Another novel in the series is in the works and the author has worked on the screenplay for a movie based on the first volume which is currently in production by Dino De Laurentiis.

Along with Max Barnard, Herbert has been devoting his time recently to developing his own home computer system which will operate his household appliances, manage his finances and help him produce his books.